"Finally, an opening to the Talmud for [...] Amy Scheinerman addresses topics tha[...] relationships and self-understanding. She deftly walks us through the logic of the passage, asking thought provoking questions along the way, and allowing us to draw our own conclusions."

> —RABBI LOUIS RIESER, teacher, scholar-in-residence, and author of *The Hillel Narratives*

"Amy Scheinerman gently and adroitly guides us through some of the most fascinating and provocative passages of talmudic literature. . . . *The Talmud of Relationships* amply demonstrates that talmudic/rabbinic literature retains its power to speak to the spiritual issues we face individually and communally, even more than a millennium and a half later."

> —GAIL LABOVITZ, associate professor of rabbinic literature, Ziegler School of Rabbinic Studies

"Amy Scheinerman does it again. She takes the most obscure Talmudic texts and makes them come alive, right before your eyes. And the best part: the 'aha' moment is not short-lived. Amy's insights will stick to your bones and add value and meaning to your life."

> —RABBI STACY OFFNER, Temple Beth Tikvah, Madison, Connecticut

"A treasure trove of insight, information, and meaning which invites us into the world of the rabbis and the Talmudic tradition. Be prepared to experience the Talmud come alive as we learn to navigate engrossing texts, and also reflect upon our own relationships: who we are and who we aspire to be."

> —RABBI NORMAN COHEN, professor of Midrash at HUC-JIR and author of *The Way into Torah*

The Talmud of Relationships, Volume 2

The Jewish Publication Society expresses its gratitude for the generosity of the sponsors of this book.

Dr. Jeffrey S. and Susan J. Aronowitz in honor of our son, Jordan Adam, the light of our lives.

University of Nebraska Press
Lincoln

The Talmud of Relationships, Volume 2 *The Jewish Community and Beyond*

RABBI AMY SCHEINERMAN

The Jewish Publication Society
Philadelphia

© 2018 by Amy Scheinerman

All rights reserved. Published by the University of
Nebraska Press as a Jewish Publication Society book.
Manufactured in the United States of America.

Library of Congress Cataloging-in-Publication Data
Names: Scheinerman, Amy, author.
Title: The Talmud of relationships /
Rabbi Amy Scheinerman.
Description: Philadelphia: Jewish Publication Society;
Lincoln: University of Nebraska Press, [2018] |
Includes bibliographical references.
Identifiers: LCCN 2017056782
ISBN 9780827613560 (pbk.: alk. paper)
ISBN 9780827614413 (epub)
ISBN 9780827614420 (mobi)
ISBN 9780827614437 (pdf)
Subjects: LCSH: Talmud—Criticism, interpretation,
etc. | Jewish way of life. | Jewish ethics. | Interper-
sonal relations—Religious aspects—Judaism.
Classification: LCC BM504.2 .S3314 2018 | DDC
296.1/206—dc23 LC record available at
https://lccn.loc.gov/2017056782

Set in Merope by E. Cuddy.
Designed by L. Auten.

To Rabbi Louis Rieser, dear friend and *chevruta* partner, who opened Talmud to me in a new and immeasurably valuable way.

CONTENTS

ACKNOWLEDGMENTS

While it is always a pleasure to acknowledge one's blessings, the opportunity to thank the people who helped bring my first books to fruition is an exceptional delight.

My thanks to Rabbi Barry Schwartz, director of the Jewish Publication Society, who invited me to write this book. Barry's timing could not have been more perfect, since this was just the project I had been contemplating and hoping would be possible. I am grateful for his encouragement and support.

My thanks to Joy Weinberg, the JPS managing editor, for her superb editing. Joy's meticulous and sensitive attention to detail, nuance, and tone are matched by her wisdom, warmth, and patience.

My thanks to the University of Nebraska Press (UNP), JPS's partner in publishing *The Talmud of Relationships*, for their vital role in this exciting project, Elizabeth Zaleski of UNP, and Michele Alperin for her excellent questions and masterful editing.

My thanks to the wonderful colleagues and communities who have invited me in to serve as their weekend scholar-in-residence, affording me the opportunity to share what I love and to learn with them.

My thanks to my husband, Edward Scheinerman, for his steadfast and unwavering support and encouragement throughout the process of writing and revising, as well as for schlepping home piles of books from the Johns Hopkins University library.

Finally, a special thanks to my dear friend, colleague, and *chevruta* partner, Rabbi Louis Rieser, who opened Talmud to me in an entirely new way, and whose friendship has been an extraordinary gift.

INTRODUCTION   *Why Talmud?*

The Hasidic master Rebbe Nachman of Bratzlav told this parable: Once a Jewish man who lived in Austria dreamed that a valuable treasure lay buried under a bridge in Vienna. Determined to find it, he packed a bag and journeyed two days and two nights until he reached the bridge. Then he stood there wondering what to do, since searching during daylight would provoke suspicious questions.

A soldier came by and asked him, "What are you looking for?"

The man told the soldier about his dream.

The soldier replied, "I feel sorry for you, you crazy dreamer! Believing in dreams is nonsense. I, too, dreamed once of a valuable treasure that lay buried in a cellar." And then, to the man's amazement, the soldier not only located that treasure in the town where this Jewish man lived, but also mentioned his name.

The soldier continued, "I have no idea where this town is or who this man is, but I would be crazy to try to find him."

The man nodded politely, turned around, and headed home. Upon his arrival he went straight down to his cellar and began digging. In time he unearthed a chest containing a great treasure. The man declared, "The treasure has always lain buried in my house, but I had to leave my home and travel far away in order to discover it was under my feet all along."[1]

It is time to unearth the treasure that lies buried in our cellars. That treasure is Talmud.

For modern, liberal Jews, Tanakh (Hebrew Scripture), and particularly the Written Torah (the Five Books of Moses), has become their central religious text. But in reality the core text of Judaism has, for a very long time, been the Talmud. While Torah continues to play a central role in the inspiration, identity, and history of the Jewish people, we are Rabbinic Jews, not biblical Jews. The Rabbis of the Talmud in the second through sixth centuries CE filtered, interpreted, and enlarged Written Torah to create our Judaism—a set of ethical and ritual traditions based on three pillars: Talmud Torah (study), worship, and *gemilut chasadim* (deeds of loving-kindness).[2]

Why Do We Need Talmud?

If Jews had a Torah, why was there a need for the Talmud? One insight is Talmud's sobriquet for Talmud itself: "Oral Torah." When the Romans destroyed the Second Temple in 70 CE, the nation of Israel was traumatized and the Land of Israel decimated. Without the sacrificial cult presided over by the *kohanim* (priests), it was unclear how the Israelites could continue to serve God. Bereft of the Temple, how could they maintain their covenant with God?

Stepping into this void, over the course of many centuries, the Rabbis shaped what we know as Judaism. The Jewish traditions of sacred texts, religious practices, ethical values, customs, and ideals—all interwoven with a cultural emphasis on learning and teaching, questioning and debating, family and community—have withstood the vicissitudes of history and traveled with Jews through time and space ever since. Rabbinic tradition and methodology proved flexible enough to adapt to the contingencies of life, sturdy enough to support the Jewish people during dark times, and idealistic enough to provide challenge and inspiration throughout.

At the core of Judaism stands a set of sacred texts—Mishnah, Tosefta, two Talmuds (one from Babylonia, one from the Land of Israel), many compilations of midrash, a wide assortment of commentaries, numerous legal codes, and works of philosophy and mysticism—that transmit tradition from generation to generation. Talmud, the edited transcript of a four-centuries-long study session that began nearly two thousand years ago, is primary among these sacred texts.

In every age Talmud is studied, debated, and internalized by a new generation of learners. Talmud invites each learner into the conversations and debates of the ancient study houses, providing a way to explore the big questions and deepest concerns of living and arrive at one's own answer.

Why I Wrote This Book

As a teenager I longed for deep ideas, intense conversation, and religious meaning. Deep ideas could be found in the literature I read in school, but it lacked religious meaning and rarely led to intense conversation.

In high school I belonged to my synagogue's youth group. The wonderful friendships I formed enlarged my life. One spring, at a weekend retreat, a rabbinical student I had never met (and whose name I regret I cannot recall) came to teach us. It was several weeks before Passover, and he brought a short text, perhaps a paragraph or two in length, pertaining to the upcoming festival.

I was mesmerized. This brief text was unlike anything I had ever read. It opened up important and meaningful conversation on many issues, each deeper and more profound than the last. After an hour of discussion and peeling away the layers, we were still going strong.

I asked the rabbinical student where the text came from.

"From the Talmud," he replied.

I had never heard of the Talmud, despite having attended religious school weekly since first grade. Feeling that I had discovered something amazingly wonderful, I asked, "Is there more of this?"

He laughed gently and said, "Yes. There are twenty volumes."

In college I came to realize that in order to study Talmud I would need to learn both Aramaic and Hebrew. I knew neither, but that memory of just a paragraph of Talmud still pulled at me.

In rabbinical school I acquired some of the tools to learn Talmud. Yet I did not have another experience like the one on that spring afternoon in high school.

For many years I struggled with Talmud, trying to wrest from it the profound sense of meaning and connection I had first experienced. It took a long time. Along the way, books and articles helped propel me and inspire me to keep learning.

Perhaps it has something to do with middle age (or perhaps I finally grew up?), but eventually things began to click into place. I think it has to do with a very special friend, Rabbi Louis Rieser. We met at a rabbinic study retreat nearly a decade ago. I was already a fan of his thinking and writing, having read several of his articles about Hillel (that would subsequently be published in *The Hillel Narratives*). We became *chevruta* (study partners) for the week, and enjoyed our learning and conversations so much that we decided to continue after the formal week of learning ended.

Learning with a partner is a time-honored way to study Talmud, but not one I had experienced in rabbinical school, which in those days followed the Western academic model ("Keep your eyes on your own paper").

Each week we would log on to Skype and begin by sharing our lives. Then we would open the Talmud and settle into learning, unpeeling layers of meaning and layering them with our personal and professional experiences as rabbis. We did not always study Talmud—the Torah commentaries of classical Hasidic masters occupied some of our time—but we always returned to Talmud, and it felt like coming home.

When we learned together, the terse sentences sprouted longer chains of meanings—implications for the way people live together and relate to one another, for the way communities function and people treat one another, and for the relationships that define and determine our lives. Some days we would look at a text and think, "It's flat, not much here," but then a single question would inspire three ideas and six more questions . . . and soon the "dull" or "inscrutable" text was a complex, magnificent three-dimensional palace of insights.

Over the years I have had the privilege of teaching Talmud locally, as well as in congregations around the country. Often I have experienced the joy of hearing other people say, "This stuff is wonderful and so meaningful!" and "I want to learn more of this!" As a teacher who knows this feeling from the inside out, it doesn't get better than that.

The purpose of this book is to share my learning and the wonder of Talmud with you. No particular background is required; my goal is to open Talmud to anyone who is interested. I hope that's you.

Why Was Talmud Written?

We can view the genesis of the Talmud through three lenses.

First, the turmoil of the first century, including the decimation of the priestly leadership in the wake of the Jerusalem Temple's destruction, created a void and gave rise to a community of scholars who ultimately authored the Talmud. Shaye Cohen, scholar of Hebrew literature and philosophy, expresses this view:

> In 70 CE, the temple was destroyed, the high priesthood and the Sanhedrin ceased to exist, and the priests lost not only their jobs but also the institutional base of their power. The Jewish community of the land of Israel no longer had a recognized social elite or "establishment," and the Jews of the Diaspora no longer had a center that bound them together. This was a vacuum the rabbis tried to fill. Ultimately they succeeded, but victory was gained only after a struggle. The rabbis were opposed by various segments among the wealthy and the priesthood and by the bulk of the masses in both Israel and the Diaspora. The local aristocracies, especially in the cities, were not going to subject themselves voluntarily to the hegemony of the new power group; the priests still thought of themselves as the leaders of the people; and the masses were indifferent to many aspects of rabbinic piety. The rabbis triumphed over their opponents among the aristocracy and the priesthood by absorbing them into their midst, or at least coming to

terms with them. The rabbis triumphed over the indifference of the masses by gradually gaining control of the schools and synagogues. The exact date of the triumph is hard to determine, but it was not earlier than the seventh century CE.[3]

Second, the Rabbis' rise was a function of their persistent political struggles. Stuart A. Cohen, scholar of Jewish political theory and practice, advances this view:

[The eventual hegemony of rabbinic Judaism in the life of the Jewish people] was not inevitable. Neither was there anything haphazard about the process whereby it occurred. In the political arena, as in others, the rabbis had to struggle for the realization of their ambitions—often from positions of intrinsic constitutional inferiority. If the enormity of their achievement is to be properly assessed, appropriate note must be taken of the persistence with which they pursued an essentially political campaign. Their avowed purpose was to confound the contrary aspirations of rival contestants, some sacerdotal, others civil, for whatever communal authority native Jewish agencies could still claim to command.[4]

Third, the Talmud is the realization of an innovative, experimental intellectual and religious project. Barry Holtz, scholar of Jewish education, offers this wonderful lens:

Consider for a moment the following thought experiment. Let us think of the Babylonian Talmud not as we usually do—not as a vast compendium of laws, legends, debates, and interpretations, but as a massive, multivolume, postmodern, experimental volume. Wilder than *Moby Dick*, beyond the imagination of James Joyce, more internally self-referential than anything dreamed up by David Foster Wallace. Hundreds of pages of dialogue, of discussions that start but never end; organized, it seems on the surface, by free association, and filled with hyperlinked cross-references across the wide expanse of its domain. It has no beginning and no conclusion. It just is. It is as if the Talmud expects that you have read it all before you've read a single page.[5]

Torah contains a wealth of ethical injunctions meant to shape how we live in community with one another—for example, business laws, civil and criminal laws, social justice laws—but many of these laws are geared for an ancient agricultural or shepherding society. The Sages (I use the term synonymously with Rabbis) sought to extend these values and priorities into their contemporary, increasingly urbanized and complex environment. They generated oral teachings, passed down from master to disciple, that included interpretation of Torah's laws for their more modern settings, as well as Rabbinic legislation, wisdom, and memories of how ritual had been conducted in the Second Temple.

Toward the end of the second century R. Yehudah ha-Nasi (Judah the Prince), living in *Eretz Yisrael* (the Land of Israel), feared that these oral traditions and teachings would be lost, and directed that they be committed to writing. The result of this herculean effort is the Mishnah (meaning "study" or "review"), a terse and compact catalog of practices and legal rulings complete with debate, minority opinions, and an occasional brief story or sermon.

Jews in the academies of *Eretz Yisrael* and Babylonia (where Jews had lived since the destruction of the First Temple and exile of 586 BCE) studied the Mishnah in depth, exploring its implications, debating the logic of its rulings, telling their own stories, providing anecdotal illustrations of principles articulated, and more. Over the next few centuries the Sages of both *Eretz Yisrael* and Babylonia produced a Gemara (meaning "learn") containing the Rabbis' questions, analyses, discussions, and debates. Actually they produced two Gemaras: one composed in Babylonia (the Babylonian Talmud, or Bavli) and the other in the Land of Israel (the Jerusalem Talmud, or Yerushalmi).

The Jerusalem Talmud, composed primarily in the academies of Tiberias and Caesarea and completed around 400 CE, is the shorter of the two Talmuds; it clocks in at seven volumes. (While the Bavli contains Gemara discussions for sixty-three tractates of the Mishnah, the Yerushalmi has Gemara for only thirty-seven tractates.) When people say "the Talmud," they are referring to the twenty-volume-long Babylonian Talmud, composed and redacted primarily in the academies of Sura and Pumbedita and completed around 600 CE, which has long enjoyed precedence. Thus far, the Bavli enjoys far more influence and attention than the Yerushalmi.

The Five Books of Moses have come to be called *Torah she-bi-khtav* (the Written Torah) and the Talmud *Torah she b'al peh* (Oral Torah) because the Rabbis made the audacious and brilliant claim that the People of Israel received the Talmud at Mount Sinai at the same time that Moses received the Torah. Unlike Torah, however, which was immediately written down, the Talmud was transmitted orally from generation to generation for fourteen hundred years until, at the end of the second century CE, R. Yehudah ha-Nasi arranged that the Mishnah be written down.

This is a remarkable claim, given that Talmud is packed with the names and teachings of the Rabbis, who lived between the second and sixth centuries (long after Sinai!). Historically, extraordinary Sages had combined the laws and values of the Written Torah, the needs of their contemporary communities, and their keen rational skills of logic and argumentation to produce a masterpiece of religious literature with enduring spiritual value. The Rabbis' larger claim was their way of asserting divine authority for their project, which was to live in covenant with God in a world without the Temple.

The first chapter and verse of Pirkei Avot (Ethics of the Ancestors) — arguably serving as the introduction to Talmud — begins with a beautiful image of *shalshelet ha-kabbalah* (the chain of tradition). Here is how Talmud explains its origin, which it locates in the same experience of revelation that gave the People of Israel the Torah:

Moses received the Torah from Sinai and transmitted it to Joshua, and Joshua [transmitted it] to the elders, and the elders [transmitted it] to the prophets, and the prophets transmitted it to the members of the Great Assembly. They said three things, "Be deliberate in judgment, raise up many students, and make a fence around the Torah." (Pirkei Avot 1:1)

According to tradition, the Great Assembly was a synod of 120 Sages, scribes, and prophets who governed Israel from the end of the biblical period of prophets and who were active from the eighth through the fifth centuries before the Common Era, through the early Rabbinic period of the first two centuries CE. Today, many scholars question whether the Great Assembly ever existed; the Rabbis may have imagined such an institution to form a bridge from the biblical prophets to the beginning of the Rabbinic period—and hence an unbroken chain for transmission of the tradition.

Whether or not the Great Assembly is historical or legendary, the opening of Pirkei Avot demonstrates that the Rabbis are deeply invested in their claim that they are the rightful heirs of the Torah tradition, the latest link in an unbroken chain of divine revelation that goes back to Mount Sinai. Moses, Joshua, the elders, the prophets, the members of the Great Assembly, and the Rabbis are all links in this chain, as is every generation after them. When Pirkei Avot 1:1 speaks of the Torah, it intends to include the Oral Torah (the Talmud) as well.

Reconciling the claim that both Written Torah and Oral Torah were given at Mount Sinai with history is less confounding when we realize that Pirkei Avot is not making a historical claim at all. Rather, it is the Rabbis' way of declaring that Oral Torah has the same *authority* as Written Torah; it is the Sages' literary assertion that their enterprise commands the same respect and religious authority as the Five Books of Moses.

The Rabbis support their claim that Talmud has "Sinai status" in a most ingenious way; they tell a time travel story. Moses, the Giver of

Torah, goes "back to the future." He doesn't find Dr. Emmett Brown or his parents, but he does find R. Akiva—Akiva b. Yosef, a *tanna* of the latter first century and early second century. Swept some fourteen centuries into the future, Moses finds himself sitting in the back row of R. Akiva's classroom. As remarkable as it is that the Rabbis imagined time travel so long ago, perhaps even more significant is that they paired R. Akiva with Moses, whom the Rabbis called *Moshe Rabbenu* (Moses, our rabbi) and who is revered as the Giver of Torah. It is no coincidence that legend holds that R. Akiva lived 120 years—like Moses.

Legend also holds that Akiva b. Yosef rose from obscurity—an unlettered shepherd who caught the eye of the daughter of his wealthy employer—and became the preeminent Sage of his generation. Quoted extensively in Mishnah, R. Akiva is attributed with systematizing halakhah (Jewish law) by developing hermeneutics (methods of biblical interpretation) to interpret the Bible in the realms of both halakhah and midrash. So great is his contribution to the development of Rabbinic Judaism, it is not unreasonable to dub R. Akiva the second Moses (as our story in chapter 1 of this volume subtly does).

With Talmud, the Sages reshaped Torah to thrive after the Second Temple's destruction. Consider the festivals observed to this day. The Written Torah (Five Books of Moses) instructs us to observe three yearly pilgrimage festivals that have deep roots in agricultural and shepherding cultures: Sukkot, Passover, and Shavuot.[6] When the Temple stood in Jerusalem, those who were able traveled to Jerusalem to celebrate these festivals. They brought sacrifices for the *kohanim* (priests) to offer on the altar in the Temple or purchased sacrifices once they arrived in Jerusalem. Each festival called for different sacrifices and celebratory rituals.

Today nearly two millennia have passed since Jews worshiped in this manner, but thanks to the Rabbis these festivals remain a vibrant and lively facet of Jewish life. Reshaping the festivals for life in exile, the

Rabbis identified them with the national myth that explains when, how, and why the People of Israel came into existence. Each yearly cycle of celebration tells the story of Israel.[7]

So, too, with other aspects of Jewish life. Without an altar on which to offer sacrifices to God, the Rabbis developed an order of daily prayers for worship and composed specific prayers to be used for all occasions. They put liturgical "flesh on the bones" of life-cycle passages mentioned in Torah, such as marriage and death, creating a rich tradition that taps into the sacred stories of the Jewish people. Hence in Talmud we find many traditions of the Passover seder, the order of prayers in the siddur (prayer book), the marriage ceremony under a chuppah (wedding canopy) with a ring and ketubah (marriage contract)—and, beyond these rituals, extensive discussions of Jewish values and ethics that inform our lives.

Taken together, the teachings, customs, practices, and laws the Rabbis developed and recorded in the Talmud provided the Jewish people with the traditions they needed not only to survive, but also to thrive.

Geography of the Talmud

Mishnah is the substrata, or foundation, of the Talmud. Specifically it is a collection of tannaitic oral teachings and descriptions of Second Temple practices from the first two centuries of the Common Era. Rabbi Yehudah ha-Nasi commissioned its writing in *Eretz Yisrael* at the end of the second century CE, lest the oral teachings be forgotten. Some modern scholars have speculated that the Mishnah was originally a set of lecture notes (which helps explain the tight and terse style of Mishnah) that came, in time, to be viewed as a sacred religious text.

On top of this foundation—and what now constitutes the bulk of the Babylonian Talmud—is Gemara. Nominally an elucidation of Mishnah, Gemara is in reality a lengthy and complex compilation of edited transcripts reflecting four centuries of conversations and debates launched and inspired by the Mishnah, along with additional notes, stories, and material. Gemara was probably written down in its present form (following a process of editing and redacting) toward the end of the sixth century CE.

The first printed edition of the Talmud—Daniel Bomberg's in Italy between 1520 and 1523—established the general formatting used to this day. A section of Mishnah is followed by the Gemara that discusses it. The commentary of the great French commentator Rashi (Rabbi Shlomo Yitzhaki) is printed on the inner margin near the binding. The commentary of the Tosafists (medieval rabbis from France and Germany, by and large Rashi's students, sons-in-law, and grandsons) is printed in the outer margin. Additional commentaries are often published at the end of each volume.

The Vilna edition of 1835 standardized the content and numbering of each folio or page (*daf*), beginning with *bet* (page 2). Initially the cover was considered the first page, but sometime afterward another explanation arose: there is no page 1 because there is no beginning or end to Talmud study—not only is it a lifelong pursuit, but discussions continue from generation to generation. Accordingly, the first page of each tractate is 2a. The recto (front side) is called *alef* (a) and the verso (reverse side) *bet* (b). Hence "BT Berakhot 25b" means Babylonian Talmud, Tractate Berakhot, page 25, verso side. The folios of the Jerusalem Talmud, abbreviated JT, are often named a, b, c, and d, but some publishers are renaming the folios using only a and b to conform to the standardized system employed for the Babylonian Talmud.

Finally, when a mishnah alone is cited, this is customarily done by chapter and the number of the mishnah within that chapter. Hence, M Berakhot 4:2 means Mishnah, Tractate Berakhot, chapter 4, second mishnah, and will be identified that way in a printed edition of the Mishnah. In the Talmud, however, M Berakhot 4:2 will be found on *daf* 28b. Hence I often cite both references for clarity—M Berakhot 4:2; 28b—to enable the reader to locate the text quickly in either publication.

The Texts in Talmud

Within Talmud we encounter a wide variety of discussions ranging from complex legal analysis, to folklore, to theological reflection and speculation. Discussions and decisions pertaining to civil law, criminal law, business ethics, and religious rites and observances are interspersed with discussions and legal dictates concerning family relationships, ethical conundrums, relations with non-Jews, and advice to scholars and community leaders. Even more: you can occasionally find a recipe, medicinal advice, magical incantations, strategies for avoiding evil spirits and dybbuks—and a dash of locker-room humor.

Talmud evinces a deep and thorough understanding of people. The Rabbis recognized the best and the worst in us—the realities of human proclivities, passions, aspirations, and potential—and from there charted a course for Jewish living. They discussed and enshrined the values that are the hallmark of Torah: love of God, family, and community; social justice, compassion, and human dignity; tzedakah (righteousness),[8] *gemilut chasadim* (deeds of loving-kindness),[9] and *derekh eretz* (decency);[10] Torah study and learning.

They also dove into the pool of theology and offered a broader array of views of God than Torah. They abstained from dictating dogma or creed, but did make generous use of metaphor, often imagining God's psyche and emotional states in starkly human terms. Particularly in the *aggadah* (stories), the Rabbis attribute to God a wide range of intense emotions, including passion, compassion, anger, and jealousy. On several occasions they depict God as dangerously irrational and potentially out of control. The Rabbis' struggle to understand the world in which they find themselves crosses paths with their struggle to understand God and divine will. Human fallibility and divine temperament sit side by side in the study house, often overlapping, and open for examination and discussion.

Embedded too in Talmud are many stories (*aggadah*, from the Hebrew root for "tell" or "recount"). Cloaked in deceptively simple exteriors, these multifaceted tales discuss and illustrate highly sophisticated and potent religious ideas. Sometimes the stories illustrate a point, other times undermine the point, and always deepen the conversation taking place. By studying and discussing them and peeling away the layers, we discover ourselves in the stories: our relationships, our challenges and dilemmas, our dreams and aspirations, our frustrations and sorrows, our ideals and successes. Talmud is filled with treasures to be savored.

Talmud is even more than this. It teaches us, by its example, that disagreement and debate are healthy and good because they generate more ideas and deeper thinking. Thus, we are free to differ over just about every issue imaginable. At the same time, *how* we engage with one another in conversation, debate, and analysis is enormously important. The Rabbis understood that disagreement can lead to a healthy generation of new ideas or it can become malicious and cruel, and thereby rupture a relationship. They taught the concept of *machloket l'shem shamayim* (a controversy for the sake of heaven) as a criterion to ensure that one remains within a healthy boundary. The motivation for the disagreement is key: if one's purpose is to trounce, demean, and demoralize one's opponent, the approach is morally wrong. Debates that deteriorate into rancor and hostility do not result in Torah learning; their only lasting effect is to damage the people involved—and, ultimately, the broader community. Pirkei Avot encapsulates this important teaching:

> A controversy for heaven's sake will have lasting value, but a controversy that is not for heaven's sake will not endure. What is an example of a controversy that is for heaven's sake? The debates of Hillel and Shammai. What is an example of a controversy that is not for heaven's sake? The rebellion of Korach and his followers.[11]

This text impugns Korach, who fomented a rebellion against Moses and Aaron in the wilderness (Numbers 16). Korach presented his claims as a valid disagreement—thus, as if he were serving heaven—when in reality his true motivation was to gain power and control over the community. In contrast Pirkei Avot holds up as exemplars Hillel and Shammai, the leaders of the two predominant schools of thought in the Jewish community in the late first century BCE and early first century CE when Oral Torah was first developing.[12] The Talmud records more than three hundred matters in which Hillel and Shammai voiced differences of opinion. Because their goal was to foster Torah learning and serve God, and they thereby conducted their disputations honestly and civilly, their disagreements are deemed appropriate. Talmud teaches:

> For three years there was a dispute between Bet Shammai and Bet Hillel, the former asserting, "The halakhah ['legal ruling'] is in agreement with our views" and the latter contending, "The halakhah is in agreement with our views." Then a *bat kol* ['heavenly voice'] issued forth, announcing, "Both these and these are the words of the living God, but the halakhah is in agreement with the rulings of Bet Hillel."
>
> If both are "the words of the living God" what was it that entitled Bet Hillel to have the halakhah fixed in agreement with their rulings? Because they were kind and humble, they studied their own rulings and those of Bet Shammai, and were even so [humble] as to mention the opinions of Bet Shammai before their own.[13]

Talmud sets the bar wonderfully high for civil conversation and debate—teaching us to ask questions, think deeply, argue passionately, reason intelligently, seek responsible answers, remain civil—and keep our sights on heaven.

It's All about Relationships

How would you identify yourself? By your profession, religion, age, ethnicity, sexual orientation, accomplishments, possessions, background, appearance, personality, or life goals? Or perhaps by your religious beliefs and political commitments? Would you describe yourself as an athlete, a Ravens fan, a woodworker? Imagine that all these categories—all the attributes and descriptors we assign to ourselves and others assign to us—are the weft or crosswise threads of the tapestry of our lives. They change as we weave through time, lending our tapestry an easily identifiable color and texture, as well as a recognizable look: "Oh, that tapestry is Sarah!" or "Anyone can see that tapestry is Abraham!" While we might recognize another by their weft threads, that is usually not enough for us to recognize ourselves.

Warp threads, by contrast, are the lengthwise threads strung tightly to the loom, holding the weaving together. They are the relationships of our lives, the people we love and who love us, those whom we take care of and those who nurture us: parents, children, partners, other relatives, friends and neighbors, teachers, colleagues—and God, however we may conceive God.

Unlike weft threads, warp threads enable us to discover who we are. In the end it is through our relationships with others that we come to know our own selves. Ralph Waldo Emerson wrote, "Other men are lenses through which we read our own minds."[14]

The talmudic stories chosen for this book all speak to our life relationships: with ourselves, with God, with our families, within the Jewish community, and beyond. I selected them because they are marvelous stories in and of themselves and because they offer us a lens through which to examine pressing concerns in our lives and issues of great importance in our world.

My hope is that as each of us works to improve our relationships through the lens of Talmud, the tapestry of our lives will grow ever more beautiful.

Using This Book

Talmud is a difficult text to read. Therefore, the traditional way to learn is with a guide (teacher) and a study partner (*chevruta*), the very same way the Talmud came into being in the study houses of Babylonia and

Eretz Yisrael. To this day, people study Talmud with a *chevruta* partner and in small groups.

This book is intended to be your *chevruta* partner (but by all means find yourself a study partner with whom to share it) or to be used as a classroom, family, or informal study text. Each chapter begins with an overview, "Why Study This Passage?," intended to orient the reader toward the theme of the story and provide the literary and historical background needed to understand and appreciate the passage. Subsequently, "A Broad View to Begin" places the passage into the larger picture of Rabbinic discussion about a moral or theological principle of concern. Next comes "Exploring the Nooks and Crannies of Our Passage" in which the passage is presented in English translation, together with detailed explanation and analysis. From there, "Continuing the Conversation" offers provocative questions arising from the passage and related texts to ponder on one's own or discuss with others. Finally, the concluding section, "Summing Things Up," places the chapter's larger relationship discussion into perspective. Some readers may wish to begin by reading this summary.

Translations and Abbreviations

Translation can be tricky business. A brochure translated from Mandarin into English, dubbed the worst-ever translation, illustrates this: "Getting There: Our representative will make you wait at the airport. The bus to the hotel runs along the lake shore. Soon you will feel pleasure in passing water. You will know that you are getting near the hotel, because you will go round the bend. The manager will await you in the entrance hall. He always tries to have intercourse with all new guests."[15]

Another example: The first week my husband and I lived in Israel as students, before we knew Hebrew, we received a hand-scrawled note from his relatives in Netanya. They had called the university switchboard and the Israeli student on duty took their message and helpfully translated it to English for us. Here's what we received: "We order you to come on

Shabbat, but you must not come." Bewildered, we decided that if they had gotten in touch that meant they wanted us to visit, so we hopped a bus and showed up Friday afternoon. Some months later, we learned that the verb *l'haz'min* means both "invite" and "order," and that *atem lo mukhrachim* means "you don't have to." Our invitation would have been better translated, "We invite you to come, but you don't have to if you don't want to."

An Italian proverb has it that *traduttore traditore*—"the translator is a traitor." While translations never fully substitute for the original text, I hope that my translations will elucidate rather than skew or obscure the Talmud's meaning. I have tried to achieve a balance between the cadence of Talmud and the needs of an English reader.

Talmud is written primarily in a terse Aramaic, sprinkled with Hebrew and punctuated with biblical verses, sayings, and proverbs. A conversation or story will often favor pronouns over names (e.g., "he said to him"). I have added names in square brackets (e.g., "[R. Yehoshua] said to [Rabban Shimon b. Gamliel]") for clarity, as well as additional explanatory verbiage (also in square brackets) to assist the reader.

Talmud does not supply citations for biblical verses; the Rabbis presume we have the entire Tanakh (Hebrew Scripture) memorized and accessible on a ROM chip in our brains. If only! Thus, they often cite only a section of a verse, and occasionally not even the most germane part of it. Moreover, the surrounding verses are sometimes equally important. It is generally a good idea to look up verses used as prooftexts to check their context and read the verses before and after them. Just in case you haven't had that ROM chip installed yet (mine is still on order), I often provide the full biblical verse plus citation, including the part of the verse not quoted by the Talmud in square brackets, to help the reader appreciate why this particular verse is used as a prooftext.

When quoting the Tanakh (Hebrew Scripture), I have generally used the New Jewish Publication Society translation[16] or the gender-sensitive adaption of the JPS Torah translation[17] except where I determined that my own translation would better convey the original Hebrew as the Sages understood it, and thereby help the reader better understand the Talmud's use of, and interpretation of, Scripture. In addition, I use my own translations in a few instances to reduce needlessly gendered language in the Prophets and Writings.

Here are three abbreviations you will see frequently in connection with talmudic citations:

M: Mishnah
BT: Babylonian Talmud (Bavli)
JT: Jerusalem Talmud (Yerushalmi)

Two additional abbreviations relate to people: The first is "R.," which connotes "Rabbi." As a title, "Rabbi" derives from *rav*, meaning "master" or "teacher." Rabbi, meaning "my teacher," came to be used by *tanna'im* (the Sages whose opinions are recorded in the Mishnah) and *amora'im* (the Sages of the Gemara) in the Land of Israel. *Rav* is the honorific title the *amora'im* in Babylonia generally used from the third century onward. The second is "b.," an abbreviation for "ben" (son) that, when used in a name, connotes "son of." Hence R. Yitzchak b. Avraham means "Rabbi Yitzchak, the son of Avraham." There is also a glossary in the back of this book; please reference it as needed.

Welcome to Talmud!

Welcome to the Talmud, a magnificent and crucially important work of Jewish sacred literature, the treasure that has been beneath our feet all along. I hope this book will whet the appetite of those of you tasting Talmud for the first time, as well as prove equally challenging, enriching, and delicious to those of you who have studied Talmud, making all of us hungry for more.

The Talmud of Relationships, Volume 2

PART 1 **SECOND SPHERE**

Relationships within the Jewish Community

1 Maintaining Self-Control

Babylonian Talmud, Tractate Menachot 44a

Ben Zoma taught: Who is mighty? The one who controls himself, as it says, *Better to be forbearing than mighty, to have self-control than to conquer a city* (Proverbs 16:32).

—Pirkei Avot 4:1

Why Study This Passage?

A meaningful relationship with God is a sine qua non for religious people. The nature of that relationship will vary greatly depending on how each person conceives God. Is God an independent power from without or the divine spark within? Is God a cosmic being or a set of sacred values and principles? When we engage with God, are we reaching beyond ourselves or looking deep within—or both? And who is the "I" in the relationship? If we could shine a light on the very core of our being, what would we find, and how would that discovery mediate our relationship with God?

In describing the human psyche, the Rabbis proposed that every person is endowed with a *yetzer*, an innate internal force that animates, motivates, and propels us in life. We possess both a *yetzer tov* (inclination for good) and a *yetzer ra* (inclination for evil). When we follow the *yetzer tov*, we do good; when we yield to the *yetzer ra*, we commit sins that harm our relationships with God and other people. These two inclinations—one drawing us toward goodness and the other tempting us with evil—are forever at odds with one another inside us because we generally want to do what is right but we are also tempted by what is forbidden. If only all pleasure and reward derived from doing the right thing!

For the *yetzer tov* and *yetzer ra* to operate in the way the Rabbis imagined, human beings must have free will and thereby the capacity to choose to follow the path of the *yetzer tov* and to distance themselves from the temptations of the *yetzer ra*. Indeed, the Rabbis affirmed time and again that we have free will and therefore bear responsibility for the choices we make.

In Pirkei Avot 2:16, R. Yehoshua b. Chananiah says that the evil inclination is one of three things that "take a person out of this world." A comment on R. Yehoshua's teaching in chapter 16 of the midrash *Avot de-Rabbi Natan*[1] gives us further insight into the Rabbis' thinking:

> The *yetzer ra* is older than the *yetzer tov* by thirteen years. In the mother's womb, the *yetzer ra* begins to develop and is born in the person. If he begins to profane Shabbat, it does not prevent him from doing so; if he commits murder, it does not prevent him from doing so; if he pursues a sexual transgression, it does not prevent him.
>
> Thirteen years later, the *yetzer tov* is born. When he profanes Shabbat, it reprimands him, saying: "Empty one! *One who profanes [Shabbat] shall be put to death* (Exodus 31:14)." If he goes to commit murder, it reprimands him, saying: "Empty one! *Whoever sheds human blood, by human [hands] shall that one's blood be shed* (Genesis 9:6)." If he pursues a sexual transgression, it reprimands him, saying: "Empty one! *[Both] the adulterer and the adulteress shall be put to death* (Leviticus 20:10)."
>
> When a man engages in sexual transgression, all his limbs obey him, for the *yetzer ra* rules over his 248 limbs [i.e., his entire body].

When he goes off to do a good deed, all his limbs begin to drag, for the *yetzer ra* within is sovereign over his 248 limbs, while the *yetzer tov* is like a captive in prison, as it is said, *[Better a poor but wise youth than an old but foolish king who no longer has the sense to heed warnings.] For the former can emerge from a dungeon to become king* (Ecclesiastes 4:13–14);[2] that is to say, the *yetzer tov*.

The three sins mentioned in *Avot de-Rabbi Natan* are not arbitrary choices: biblically each is a capital crime. The midrash thereby asserts that these mitzvot are not obvious to a child; nor does a child have the moral sense or sophistication to avoid them prior to age thirteen, when a keener moral sense blooms and, accordingly, the child becomes obligated by the mitzvot (which is what becoming bar mitzvah or bat mitzvah means). The midrash quotes Ecclesiastes 4:14, which it understands metaphorically: the "poor but wise child" is the *yetzer tov* that emerges from "prison" at the age of thirteen; the "old but foolish king" is the *yetzer ra* that "rules" over his behavior to his detriment.

The midrash proceeds to focus on the sin of sexual transgression, citing Joseph's ability to resist Potiphar's wife, R. Tzaddok's ability to resist a beautiful maidservant that a Roman matron tempted him with while he was a captive in Rome, and R. Akiva's ability to resist two beautiful women "bathed and anointed and outfitted like brides [who spent the night] thrusting themselves at him."

The examples of Joseph, R. Tzaddok, and R. Akiva reveal yet another aspect of Rabbinic thinking on this matter: The Rabbis identified the *yetzer ra* as the male sexual urge and aggression, which they held to be a cause of much pain and violence in the world. At the same time, without the sexual urge, generativity and civilization would end, as the self-sustaining order of God's Creation would come to a grinding halt. Without the *yetzer ra*, "a man would not build a house, marry a woman, or father children."[3]

In time, the Rabbis came to speak of one undifferentiated *yetzer*, which we might term the "life force," the metaphysical energy that flows through us, animating our lives and fueling our will and desires. "Ben Zoma said, . . . Who is mighty? The one who conquers his *yetzer*, as it is written, *Better to be forbearing than mighty, to have self-control than to conquer a city* (Proverbs 16:32)."[4] No wonder they both feared and admired the *yetzer*.

Joseph, R. Tzaddok, and R. Akiva were exemplary righteous individuals. How is an ordinary person to avoid the power of his or her *yetzer ra*?

R. Shimon b. Elazar tells us: "The *yetzer ra* is like iron that is held in a flame. So long as it is in the flame, one can make of it any implement he pleases. So, too, the *yetzer ra*. Its only remedy is in the words of the Torah, for they are like fire, as it is said, *If your enemy is hungry, give him bread to eat; if he is thirsty, give him water to drink. You will be heaping live coals on his head, and Adonai will reward you* (Proverbs 25:21–22). In other words, feed the *yetzer ra* plenty of Torah.

Sexual desire, closely associated with the *yetzer*, can be overwhelming, and also sanctifying. In a permitted context, the Rabbis readily endorse sexuality and sexual pleasure. Taming and properly channeling the sexual urge is one of the greatest challenges many people face. God does not abandon us to this challenge, however. The mitzvah of tzitzit, fringes worn on the corners of one's garment, is intended to help the wearer fulfill his or her covenantal obligations.[5]

The delightful story in this chapter, told in Tractate Menachot 44a, demonstrates the reward for obeying the commandment of tzitzit in one's lifetime and speaks stunningly to the power of tzitzit to help people channel their *yetzer* toward good rather than sin. A young scholar's intense sexual desire steers him to the most beautiful and expensive prostitute known. Just in time, his tzitzit rescue him from committing sin. By itself, the story is a carefully crafted marvel with high literary value. In its talmudic context—a discussion of the mitzvah of tzitzit —it takes on much greater depth and meaning, conveying an important message about where and how we encounter God in our lives and what it means to have a relationship with God.

A Broad View to Begin

The story is situated within a discussion of the mitzvot of tzitzit (fringes), tefillin (phylacteries), and mezuzah—outward signs or technologies that serve as reminders attached to one's clothing, body, and home of the mitzvot that are to guide one's life, spurring one to do what God requires and instilling self-restraint to avoid succumbing to the *yetzer ra*. Torah instructs the Israelites to tie special fringes, tzitzit, to the corners of their garments, and attach a thread of blue (*p'til tekhelet*) to each: *That shall be your fringe; look at it and recall all the mitzvot of Adonai and observe them, so that you do not follow your heart and eyes in your lustful urge* (Numbers 15:39). A more precise translation of the last phrase of the verse is "and go whoring after them," referring to any human desire that is forbidden.

Tzitzit, then, are intended to serve as a constant reminder of the mitzvot, both positive (what we are obligated to do) and negative (what we may not do). *Thus you shall be reminded to observe all My mitzvot and be holy to your God* (Numbers 15:40). R. Eliezer b. Yaakov teaches that one who observes the mitzvah of tzitzit, together with tefillin and mezuzah, is fully guarded from sin, as reflected in Ecclesiastes 4:12: *A threefold cord is not quickly broken.*[6] The tzitzit, worn visibly while awake, are a first-line reminder or warning.

Perhaps the tzitzit provide a visual reminder that "God is watching." Abundant psychological evidence demonstrates that many people behave differently—better—when they believe they are being observed.[7] Ara Norenzayan, who explores the psychology of prosocial religions, writes: "The trial-and-error processes of cultural evolution stumbled on *supernatural monitoring*, a principle that piggybacks on preexisting capacities for social monitoring. If watched people are nice people, watchful deities—Big Eyes in the Sky—could encourage cooperation, even when no one is watching."[8]

Our story illustrates the claim that tzitzit protects the wearer from sin by reminding him or her of the mitzvot, and especially, as Torah expressed it so graphically, from that which our hearts and eyes "go whoring after." In fact, the story is a literal enactment of that phrase.

The redactors of the Talmud chose to place this story immediately following a comment about the expensive cost of the dye to make *tekhelet*, as if the point were, "Speaking of expensive, let me tell you a story about the most expensive prostitute in the world!" But the story turns out to be about the religious power of tzitzit. The meaning ascribed to the *tekhelet*, therefore, sets the spiritual tone for the story.

> It was taught: R. Meir used to say: Why is blue specifically singled out among the other colors [for the mitzvah of *tekhelet*]? Because blue resembles the color of the sea, and the sea resembles the color of the sky, and the sky resembles the color of [some editions add: a sapphire, and a sapphire resembles the color of] [God's] Throne of Glory, as it is said, *Under his feet there was the likeness of a pavement of sapphire [like the very sky for purity]* (Exodus 24:10), and it is also written, *[Above the expanse over their heads was] the semblance of a throne, in appearance like sapphire* (Ezekiel 1:26). . . . Our Rabbis taught: The *chilazon* resembles the sea in its color, and a fish in its shape. It appears only once every seventy years, and, with its blood, one dyes the blue thread; therefore, it is very expensive.[9]

The dye for *tekhelet* is produced from an exceedingly rare mollusk called a *chilazon*, which explains why it is very expensive. It requires both a substantial financial investment and considerable manufacturing effort, as R. Shmuel b. Rav Yehudah's recipe on 42b reveals. But even more significant for the Rabbis, *tekhelet* has a mystical quality. The two verses Talmud quotes layer additional meaning onto its color. In Torah's account of the Revelation at Mount Sinai, we are told that Moses, along with his brother, Aaron, two nephews, and seventy elders of Israel, ascends Mount Sinai where (yes, Torah really says this), *they saw the God of Israel: under [God's] feet there was the likeness of a pavement of sapphire, like the very sky for purity* (Exodus 24:10). Although they see God, it is the pavement beneath God that is described. It is a glistening, sparkling sky blue, comparable to sapphire.

The prophet Ezekiel also sees God. Ezekiel 1 includes a detailed description of God's chariot, which comprises a mélange of faces (human, lion, ox, eagle), wings, and legs. A sapphire-blue expanse (*raki'ah*, the same word used in Genesis 1:6 to connote "sky" or "heaven") stretches above the heads. *Above the expanse over their heads was the semblance of a throne, in appearance like sapphire; and on top, upon this semblance of a throne, there was the semblance of a human form* (Ezekiel 1:26).

The Talmud understands the blue thread that runs through the tzitzit to recall the two times that prophets of Israel had such close encounters with God: they glimpsed the pavement under God's feet and God's Throne of Glory. Perhaps the Rabbis also had in mind that when God sits on the dazzling blue Throne of Glory, or looks down at the sapphire pavement, God is reminded of the blue thread worn by Jews as a token of their commitment to God's covenant, and rewards their compliance with blessings.

Exploring the Nooks and Crannies of Our Passage

Talmud segues from the discussion on *tekhelet*—rare, expensive, and evocative of God and heaven—with this comment about the divine rewards bestowed on those who observe the mitzvah of tzitzit, which includes the thread of *tekhelet*:

> R. Natan said, "There is no mitzvah in the Torah so minor that its observance is not rewarded in this world. And concerning its reward in the world to come, I do not know how great it is. Go and learn this from the mitzvah of tzitzit."

Recall that Torah instructs Jewish men to wear tzitzit to serve as visual reminders not to let their hearts and eyes "go whoring after" what is forbidden. That is precisely—literally—what a young student does in this tale.

> There was once a man who was meticulous in the observance of the mitzvah of tzitzit. He heard that there was a prostitute in one of the towns by the sea who charged four hundred gold *dinarim* for her services. He sent her the fee and set an appointed time to meet her. When he arrived at the appointed time, her maid came and told her, "That man who sent you four hundred gold *dinarim* is here waiting at the door." She replied, "Let him come in." When he came in, she had prepared for him seven beds [one atop the other]: six of silver and the uppermost one of gold. Between the beds were six silver ladders, and a golden ladder led to the uppermost one. She then went up to the top bed and lay down on it naked. In his desire, he went up after her to sit naked with her, but suddenly the four tzitzit struck him across the face.
>
> He got down and sat on the ground. She also got down and sat on the ground.

Consider how much planning was involved here. This woman is not an ordinary prostitute; a man must wait a long time to secure an appointment, and she commands an exceedingly high fee to be paid in advance at the time the appointment is set. We never learn her name, but historically there were many such women in the Roman Empire. Elite courtesans served the power brokers of Rome and, as a result, were wealthy in their own right. (Note that she has a servant who waits on her.) Cytheris, who lived in the first century BCE, was just such a courtesan. She was educated, artistic, and charming—a frequent dinner guest among the highest echelons of Roman society. She was the favored companion of Mark Antony until he fell in love with Cleopatra. Ovid and others penned erotic elegies to such women.[10]

How long would it take for a young Torah scholar to amass the four hundred gold *dinarim* required for her fee?[11] The high fee mirrors the intensity of his desire; waiting enhances his anticipation. By the time the appointed day arrives, his desire has reached fever pitch. The courtesan's maid escorts him into her elegant boudoir. She has prepared lavishly for him. Certainly seven beds of silver and gold, stacked one on top of the other, is hyperbolic, but it might help here to picture famous paintings of odalisques by Ingres, Delacroix, Renoir, Matisse, and others; although odalisques were concubines, the opulent décor of their chambers supplies a sense of what the young man would have seen. Perhaps Manet's painting *Olympia* serves us even better, both because Olympia herself is a wealthy courtesan with her own servant and because she, like the woman in this story, is self-aware and confident.

The woman ascends the seven beds and lies down naked, seductively waiting for the young man to join her. He ascends posthaste—the reader can imagine him vaulting up the ladders—yet before he can fully disrobe, the tzitzit fly up from his garment and slap him across the face: Wake up! Do you realize where you are and what you're about to do! Awaken from this fantasy and come back down to earth!

Are the flying tzitzit dramatic or humorous—or both? Talmud leaves the reader to decide. Perhaps the animated tzitzit convey the sense that God is watching. A story is told of the Chofetz Chaim, Rabbi Israel Meir ha-Kohen Kagan (1839–1933), who was once traveling home in a horse-drawn cart. His driver, unaware of his passenger's identity and importance, stopped the cart along the road next to an apple orchard. "Look out for me," he said. "I'm going to get a few apples. Let me know if someone sees." Jumping out of the cart, he headed into the orchard.

The rabbi called out, "Someone sees!" and the driver quickly scurried back to the cart. They drove on farther and came to another apple orchard.

Again, the driver jumped down and told his passenger to serve as lookout. Once again, no sooner had the driver set foot in the orchard than the Chofetz Chaim called out, "Someone sees!" and the driver came running back.

This time the driver looked around and, not spotting a soul, said to the Chofetz Chaim, "I don't see anyone. No one was watching me. Why did you tell me twice now that someone sees when there isn't anyone around?"

The rabbi replied, "Someone always sees. Even when other people cannot see what we do, God sees and knows. And so do we in our hearts."

As God sees, the young man sees himself through God's eyes. And he is not alone. The woman observes his behavior and is determined to understand it.

> She said to him, "[I swear] by the Roman Emperor that I will not leave you until you reveal to me what blemish you found in me!" He said to her, "[I swear by the temple] worship that I have never seen a woman as beautiful as you. However, there is one mitzvah that we were commanded by our God, and tzitzit is its name. Concerning this mitzvah, it is twice stated in the Torah, *I am Adonai your God* [meaning] I am the One who will exact retribution in the future, and I am the One who will reward in the future. Now the [tzitzit] appeared to me as four witnesses [testifying against me]."

The woman is shocked. No one has ever rejected her. After all, she is the most beautiful, desirable, enticing, and erotic woman in the world. What man can resist her? Even more, *how* did this man resist her? Her first thought is that the young man has found fault in her. Even she, who enthralls the elite and commands both their wealth and attention, is human and vulnerable.

The enormous cultural chasm between them is evident in the use of the expressions, "By the Roman Emperor!" and "By the temple worship!" The woman is entrenched in the pagan world of Rome and its idolatrous cults; for her, the Roman Emperor is the most fearsome power in the world. The young man is a student of Torah and devoted to the temple sacrifices (although this story postdates the Jerusalem Temple's destruction, the Rabbis nonetheless longed for the Temple to be rebuilt); God is the ultimate power in the universe.

As the man and woman sit together on the floor naked, their fundamental religious and cultural differences are evident as well. The reader is led to believe that the woman is merely an object to this man, and he merely a customer to her. Therefore, a genuine relationship between them is impossible. But is it?

It would seem that all is revealed, yet the woman perceptively says she will not permit the young man to leave until he reveals *himself* to her. She senses that there is much more to him than meets the eye.

> She said, "I still will not let you leave until you provide me with your name, the name of your city, the name of your teacher, and the school in which you study Torah." He wrote down all the information and placed it in her hand.

This woman of confidence, authority, and power, accustomed to issuing orders and being obeyed, is drawn to this young man; but what is his formidable commitment that overpowers her allure? She must know, but, as we will soon see, she wants to know it intimately, just as she wants to know him intimately. His rejection of her has drawn her to desire him on a much deeper level. No longer is their relationship a business transaction where sex is a commodity. She wants to understand who he is at the core: what is the Torah that makes him tick?

The woman demands the man's personal information in writing. Why add this detail about writing down his personal information? This is the Rabbis' way of signaling us that the young man is not merely giving her his business card; he is giving her his own personal "torah": his name, town, and especially the name of his Rabbi and school, are key to truly understanding his being. The image of the young student handing the woman his torah evokes the image of God giving the Torah to Moses on Mount Sinai—face to face. The image created is one of a covenant forged between the two.

As receiving God's Torah was a transformative experience for Israel, so is receiving this man's torah transformative for the woman. She transforms herself, leaving the world of Roman culture and her life as a prostitute. She escapes her Egypt, redeemed by the young man's torah.

> She arose and sold all her possessions. [She gave] a third of her money to the government, a third to the poor, and she took a third with her, as well as the bedding, and went to the *bet midrash* of R. Chiyya. She said to him, "Rabbi, instruct me and convert me." He said to her, "My daughter, perhaps one of the students has caught your eye?" She pulled out the writing and gave it to him. He said to her, "Go and possess what you have purchased."

The next step in the woman's self-transformation is to sell her material possessions, all the trappings of her life as a Roman courtesan. The manner in which she distributes her wealth tells us a great deal about her character. She gives a portion to the government, a nod to her past and an expression of gratitude to the society that supported her in her lifestyle. She donates a third to tzedakah, demonstrating that she is already subscribing to Jewish values and looking ahead to her future life commitments.[12] She retains a third of her wealth to fund her travel and living expenses as she sets out in quest of a life with the young man who turned her world upside down. The one and only physical item of her past that she keeps is the lavish and luxurious bedding she prepared for him that was not used when the tzitzit fulfilled their purpose.

When the woman arrives at the *bet midrash* of R. Chiyya bar Abba, she demands that he teach her in preparation for conversion. The woman's imperious manner catches R. Chiyya's attention, and seeing the woman before him, he undoubtedly recognizes her background. Reading the note she carries, written by the hand of his own student, he deduces what has transpired. Comprehending that this woman is drawn to his student's deep devotion to Torah and mitzvot, R Chiyya acknowledges this by saying that she has already "purchased" the right to convert by having *sold* all her possessions and left her previous life to follow him and become a Jew. Alternatively, he may have meant: "Certainly, I will help you convert so that you can possess the man you have already married in your heart [i.e., fallen in love]." R. Chiyya's response is a pun: "What you have purchased" comes from the root *lamed-kof-chet*, which is used for both "purchase" and "marriage." His rejoinder is especially curious because traditionally the man "acquires" the woman in marriage; here she is the agent and the man is the acquisition.

There is yet another beautiful pun implicit in the story: the Aramaic term *z'chi* (verb, "possess") also means "become pure." R. Chiyya is more than willing to consider her change of heart sufficient to erase the "blemish" of prostitution in her background. Her love of Torah and the young man purifies her.

The Rabbis compose an uncharacteristically romantic closing for the story: The sole material possession the woman has retained is the sumptuous bedding she prepared but never used—never consummated—with the young student. Now that she has converted, the bedding adorns their bridal bed, where they will consummate their sanctified love for one another.

The very same bedding that she had prepared for him illicitly she now prepared for him lawfully.

While this would have been a lovely note on which to end the story, it closes with a tagline that matches its opening. Recall that the story began: "R. Natan said, 'There is no mitzvah in the Torah so minor that its observance is not rewarded in this world. And concerning its reward in the world to come, I do not know how great it is. Go and learn this from the mitzvah of tzitzit.'" The Rabbis now comment:

Such is the reward [for observing the mitzvah of tzitzit] in this world. Who knows how great is the reward in the world to come!

We have returned to the subject and purpose of the story: the illustration of the singular importance of the mitzvah of tzitzit, because it serves to remind one throughout the day of all the other commandments incumbent on a Jew.

The story of the young student and the courtesan illustrates this principle in a fascinating way: delving into a rich and evocative male fantasy of winning the heart and mind of an extraordinarily beautiful, desirable, and sexually experienced woman. This young student is alone among men in being pursued ardently and arduously by the very woman other men must wait a long time, and expend exorbitant amounts of money, to bed. What is more, she renounces her life and status in Roman society in favor of becoming a Jew; she relinquishes the material riches she has amassed in favor of becoming his wife and lover forever after. Could a young man imagine a more exquisite reward in *olam ha-zeh* (this world)? How much greater, the Rabbis postulate, is the reward in *olam ha-ba* (the world to come)?

On the surface, this is a charming tale about a young man whose tzitzit dramatically (and humorously) save him from sin—who then is rewarded in kind with precisely the prize he chose to forego in deference to Torah's standards of behavior. But it is also far more.

Underscoring the message about commitment to the mitzvot is a subtler story about finding God not "out there" but in one's core sense of self and one's religious commitments. The young man must look within himself to find the commitment and corresponding willpower that for him bespeaks God. This is the personal "torah" that he writes down for the woman, chiefly his teacher and the school where he studies Torah. The woman comprehends, appreciates, and admires the depths of his spirituality. In fact, she is so utterly taken by it, she gives up everything to join the Jewish community and participate in his spiritual venture.

Considering the story's placement, immediately following the Gemara's discussion of *tekhelet*, perhaps there is yet another layer of meaning. When the young man's tzitzit fly up and slap him across the face, the reader imagines a sky-blue thread of *tekhelet* running through them. The courtesan's services are costly because they are valuable and greatly prized. So, too, is the *tekhelet* costly—required by Torah and exceedingly rare—but why? Its religious value lies in its meaning and connotations: *tekhelet* reflects the visions of God that Moses beheld and Ezekiel expressed through commitment to the mitzvot. The Rabbis do not hope to behold God directly, as Moses and Ezekiel did. They cannot even offer sacrifices on the temple altar, which once constituted Israel's nexus with heaven, because it was torn down in 70 CE. But they can keep the mitzvot, tangible acts that provide a "vision" of the Divine. On this deeper level, the story is about securing a glimpse of God through the mitzvot.

Continuing the Conversation

1. *Whence Strength?*

The courtesan sees that the young Torah scholar's source of strength is his self-restraint. He can control his *yetzer ra*. He explains to her that he does so with the aid of the tzitzit. To what degree is self-control a measure of strength? What helps you gain a greater measure of self-control?

Here are some thoughts on self-control from a variety of sources. Do you agree or disagree with each?

> "You have power over your mind, not over outside events. Realize this and you will find strength." (Marcus Aurelius, 121–180 CE)
> "Those who restrain desire do so because theirs is weak enough to be restrained." (William Blake, 1757–1827)
> "One can be the master of what one does, but never of what one feels." (Gustave Flaubert, 1821–1880)
> "To handle yourself, use your head; to handle others, use your heart." (Eleanor Roosevelt, 1884–1962)
> "I am very happy because I have conquered myself and not the world. I am very happy because I have loved the world and not myself." (Sri Shinmoy, 1931–2007)

2. The Role of Ritual

The Jewish ritual of tzitzit is multifaceted. First, it serves to remind the wearer to fulfill God's commandments (much as once a red string tied around the finger served as a reminder, or as an alarm set on a smartphone does today). Second, wearing tzitzit is a mitzvah in and of itself. Third, tzitzit are a visible sign of Jewish identity. Thus, people wear tzitzit as a reminder, for the sake of the mitzvah, and to mark themselves as Jews. If you do or were to wear tzitzit, how would you prioritize these three reasons for doing so, and why?

While some people believe rituals are ineffectual superstitious behaviors, Francesca Gino and Michael Norton of the Harvard Business School write in *Scientific American*: "Recent research suggests that [religious and secular] rituals may be more rational than they appear. Why? Because even simple rituals can be extremely effective [for example, in facing loss, reducing anxiety, achieving focus, and alleviating disappointment].... Despite the absence of a direct causal connection between the ritual and the desired outcome, performing rituals with the intention of producing a certain result appears to be sufficient for that result to come true."[13]

What is the place and purpose of ritual in your life? Do you practice rituals that have produced a desired result?

Rabbi Bradley Artson, addressing many modern Jews' perception that a dichotomy exists between rituals and social justice, notes that Leviticus 19 and 20 interweave a variety of mitzvot that are often separated into "ritual" and "social justice" concerns, thus testifying that Torah does not recognize this dichotomy. Neither should we, Artson argues, because ritual and ethics not only complement one another, they reinforce one another:

> Ritual requires ethics to root it in the human condition, to force it to express human needs and to channel urges, to serve human growth and to foster insight. Ethics requires ritual to lend substance to lofty ideals, to remind, on a regular basis, of ethical commitments

already made, and to create a community of shared values and high standards. Ritual without ethics becomes cruel. Ethics without ritual becomes hollow.

One of Judaism's central insights is to fuse ritual and ethics into a single blazing light—the *mitzvah* (commandment)—and then to reorient that new composite creation—holiness—to reflect the very nature of God. Our standard is no longer tailored to concede our own imperfections or to cater to our mendacity.

Ethics alone make man the measure of all things. Ritual alone surrenders the intellect to the power of unregulated passion. As many people have perished from emotion unleashed as from an unfeeling mind. The two need each other to teach restraint, balance, and compassion. By blending ritual and ethics, we shift the focus from our perspective to God's. "You shall be holy, for I, Adonai your God, am holy."[14]

Do you agree? How can ritual and ethics be complementary and reinforcing in your life?

3. *The* Chilazon

The *chilazon* is the creature used to make the dye for *tekhelet*, the blue thread of the tzitzit. On the same *daf* of Talmud, just prior to the story in this chapter, Talmud tells us: "Our Rabbis taught: The color of the *chilazon* resembles the sea, its shape resembles a fish, it comes up once in seventy years, and one uses its blood to dye the *tekhelet* and therefore its blood is very expensive."[15] The courtesan is like the *chilazon* in several ways. She lives *near* the sea, just as the *chilazon* lives *in* the sea. She, too, is very expensive and is rarely encountered, since few men could hope to be with her even once in a lifetime. At the same time, she is the antithesis of *tekhelet*: she draws one away from the mitzvot, at least until she, herself, is drawn to them.

What other things, people, or experiences in our lives are exotic and enticing, but also dangerous? Do we sometimes choose to view them from the *"chilazon* angle," seeing good where it does not exist and ignoring the danger? Are there aspects of our lives that are both good in the proper measure, but dangerous when not held in check?

4. The Reward for Fulfilling a Mitzvah

The story of the young student ostensibly claims that God rewards those who perform the mitzvot. However, a teaching of the early second-century Sage Shimon ben Azzai expresses a different view:

> Ben Azzai says: Run to perform a minor mitzvah and flee from sin, for one mitzvah leads to another mitzvah, and one sin leads to another sin. Thus, the reward for [performing] a mitzvah is a mitzvah, and the punishment for [committing] a sin is a sin.[16]

According to Ben Azzai, one should not expect material reward for performing a mitzvah. Rabbi Shmuel de Uzeda (born c.1540), a disciple of Rabbi Isaac Luria,[17] explains Ben Azzai's teaching in *Midrash Shmuel*, a collection of midrashic commentaries he edited on Pirkei Avot:

> Rabbenu Yonah[18] teaches two reasons why one mitzvah leads to the fulfillment of another: Fulfilling one mitzvah reinforces good habits and causes one to have divine assistance. Furthermore, he writes that it would be inappropriate to expect reward in this world for the fulfillment of mitzvot—the essential reward for mitzvot is given in the next world. In this world, however, we are rewarded for having fulfilled mitzvot by being given the opportunity to fulfill even more mitzvot.[19]

What do you believe are the rewards for fulfilling mitzvot? Have you found that fulfilling one mitzvah has led to your fulfilling others? Do you believe the opportunity to fulfill even more mitzvot in this world is, in fact, its own reward?

5. Tekhelet and Mysticism

People throughout the ages have sought to glimpse, encounter, or experience God. One strategy for achieving this goal is mysticism. The Rabbis note that when Moses and Ezekiel saw God, each concurrently beheld a dazzling shade of sapphire blue. The Rabbis mention this striking shade of blue in a famous story in the Bavli that is understood as a warning about the dangers of delving into the deep and roiling waters of mysticism in order to elevate one's ontological level in an effort to glimpse God (often described as "seeing God's chariot").

The story concerns four Rabbis who enter a *pardes* (orchard), a metaphor for mysticism.

> The Rabbis taught [in a *baraita*]: There were four who entered the *pardes* ['orchard'] and these are them: Ben Azzai, Ben Zoma, Acher [Elisha b. Abuyah], and R. Akiva. R. Akiva said to them, "When you arrive at the pure marble stones, do not say, 'Water! Water!' because it says, *One who speaks untruth shall not stand before my eyes* (Psalm 101:7)." Ben Azzai glanced and died. Concerning him, it says, *The death of his faithful ones is grievous in [God's] sight* (Psalm 116:15). Ben Zoma glanced and was stricken. Concerning him, Scripture says, *If you find honey, eat only what you need, lest, surfeiting yourself, you throw it up* (Proverbs 25:16). Acher mutilated the roots. R. Akiva emerged whole. (BT Chagigah 14b)

Of the four Sages who immerse themselves in mystical practice and speculation, only R. Akiva emerges unscathed. Apparently he issued a warning to his colleagues but they either did not, or could not, comply. Ben Azzai lost his life, Ben Zoma lost his mind, and Elisha b. Abuyah lost his Jewish grounding and became a heretic.

R. Akiva describes his vision in terms of pure marble and water, reflective of both the heart of the sea and the vault of heaven: God within and God "out there." Do you think that the young Torah scholar would say that God is outside him, watching him from a realm beyond our world and commanding from on high? Or would he say that to find God, one must look deep within, into one's heart and soul? In what ways does the story support both images?

Does either image fit your understanding of God in your life? Are there other images that resonate with you?

Summing Things Up

The talmudic story of the young student and the courtesan combines the themes of loyalty to God's mitzvot and the reward that comes from performing them, against the backdrop of one of the biggest challenges presented by human nature: the *yetzer ra* that perpetually threatens to give in to myriad temptations to violate God's will. The Rabbis uphold tzitzit—and the commitment to God's mitzvot that they represent—as an important and effective ritual or technique to help one reverse course and reclaim self-control even in the most extreme situation. The process, in turn, of recalling one's commitment and exerting self-control is, for the Rabbis, an experience of the Divine, whether one conceives of God as the commanding power from without or the divine spark within.

2 Respecting Human Dignity

Babylonian Talmud, Tractate Berakhot 27b–28a

R. Eliezer says, "Let your neighbor's dignity be as precious to you as your own."

—Pirkei Avot 2:10

Why Study This Passage?

Reams have been written on "leadership style." A recent search on amazon .com netted more than twenty-five hundred book offerings, from leadership for introverts to spiritual leadership, from leadership through coaching to toxic leadership, from being a "kick-ass boss" to "the servant leader." Business schools devote entire courses to the subject. Surrounded by all this new material, many do not realize that some of the earliest, richest discussions of leadership style can be found in talmudic narratives.

Talmud would support, for example, this oft-quoted remark by the nineteenth-century British historian, politician, and writer Lord John Dahlberg-Acton: "Power tends to corrupt, and absolute power corrupts absolutely. Great men are almost always bad men."[1] As the Talmud teaches, truly great leaders empower others—and those who are in positions to exert power and authority, but do not temper it with self-awareness, self-control, and humility are in grave danger of abusing others.

An appropriate use of power is inextricably bound up with an understanding of, and attentiveness to, human dignity. The deployment of authority at others' expense can not only diminish each individual's dignity, but also reduce the morale and well-being of families, institutions, and communities.

On a steamy tropical day in 2003, psychologist Donna Hicks, an associate at the Weatherhead Center for International Affairs at Harvard University, stood before a room filled with military and civilian leaders in Colombia, a country so steeped in conflict and hostility after decades of civil war that the people in the room avoided eye contact with one another. She and her partner, Ambassador José María Argueta, had planned to run a communications skills workshop. Dr. Hicks recalls:

> The president of the country walked into the room. He had come only to introduce us and intended to leave for a meeting in the capitol shortly thereafter. "Dr. Hicks," he said, "thank you for coming to conduct this communications workshop with my colleagues. Could you tell us a little about what you plan to do for the next two days?"
>
> "Mr. President," I responded, "with all due respect, I have a feeling that a communications workshop is not what is needed here. The rifts in the relationships in this room are deep. My experience with parties in conflict is that when relationships break down to this extent, both sides feel their dignity has been violated. With your permission, I would like to shift the focus of the workshop to address issues of dignity."
>
> Looking taken aback but remaining in control, the president turned to his scheduler and said, "Cancel my meetings in the capitol. I'll be staying for this workshop."

Hicks reports that her experience confirmed the paramount importance of dignity in repairing relationships, both on a global and a personal level.

At the end of the workshop . . . [one] of the most resistant and unapproachable generals in the room, who had refused to look me in the eye for two days, came up to me and said, "Donna, I want to thank you. Not only did you help the relationships in this room—I think you also saved my marriage."[2]

Today, the Western understanding—not yet accepted everywhere around the globe—is that while respect is earned, dignity is a birthright emerging from one's innate value and worth as a human being.[3] This conception of human dignity as a birthright has been long in the making.

Plato (fifth century BCE) and Aristotle (fourth century BCE), who laid the foundations of Western thought, were not proponents of universal human dignity. Both believed that human nature makes most people unworthy of freedom, and hence suited to serve as slaves. Aristotle maintained that human worth is a function of one's ability to reason; therefore, not all people are invested with the same dignity.

The European Renaissance of the fourteenth century, and the Enlightenment that followed on its heels, may have birthed the idea of intrinsic human dignity, but a robust view of inherent human dignity was not fully articulated until much later.

The seventeenth-century English political philosopher Thomas Hobbes held that a human being's worth is a function of personal work output: "The 'value,' or 'worth,' of a man is, as of all other things, his price; that is to say, so much as would be given for the use of his power; and therefore is not absolute but a thing dependent on the need and judgment of another. . . . The public worth of a man, which is the value set on him by the commonwealth, is that which men commonly call 'dignity.'"[4]

In the eighteenth century the philosopher and proponent of deontology (religious moral duty) Immanuel Kant (1724–1804),[5] writing in *Groundwork for the Metaphysics of Morals*, promulgated the "categorical imperative," an unconditional guiding principle for obligatory moral behavior, with these formulations:

Act only according to that maxim[6] whereby you can at the same time
will that it should become a universal law without contradiction.
(*Groundwork* 4:421)

Act in such a way that you treat humanity, whether in your own person
or in the person of any other, never merely as a means to an end but
always at the same time as an end. (*Groundwork* 4:429)

Therefore, every rational being must so act as if he were through his
maxim always a legislating member in the universal kingdom of
ends. (*Groundwork* 4:438)

One hundred fifty years after Hobbes, Kant pronounced that all rational
beings possess dignity *if* they are capable of autonomous reasoning and
moral behavior. Here, too, human dignity was predicated on the individual's circumstances and capacity; it was still not viewed as a birthright.

Since the twentieth century, particularly in the aftermath of the cataclysm of the Second World War, human dignity has come to be identified
with human rights, an equation the United Nations General Assembly
enshrined when it adopted the Universal Declaration of Human Rights
in Paris in 1948. Its preamble begins, "Whereas recognition of the inherent dignity and of the equal and inalienable rights of all members of the
human family is the foundation of freedom, justice and peace in the
world," and Article 1 asserts, "All human beings are born free and equal
in dignity and rights. They are endowed with reason and conscience and
should act towards one another in a spirit of brotherhood."[7] Thus today
the common current running through Western thought is that human
dignity is *intrinsic* to the individual—as a birthright *and* deriving from
that person's ability to work, think, reason, and act in accord with his or
her desires, values, and conscience.[8]

Torah, in contrast, understands human worth as *extrinsic*, deriving
from God. Human beings are created *b'tzelem Elohim* (in the image of
God), lending every person an aspect of the divine.[9] The very term for
human dignity in Rabbinic parlance, *k'vod ha-briot* (honor of the created

ones), points back to the Creator, the source of, and reason we have, human dignity. The fact that human dignity is derivative of divine dignity establishes its importance. Consequently, degradation of a human being is tantamount to degradation of the divine image.[10]

A stark illustration is found in the Rabbis' understanding of Deuteronomy 21:22–23. Torah requires that an executed prisoner's body, if hung on a pole (as was commonly done in the ancient Near East), must be removed before nightfall and buried the same day;[11] to do otherwise, Torah warns, would desecrate the land itself. *Midrash Tanna'im* to Deuteronomy 21:23 reflects: "There were once twin brothers who were identical in appearance. One was appointed king, while the other became a thief and was hanged. When people passed by and saw the criminal hanging they exclaimed, 'The king is hanging.'" Midrash Deuteronomy Rabbah 4:4 on Deuteronomy draws a similar analogy: "When an icon [of the king] is paraded in front of people, what do they say? Give honor to the icon of the king." The midrash teaches that we are all icons of God and therefore an affront to *any* human being is de facto an affront to God. The dignity accorded a criminal is also dignity accorded God because even a criminal is *tzelem Elohim*. Therefore, midrash *Mekhilta de-Rabbi Yishmael* can confidently declare, "God cares about the dignity of human beings."[12]

The second-century Sage Ben Zoma delved into the question of dignity by asking, "Who is honored?" (Ben Zoma used the Hebrew term *m'khubad*, from the word *kavod* meaning "honor," "dignity," or "glory.")

Who is honored? Those who honor all those created [i.e. people], as it is written, *For I honor those who honor Me, but those who spurn Me will be dishonored* (1 Samuel 2:30). (Pirkei Avot 4:1)

The Rabbis ponder the meaning and implications of their understanding that human dignity is a halakhic, covenantal requirement. They conclude that while *k'vod ha-briot* does not justify abrogating Torah law, the Rabbis can and must waive Rabbinic authority for the sake of human dignity. From Tractate Berakhot in the Bavli:

> Come and hear [from a *baraita*]: Human dignity is so great [i.e., important] it supersedes even a negative commandment of the Torah (BT Menachot 37b). Why should it? Let us rather say: *No wisdom, no prudence, and no counsel can prevail against Adonai* (Proverbs 21:30). Rav bar Shaba explained [the *baraita*] before R. Kahana to refer to the prohibition, *[You shall act in accordance with the instructions given you and the ruling handed down to you;] you must not deviate [from the verdict that they announce to you either to the right or to the left]* (Deuteronomy 17:11). They [i.e., his colleagues] laughed at him, [saying,] "The negative commandment, *you must not deviate*, is itself from the Torah!" R. Kahana said: "If a great man [like Rav bar Shaba] makes a statement, you should not laugh at it. All the ordinances of the Rabbis were based on the negative commandment *you must not deviate*, but for the sake of human dignity the Rabbis allowed [Rabbinic decrees to be waived]. (BT Berakhot 19b)

Here the Rabbis cite a *baraita* from Tractate Menachot asserting that human dignity is so important to God, even negative commandments (prohibitions) are to be set aside when they conflict with human dignity. The Gemara questions this claim, citing Proverbs 21:30, here understood to say that Rabbinic decisions cannot override God's law in the Torah. Rav bar Shaba explains the *baraita* in light of Deuteronomy 17:11 to mean that Rabbis have the authority to render decisions that must be upheld concerning Torah law. The students listening to his exposition laugh because he bases his claim that that the Rabbis can supersede Torah law on a law from the Torah. R. Kahana, in whose classroom this exchange takes place, chastises them for laughing at a "great man" and points out that *all* Rabbinic decisions are grounded, one way or another, in the commandment of Deuteronomy 17:11, which instructs people to follow the rulings of the judges in their generation. For the sake of human dignity, R. Kahana asserts, the Rabbis permit their own decrees to be overridden.[13] The Rabbis even find occasions for Toraitic legislation to defer to human dignity.[14]

Our passage recounts a conflict between Rabban Gamliel and R. Yehoshua b. Chananiah concerning whether evening prayers (*Ma'ariv*) are optional or obligatory. Rabban Gamliel, the *nasi* (president) of the Sanhedrin, exerts his authority and imposes his view on his elder colleague, R. Yehoshua. His heavy-handed approach is the subject of this passage that explores how leaders can overexert their authority at the expense of human dignity.

The passage affords us a front-row seat in the *bet midrash*, but we might just as soon imagine a control room, situation room, or boardroom—anywhere powerful people come into conflict and seek to work out their disagreements without damaging the institution that affords them their position of authority.

The Rabbis, like all leaders, face a constellation of concerns: their own values, goals, ideologies, and egos, and those of their colleagues, as well as the needs of the constituency and society they serve. Conflicts of philosophy, agenda, and personality abound. How is one to determine when someone has overstepped appropriate boundaries, even an individual who has the authority to do so? How should others respond? Should the authority figure be taken to task, censured, removed from his or her position? And if there is to be a response of this type, how should it be conducted? Must power lead inexorably to corruption, or can powerful people find a moral path?

A Broad View to Begin

It is helpful to understand the historical context for this story. Following the disastrously unsuccessful Jewish revolt against Rome that culminated in the destruction of the Second Temple in 70 CE, the Romans stripped the Jews of all remaining political power. They also renamed *Eretz Yisrael*

"Palestine," in an attempt to erase one thousand years of Jewish history by harkening back to the Philistines who had lived in the land during the time of King David. The Talmud records that the religious leader of the Jewish community, Rabban Yochanan b. Zakkai, nonetheless sought and received the permission of Vespasian, the Roman general during the revolt of 66–70 CE and soon after the emperor of Rome, to establish an academy north of Jerusalem in Yavneh.

The Romans granted the Jews authority to manage their own internal affairs. The Sages who assumed this authority over the Jewish people are called *tanna'im*. Their organization was loose and informal during this period. A recognized Sage would gather a circle of disciples around him, teaching and debating, generating and passing along the very oral tradition they were championing. The *tanna'im*[15] organized themselves around four primary functions: studying and interpreting Torah, recording received oral traditions and expanding their scope of application, serving as judges over religious and some civil matters for the Jewish population of *Eretz Yisrael*, and establishing a communal structure and hierarchy in preparation for reclaiming Jewish sovereignty when the opportunity would present itself.

The primary position in the Sages' hierarchy was *nasi*, president of the Sanhedrin; the *nasi*'s title was Rabban. Hillel was deemed the first *nasi*, though Gamliel the Elder, it appears, is the first leader titled Rabban. The *nasi*-ship was inherited in successive generations with two exceptions, noted here (*):

Hillel ha-Zaken (Hillel the Elder), b. c. 110 BCE, d. 10 CE
Shimon b. Hillel
Gamliel the Elder (Gamliel I), d. 50 or 52 CE
Shimon b. Gamliel, died during First Revolt against Rome
*Yochanan b. Zakkai, 30–90 CE
Gamliel II (Gamliel of Yavne), *nasi* from 70 to c. 80 CE, and Elazar b.
    Azariah, who shared the *nasi* position with Gamliel II for a time

Shimon b. Gamliel II (Gamliel of Yavne)
*Yehudah ha-Nasi, 135–c. 217

Hillel's grandson was Rabban Gamliel the Elder; Rabban Gamliel's grandson, also named Gamliel—often called Rabban Gamliel II or Gamliel of Yavne to distinguish the two—served as *nasi* of the Sanhedrin after the Second Temple's destruction. A descendant in the Davidic line, Rabban Gamliel II was considered the rightful heir to occupy the primary seat of Jewish authority and rule as the patriarch.

The Rabban Gamliel in this story is Gamliel II of Yavne. He faced nearly insurmountable challenges. Jerusalem lay in ruins, the country was decimated, and the population was demoralized and impoverished by the wars with Rome. Political divisions ran deep, threatening the community's viability. To consolidate his power for the purpose of unifying the community under the Sanhedrin's authority, he took some drastic steps, including temporarily excommunicating his own brother-in-law, R. Eliezer b. Hyrcanus (husband of his sister, Ima Shalom) over a halakhic disagreement that threatened his authority.

The Talmud story recounts an occasion when Rabban Gamliel asserted his authority over the beloved, respected Sage R. Yehoshua b. Chananiah, the *av bet din* ("head of court," second in authority). There is a backstory to this incident, a prior occasion when Rabban Gamliel and R. Yehoshua had disagreed about how to calculate the Jewish calendar and therefore had disputed over the proper day for celebrating Yom Kippur (see chapter 3 of this volume). Rabban Gamliel had ordered R. Yehoshua to violate the prohibitions of Yom Kippur on the day R. Yehoshua calculated to be the holy day—as a sign that R. Yehoshua had submitted to Rabban Gamliel's authority. R. Yehoshua acquiesced, leading Rabban Gamliel to greet him warmly, rise to embrace him, and address R. Yehoshua as "my teacher, who is greater than I in the wisdom of Torah." Now, witnessing yet another incident in which R. Yehoshua's dignity is undermined, his colleagues in the Sanhedrin are spurred to take drastic action.

The story provides a view into the power struggle of religious leaders caught up in the realpolitik of the late first century. Both their egos and their ideals are in full evidence. And far more is at stake than who will be the last Rabbi standing in the Sanhedrin at the end of the day.

Exploring the Nooks and Crannies of Our Passage

The passage begins with a question concerning the *Amidah* prayer. The *Amidah*, recited thrice daily, is a Rabbinic innovation that parallels and thereby recalls the sacrificial service that ended with the Second Temple's destruction. To retain the people's strong connection to God and the rhythms of Jewish life specified in Torah, the Rabbis instituted prayers corresponding to the times when sacrifices had been offered.[16] Midrash *Avot de-Rabbi Natan* (chapter 4) claims that the process began in Yavne soon after 70 CE and under the direction of Rabban Yochanan b. Zakkai, who persuaded his colleagues that substituting prayer for burnt offerings would constitute legitimate worship of God by quoting Hosea 6:6, *I desire goodness, not sacrifice; obedience to God, rather than burnt offerings.*[17]

In time, prayer was established as the appropriate mode both to worship God in the absence of the Temple and to remember the sacrifices offered on the altar. *Shacharit* (morning prayers) recalls the morning *tamid* (daily sacrifice). *Mincha* (afternoon prayers) are recited during the interval when the afternoon *tamid* was offered.*Musaf*, which means "additional," recalls the *Musaf* sacrifice offered on Shabbat, holy days, and Rosh Chodesh (the new moon).[18] But what is the status of *Ma'ariv* (evening prayers)? Torah does not require an evening *tamid* offering, so the prayer corresponds to the overnight burning of the leftovers of offerings made throughout the day—but, since this was not a separate sacrifice in and of itself, it was unclear whether *Ma'ariv* prayers ought to be obligatory.

Mishnah Berakhot 4:1 discusses a number of opinions concerning the time intervals when *Shacharit* and *Mincha* may be recited. Specifically, how late in the day may the prayers be said?

Shacharit may be recited until noon. R. Yehudah says until [the end of] the fourth hour of the day. *Mincha* may be recited until nightfall. R. Yehudah says: until *p'lag ha-mincha* (the middle of the afternoon). *Ma'ariv* has no fixed time. And *Musaf* may be recited all day long. R. Yehudah says until [the end of] the seventh hour of the day.

End times are thus specified for *Shacharit*, *Mincha*, and *Musaf*: *Shacharit* must be recited by noon, *Mincha* from midday until nightfall, *Musaf* during the daytime. However, concerning *Ma'ariv*, the mishnah tells us, "*Ma'ariv* has no fixed time." The *tanna'im* do not assign *Ma'ariv* an end point, because it does not correspond to a sacrifice. The Gemara picks up the discussion by asking precisely what "has no fixed time" means.

[The mishnah said:] The evening prayer has no fixed limit. What is the meaning of "has no fixed limit"? Shall I say it means that if a person wants he can say the *Tefillah* [i.e., the *Amidah*] any time in the night? Then let it state: "The time for the evening *Tefillah* is the whole night!" But what, in fact, is the meaning of "has no fixed limit"? It is equivalent to saying: The evening *Tefillah* is optional. For Rav Yehudah said in the name of Shmuel, "With regard to the evening *Tefillah*, Rabban Gamliel says it is compulsory, but R. Yehoshua says it is optional." Abaye says, "The halakhah ['law'] is as stated by the one who says it is compulsory." Rabbah says, "The halakhah follows the one who says it is optional."

The disagreement between Rabban Gamliel and R. Yehoshua arises over the correct interpretation of the mishnah's statement, "The evening prayer has no fixed limit." It suggests that one may recite *Ma'ariv* at any time from sundown until sunup. Gemara therefore begins the discussion by asking why the mishnah does not say "the whole night" if that is its intent. At this point Gemara presumes that "no fixed limit" connotes something else and proceeds to answers its own question: "no fixed limit" means that the *Ma'ariv* prayers are optional.

This interpretation provokes considerable dispute. Rabban Gamliel and R. Yehoshua, both *tanna'im* living in the Land of Israel in the last half of the second century, come to opposite conclusions: Rabban Gamliel considers *Ma'ariv* compulsory; R. Yehoshua b. Chananiah believes it is optional. The Gemara, furthermore, wants us to know that this dispute was not settled quickly. Both Abaye and Rabbah, early fourth-century *amora'im* in the Babylonian academy at Pumpedita, held differing opinions as well. Apparently, the issue remained an open question for a long time.

> The Rabbis taught [in a *baraita*] that there was an incident: A certain student came before R. Yehoshua and asked him, "Is the evening *Tefillah* compulsory or optional?"
>
> He replied, "It is optional."
>
> [The student] then presented himself before Rabban Gamliel and asked him, "Is the evening *Tefillah* compulsory or optional?"
>
> [Rabban Gamliel] replied, "It is compulsory."
>
> He said, "But did not R. Yehoshua tell me it is optional?"
>
> [Rabban Gamliel] said, "Wait until the champions enter the *bet midrash* ['house of study']."

An as yet unnamed student privately solicits R. Yehoshua's opinion, then goes straightaway to the Sanhedrin, where he publicly asks Rabban Gamliel the very same question. It seems this student is already familiar with Rabban Gamliel's view. Perhaps he raises the issue for public discussion so it can be settled once and for all, but we cannot ignore the possibility that he might be looking to stir up trouble.

> When the champions came in, someone rose and inquired, "Is the evening *Tefillah* compulsory or optional?"
>
> Rabban Gamliel replied, "It is compulsory."
>
> Rabban Gamliel said to the Sages, "Is there anyone who disputes this?"
>
> R. Yehoshua replied to him, "No."

[Rabban Gamliel] said to [R. Yehoshua], "Did they not report to me that you said it is optional?"

[Rabban Gamliel] said to [R. Yehoshua], "Yehoshua, stand up and let them testify against you!"

R. Yehoshua stood up and said, "Were I alive and he [the witness] dead, the living could contradict the dead. But given that he is alive and I am alive, how can the living contradict the living [i.e. how can I deny his claim]?"

Armed with evidence that R. Yehoshua is promulgating a view that contradicts his own, Rabban Gamliel orchestrates a showdown in the Sanhedrin, the heart of Rabbinic society. He refers to the students of Torah and Rabbis in the Sanhedrin as ba'alei t'risim ("champions" or "shield bearers"), a term that carries connotations of warrior or gladiator. What fascinating imagery for a group of Torah scholars! The Rabbis see themselves as heroes fighting for the survival of the Jewish nation, yet some of their battles are fought internally with one another. Rabban Gamliel waits for the "champions" at the entrance into the house of study—the arena where "armed" battle will ensue, words and arguments serving as weaponry.

Why is Rabban Gamliel spoiling for a fight? His public challenge suggests he might harbor personal animosity toward R. Yehoshua. Alternatively, he might view the circumstances as an opportunity to promote his own authority over that of the illustrious, beloved elder statesman who was one of two primary disciples of his own predecessor, Rabban Yochanan b. Zakkai. Elsewhere Rabban Gamliel has locked horns with the other primary disciple, R. Eliezer b. Hyrcanus, going so far as to excommunicate him when R. Eliezer refused to accede to the majority on a halakhic matter.[19]

Rabban Gamliel issues a ruling: Ma'ariv is mandatory. He proceeds to ask if anyone present disputes his view, knowing full well that R. Yehoshua has privately expressed a contradictory opinion. R. Yehoshua replies in the negative; he will not contravene Gamliel's authority in the Sanhedrin.

At this point, Rabban Gamliel could have accepted R. Yehoshua's public reply without further ado—yet he does not. His motivation and agenda are thereby in question. Why doesn't Rabban Gamliel choose the path of peace and avoid conflict? This question will hover over the remainder of the story.

R. Yehoshua's forthcoming response is telling: he acknowledges the truth only because he has no choice; a living witness denies him the possibility of evading a confrontation. As for his stating his personal opinion on the status of *Ma'ariv* outside the academy, this need not, strictly speaking, be seen as undermining Gamliel's position, since it appears that no decisive ruling on *Ma'ariv* has, as yet, been issued—as we've learned, the Gemara says that the issue is still a matter of disagreement in the fourth century.

However, R. Yehoshua, as we will soon learn, has tangled before with Rabban Gamliel and experienced firsthand the *nasi*'s capacity to fiercely protect his authority. Hence, R. Yehoshua might want to avoid another personal clash with Rabban Gamliel. Alternatively, R. Yehoshua may be motivated by the belief that a public showdown is not in the best interests of the community of scholars and the broader Jewish community.

Rabban Gamliel remained sitting and expounding and R. Yehoshua remained standing on his feet, until all the people there began to murmur and said to Chutzpit the Translator, "Stop!" and he stopped.

They then said, "How long is [Rabban Gamliel] to go on insulting [R. Yehoshua]? Last year on Rosh Hashanah he insulted him. He insulted him in the matter of the firstborn in the affair of R. Tzaddok. Now he insults him again! Come, let us depose him! Whom shall we appoint instead? We can hardly appoint R. Yehoshua, because he is one of the parties involved. We can hardly appoint R. Akiva, lest Rabban Gamliel bring a curse upon him because [R. Akiva] has no ancestral merit. Let us then appoint R. Elazar b. Azariah, who is wise and rich and the tenth in descent from Ezra.[20] He is wise, so if anyone puts a question to him he will be able to answer it. He is rich, so if occasion arises to pay homage at the Caesar's court,[21] he will be able to do so. He is tenth in descent from Ezra and therefore has ancestral merit, so [Rabban Gamliel] cannot punish him."

Rabban Gamliel had commanded R. Yehoshua to rise and face the accusation that he had expressed an opinion on halakhah that conflicted with Rabban Gamliel's view and had either de facto challenged the *nasi*'s authority or could be construed as doing so. He now compels R. Yehoshua to stand before him for a very long time while he lectures him, thereby humiliating the highly esteemed elder Sage. Moreover, this is not the first time Rabban Gamliel has publicly insulted R. Yehoshua. The Sages remind one another of two previous occasions.[22] Now those present at the Sanhedrin are furious. They resolve to depose Rabban Gamliel.

The Rabbis now consider who will replace the *nasi*. Ideally the Sanhedrin functions as a democracy, so the Rabbis caucus to identify a unifying figure to serve as president. The *nasi* position is reserved for a direct descendant of Hillel; only once in the past, with Yochanan ben Zakkai, had it been filled by someone not from the line.[23]

First the Rabbis consider R. Yehoshua but dismiss him just as quickly. Such a move would be unseemly; it would appear to those outside the Sanhedrin that R. Yehoshua had instigated a coup d'état.

They next consider R. Akiva, who is brilliant, charismatic, and revered as a peacemaker, but fear that R. Akiva's humble origins are insufficient to protect him from Rabban Gamliel's wrath and power.

The third candidate proposed is R. Elazar b. Azariah, whose admirable and pragmatic qualifications include wisdom and erudition sufficient to fulfill the teaching role, wealth required to serve as a diplomat and pay Roman extortion when necessary, and ancestral merit that will protect him from Rabban Gamliel. He is accordingly invited to become the *nasi*.

They went and said to [R. Elazar b. Azariah], "Will the master consent to become head of the academy?"

He replied, "I will go and consult the members of my family."

He went and consulted his wife. She said to him, "Perhaps they will depose you [later on]."

He replied to her, "[There is a proverb:] 'Let a man use a cup of honor for one day even if it be broken the next.'"

She said to him, "You have no white hair."

He was eighteen years old that day, and a miracle was wrought for him. Eighteen rows of hair [on his beard] turned white. That is why R. Elazar b. Azariah said, "Behold I am like one who is seventy years old,"[24] and he did not say, "[I am] seventy years old."

We can appreciate R. Elazar b. Azariah's hesitancy when, in the wake of Rabban Gamliel's deposition, a delegation of Rabbis invites him to become the *nasi*, a position that is the rightful inheritance of Rabban Gamliel, a direct descendant of Hillel. R. Elazar is only eighteen years old. One might think that such an offer would feed a young scholar's ego, but it is a sign of his maturity and wisdom — confirming his colleagues' positive assessment — that he consults his family before responding. His wife expresses two concerns. She sagely warns him that the offer will extend only until the political brouhaha that caused the rift between Rabban Gamliel and the Sages is repaired, after which Rabban Gamliel will be restored to his erstwhile position. Where will that leave R. Elazar? R. Elazar responds that being honored for even one day is worthwhile. Her second concern is that at the tender age of eighteen R. Elazar does not look the part of a Sage, let alone a wizened *nasi*. In response comes a miracle: suddenly he sprouts white hair. Voila! He looks like an elder and thereby will command greater credibility as *nasi*.

It was taught [in a *baraita*]: On that day, the doorkeeper was removed and permission was given to [all] the students to enter, for Rabban

Gamliel had issued a proclamation [saying]: No student whose inside [i.e., thoughts and feelings] does not correspond to his exterior [i.e., behavior] may enter the *bet midrash*.

On that day, many benches were added. R. Yochanan [bar Nafcha] said, "There is a difference of opinion on this matter between Abba Yosef b. Dostai and the Rabbis. One says that four hundred benches were added, and the other says seven hundred."

Rabban Gamliel became dispirited and said, "Perhaps, heaven forbid, I withheld Torah from Israel!" He was shown in his dream white casks full of ashes. This, however, really meant nothing; it was only shown to set his mind at ease.

In his first act as *nasi*, R. Elazar throws open the doors of the *bet midrash* to welcome all who wish to study with the Sages. Apparently Rabban Gamliel had restricted access to those who met his high standards. Admitting only people possessed of intelligence, wisdom, and character might serve to raise the Sanhedrin's standing, authority, and prestige in the broader community, yet a primary purpose of the Sanhedrin is to create and disseminate Oral Torah to the people, and from this vantage point severely restricting public access is counterproductive. Indeed, hundreds now flock to the academy.[25]

Seeing people flooding into the *bet midrash*, Rabban Gamliel worries that his restrictive standards prevented the growth of Torah learning in the community. However, in a dream that he understands to be a communication from heaven, he sees casks of white ashes, which he interprets to mean that the people he barred from studying with the Sages were, indeed, as unworthy as he deemed them to be. The Gemara editorializes that Rabban Gamliel's restrictive policy was wrong, but heaven supplied the dream nonetheless to allay his guilt and ease his mind.

It was taught [in a *baraita*]: Eduyot[26] was formulated on that day. Wherever the expression "on that day" is used, it refers to that [specific] day.

There was no halakhah about which any doubt existed in the *bet midrash* that was not fully elucidated.

As soon as R. Elazar assumes the position of *nasi*, the Sages waste no time instituting what they consider long-overdue change. A backlog of halakhic issues, unresolved disputes within the *bet midrash,* are decided, giving rise to a new tractate, Eduyot, a mishnaic catalog of Rabbinic disputes.

The Talmud describes this burst of activity as happening "on that day"—on R. Elazar's first day—a literary telescoping technique that dramatizes the momentous change in policy.

Even Rabban Gamliel did not absent himself from the *bet midrash* for a single hour, as we learned:[27]

On that day Yehudah, an Ammonite proselyte, came before them in the *bet midrash*. He said to them, "Am I permitted to enter the congregation [i.e., marry a Jewish woman]?"

Rabban Gamliel said to him, "You are forbidden to enter the congregation."

R. Yehoshua said to him, "You are permitted to enter the congregation."

Rabban Gamliel said to [R. Yehoshua], "Is it not already stated, *No Ammonite or Moabite shall be admitted into the congregation of Adonai; [none of their descendants, even in the tenth generation, shall ever be admitted into the congregation of Adonai]* (Deuteronomy 23:4)?"

R. Yehoshua said to him, "Do Ammon and Moab still reside in their original homes? Sennacherib, king of Assyria, long ago went up and mixed up all the nations [resettling conquered peoples in different lands], as it says, *I have erased the borders of peoples; I have plundered their treasures, and exiled their vast populations* (Isaiah 10:13). [Moreover] whatever separates [from a group] is assumed to have separated [i.e., originated from] the majority [i.e., in the absence of proof that he was an Ammonite or Moabite, we presume this man came from one of the other nations]."

Rabban Gamliel said to him, "But it has already been stated, *But after-ward I will restore the fortunes of the Ammonites—declares Adonai* (Jeremiah 49:6); so they have already returned!"

R. Yehoshua said to him, "And has it not [also] been stated, *I will restore My people Israel* (Amos 9:14)—yet they have not returned."

They immediately permitted [Yehudah] to enter the congregation.

Rabban Gamliel remains in the *bet midrash* after being deposed. He does not "collect his marbles and go home," testifying to his commitment to the institution, above and beyond his ego's concerns. What is more, Rabban Gamliel evidently can see beyond his interpretation of the dream of white ashes. He comes to understand the need to tone down his autocratic leadership style. Gemara supplies evidence of his evolving approach in the discussion with R. Yehoshua on the status of Yehudah the Ammonite proselyte.

The debate about Yehudah the Ammonite is also found in M Yadayim 4:4. In the context of the conflict between Rabban Gamliel and R. Yehoshua, it demonstrates a return to civility and mutual respect; the halakhic question posed—whether Yehudah may marry a Jewish woman—is decided by reason, not power.

Yehudah the Ammonite is a proselyte whose very name is a marvelous word play: Yehudah means "Jew." What is more, he is called "the Ammonite," an ancient nation that was among Israel's arch nemeses. Deuteronomy 23:4 explicitly forbids Ammonites (and Moabites) from becoming part of the Jewish nation. Here, however, we have a strange situation: Yehudah has already converted and now wants to marry a Jewish woman. Rabban Gamliel interprets the verse in Deuteronomy to mean that an Ammonite or Moabite man may not marry a Jewish woman even *after* converting to Judaism.

R. Yehoshua offers a clever rebuttal, arguing that long ago, in the eighth century BCE, after King Sennacherib of Assyria attacked the Northern Kingdom of Israel, he settled together the populations of numerous small city-states he conquered. As a result, in Rabban Gamliel and R. Yehoshua's day (more than eight hundred years later), it is no longer possible to accurately identify anyone as an Ammonite or Moabite. The verse from Isaiah suggests divine imprimatur to this understanding of history. Therefore, R. Yehoshua explains, we now operate by the principle that a person of unproven background has the same ethnic identity as the majority population in the locale where he resides. Hence, Yehudah is not considered an Ammonite and is free to marry a Jewish woman.

Rabban Gamliel objects that the mingling of nations was not intended to be permanent: God promised to separate the Ammonites from the mixture and restore their nationhood, as Jeremiah attested. R. Yehoshua retorts, in effect: "God also promised to restore the nation of Israel, but that didn't occur either." Rabban Gamliel might have countered that the prophetic prediction might yet be fulfilled, but he does not. Checking his superior authority, he raises no further objection.

R. Yehoshua's line of reasoning protects the dignity of Yehudah the Ammonite. In conceding the disagreement, Rabban Gamliel treats both R. Yehoshua and Yehudah the Ammonite with due respect.

> Rabban Gamliel said [to himself]: This being the case, I will go and appease R. Yehoshua. When [Rabban Gamliel] reached [R. Yehoshua's] house he saw that the walls were black. [Rabban Gamliel] said to him, "From the walls of your house it is apparent that you are a charcoal burner."
>
> [Rabbi Yehoshua] said to him, "Alas for the generation of which you are the leader, for you know nothing of the troubles of the scholars of Torah, their struggles to support and sustain themselves!"
>
> [Rabban Gamliel] said to him, "I have spoken excessively against you. Forgive me."
>
> [R. Yehoshua] paid no attention to him.
>
> [Rabban Gamliel said,] "Do it out of respect for my father."
>
> [R. Yehoshua] was appeased.

Having learned the lessons his deposition was intended to teach about respecting human dignity and not humiliating others in public, Rabban Gamliel goes to R. Yehoshua's home to apologize. Upon entering the house, Rabban Gamliel realizes that his colleague lives in dire poverty, barely eking out a living as a charcoal burner. R. Yehoshua bemoans the wealthy Rabban Gamliel's failure to learn about the Sages' struggles and suffering—more evidence that Rabban Gamliel has not fully attended to the dignity of his colleagues.

R. Yehoshua ignores Rabban Gamliel's apology until the latter requests it for the sake of "his father"—perhaps meaning his father, Rabban Shimon b. Gamliel, but more likely meaning his great-great-grandfather, Hillel the Elder. This is tantamount to evoking the well-being of the nation of Israel, which (from the Rabbis' perspective) depends on the line of Hillel for leadership and unity. R. Yehoshua accedes and forgives.

> They said, "Who will go and tell the Rabbis?"
>
> A certain laundryman said to them, "I will go."
>
> R. Yehoshua sent [a message] to the *bet midrash* saying: Let he who is [appropriate] to wear the mantle [of the *nasi*] wear it. Shall he who is not [appropriate] to wear the mantle [i.e., R. Elazar b. Azariah] say to him who is appropriate to wear it [i.e., Rabban Gamliel], "Remove your mantle and I will put it on"?
>
> R. Akiva said to the Rabbis, "Lock the doors so that the servants of Rabban Gamliel do not come and upset the Rabbis."

The debacle is not yet resolved, because Rabban Gamliel must now be restored to his rightful position as *nasi*: his deposition was motivated by the Rabbis' desire to protect R. Yehoshua's dignity, and Rabban Gamliel's apology has accomplished that.

At this point the focus shifts to R. Elazar b. Azariah: If he is unceremoniously dismissed, what happens to *his* dignity? The precariousness of the situation is further compounded by the realization that some

Rabbis in the Sanhedrin still harbor anger and resentment toward Rabban Gamliel and will oppose his restoration as *nasi* despite the fact that due to his family lineage he "wears the mantle" of the office.

To reach a resolution acceptable to all, R. Yehoshua sends a message to the Rabbis asking them to restore Rabban Gamliel as *nasi*. He reminds them that the position is one of inheritance, and R. Elazar lacks the genealogical credential.

R. Akiva, however, is apparently not prepared to acquiesce. He orders the doors barred to prevent the servants of Rabban Gamliel from forcing their way into the academy.

Tensions are running high and tempers are flaring. R. Yehoshua's proposed resolution could well result instead in another conflagration. To prevent such a calamity, R. Yehoshua returns to the *bet midrash* to speak directly with his colleagues. He alone is positioned to address them on the matter of Rabban Gamliel's restoration, because his dignity was the one impugned. What is more, the diplomatic qualities of his presence and persona are needed.

> R. Yehoshua said, "It would be better for me to go to them."
>
> He came and knocked on the door. He said to them, "Let the sprinkler, son of a sprinkler [i.e., a priest, son of a priest, who sprinkles the waters of purification], sprinkle. Shall he who is neither a sprinkler nor the son of a sprinkler say to a sprinkler, son of a sprinkler, 'Your water is cave water and your ashes are oven ashes'?"
>
> R. Akiva said to him, "R. Yehoshua, are you appeased? We have done this entirely for your honor. Tomorrow morning you and I will go early to speak with him."

R. Yehoshua explains that certain roles are acquired through birth. A "sprinkler" refers to a *kohen* (a biblical priest descended from the line of Aaron); only a *kohen* was authorized to sprinkle the ashes of the red heifer on someone to purify that individual (Numbers 19:1–10). One who is not born a *kohen* cannot impugn the *kohen* by claiming that the priest conducts the purification ritual incorrectly, using "cave water" (rather than free-running "living water") or ashes gathered from an ordinary cooking oven (rather than the purifying ashes of a red heifer). The point is that to be a priest, one must be born into a priestly family. R. Elazar b. Azariah, we recall, is descended from the priest-scribe Ezra. He *is* a *kohen*. R. Yehoshua's comment subtly reminds his colleagues that R. Elazar, albeit a brilliant Sage and by birth a *kohen*, is nonetheless not qualified to be *nasi*, because he is not descended from Hillel the Elder.

R. Akiva, however, does not respond to R. Yehoshua's argument about Rabban Gamliel's family lineage as determinative of his right to serve as *nasi*. He wants to know if R. Yehoshua's dignity has been respected. The concern about R. Yehoshua's dignity is, after all, what precipitated the deposition. It is only when R. Akiva and his colleagues are satisfied that R. Yehoshua has been appeased that they agree to restore Rabban Gamliel as *nasi*.

But it's never simple.

They said, "How shall we do this? Shall we depose [R. Elazar b. Azariah]? We have a tradition that in matters of sanctity, we elevate but do not lower.[28] If we let one master preach on one Shabbat and the other master on the next, this will cause jealousy. Rather, let Rabban Gamliel teach three weeks and R. Elazar b. Azariah one week."

And it is in reference to this [arrangement] that a master said [in a *baraita*[29]]: Whose week was it? It was the week of R. Elazar b. Azariah.

And the student [who started the incident] was R. Shimon b. Yochai.

The Rabbis recognize that restoring Rabban Gamliel as *nasi* compromises R. Elazar's dignity, even if he expected to be demoted. They cite the principle that we may elevate something or someone to a higher level of sanctity, but we do not decrease their sanctity. This is the reasoning behind the famous decision to light the Chanukah menorah according to the reasoning of Bet Hillel: adding one candle each night, we increase in sanctity.[30]

Retaining both Rabban Gamliel and R. Elazar with equal authority, however, is not a viable solution, the Rabbis realize, because it would engender jealousy and power struggles and, furthermore, demean Rabban Gamliel, who is heir to the position and by rights should occupy it. In an effort to protect the dignity of both Rabban Gamliel and R. Elazar b. Azariah, the Sages arrive at a compromise: a 3-to-1 arrangement.

Finally, we are told that the disciple who initiated this sequence of events by reporting R. Yehoshua's opinion to Rabban Gamliel was R. Shimon bar Yochai. This is an interesting detail to reveal, leaving us wondering if R. Shimon was seeking to stir up trouble. We will meet R. Shimon again in chapter 6 of this volume and discover just how complicated a personality he is.

Continuing the Conversation

1. Is Dignity Intrinsic or Extrinsic?

In Western secular thought, human dignity is intrinsic; if one meets certain criteria (ability to work, think, reason, and live within specified behavioral boundaries), one thereby deserves liberty. Therefore, dignity is contingent on qualities that people deem worthy of dignity. In Jewish thought, by contrast, human dignity inheres in every individual because all people are *tzelem Elohim* (the image of God), a quality and status that God bestows and people cannot revoke. Which way of viewing human dignity do you relate to more and why? What are the implications for each way of thinking for matters such as human trafficking, poverty, allocation of medical care and resources, racism, and treatment of refugees?

2. Aristocracy or Meritocracy?

Long ago, Israel was led by *kohanim* (priests) who inherited their status by birth. Much later, communities were led by Rabbis who earned their status through scholarship. Our story is located in the period of transition from the priestly aristocracy to the Rabbinic meritocracy. Rabban Gamliel is a bridge: he holds his position both by dint of family heritage and scholarly accomplishment. The miracle of white hair wrought for R. Elazar b. Azariah can be seen as a literary expression of divine affirmation of his qualifications to serve as *nasi*.

Is this also divine affirmation of the Rabbis' plan to depose Rabban Gamliel and replace him with the young R. Elazar? Or is this a way of claiming that God prefers meritocracy to aristocracy? What are the advantages and disadvantages to each system?

3. Death and Dignity

The Talmud teaches (BT Mo'ed Katan 27a–b) that at one time Jews would bring food and drink to houses of mourning. If the mourning family were wealthy, food was brought in gold and silver baskets and drinks in expensive, white glasses; if the family were poor, food was delivered in plain wicker baskets and drinks in cheaper, colored glasses. As a result, poor families felt ashamed. The Sages therefore decreed that everyone should be served in wicker baskets and colored glasses out of deference to the poor.

The Talmud further tells us that at one time the expense of providing for proper burial of a loved one was so exorbitant that families unable to afford the cost would abandon the corpse. Therefore, Rabban Gamliel "disregarded his own dignity," issuing instructions that when he died he was to be wrapped in simple, modest linen shrouds. Afterward, everyone did the same.

Whose dignity do these changes in practice protect: the deceased, the living, or both? Do practices that favor simplicity and modesty come at the expense of the dignity of others? What rituals and practices today support us in upholding the dignity of all human beings? By contrast, when are we most likely to fail to honor each person as created in God's image?

4. The Ingredients for Dignity Stew

The Talmud teaches that certain kinds of behaviors convey to others that we honor their dignity:

> For three years, there was a dispute between Bet Shammai ['the School of Shammai'] and Bet Hillel ['the School of Hillel'], the former asserting, "The halakhah is in agreement with our views," and the latter contending, "The halakhah is in agreement with our views." Then a heavenly voice announced: "Both these and these are the words of the living God, but the halakhah is in agreement with the rulings of Bet Hillel." If both [opinions, that is, of Bet Shammai and Bet Hillel] are "the words of the living God," what was it that entitled Bet Hillel to have the halakhah fixed in agreement with their rulings? Because they were kind and humble, they studied their own rulings and those of Bet Shammai, and mentioned the opinions of Bet Shammai before their own." (BT Eruvin 13b)

How do kindness and humility relate to human dignity?

Have you ever had the experience of seeing a matter very differently than someone else and then concluding that both opinions are, in effect, "the words of the living God"? How did—or might—this change your view of the dispute and the other person?

5. Human Dignity on the Rise

As the proverb has it: "Give a person a fish and you feed them for a day; teach them to fish and you feed them for a lifetime." Similarly, Moses Maimonides wrote that the highest level of tzedakah one can perform to help sustain another person is to provide an interest-free loan, form a partnership, or assist him or her in finding employment or in establishing a business—all means to freeing the person from dependence on others.[31]

Independence and empowerment are critical components of human dignity; conversely, poverty, disability, racism, and/or a lack of human rights can derail it.

Has your dignity ever been compromised because of dependence, poverty, disability, racism, and/or a lack of human rights? Have you witnessed this happening on societal and global levels? What do you believe are the best means to restore and support human dignity, on a personal level and worldwide? Are there any organizations you uphold as exemplars?

Summing Things Up

Rabban Gamliel may have had good reason to rule with a strong hand: Israel was weakened by the war with Rome and the loss of the Temple; the community was scattered, disillusioned, and divided. Yet, imposing his authority at the expense of R. Yehoshua's dignity angered and alienated his colleagues and threatened his leadership position.

When people invested with power and authority seek to impose their will in group settings, their pronouncements may come at the expense of their opponents' dignity. Leaders bear a special responsibility to treat others with dignity, both because they set the agenda, priorities, and tone for the community, and because they are role models by virtue of their positions.

Balancing power and authority with respecting others' dignity, especially under adverse conditions, can be challenging. Yet, time and again the Rabbis emphasize the fundamental importance of promoting and protecting human dignity in all we do. Dignity is a divine endowment, they explain, and respecting it is our human obligation.

3 Creating Consensus in Community

Mishnah Rosh Hashanah 2:8-9 and Babylonian Talmud, Gemara Rosh Hashanah 25a-b

R. Eliezer taught: Cherish your colleague's honor as your own, do not be easily provoked to anger, and repent one day before you die.

—Pirkei Avot 2:15

Why Study This Passage?

After 70 CE, the Rabbis were engaged in a project of spiritual survival and renewal—to snatch a Jewish religious victory out of the jaws of political defeat at the hands of the Romans. The Romans' destruction of the Temple and Jerusalem had been a calamity not only of epic proportion but also cosmic significance. The world, as Jews experienced it, had turned inside out; their reality was scrambled. The enterprise of the *tanna'im*, the Sages of the Land of Israel in the first and second centuries, was to wrest a sense of order and meaning out of chaos and catastrophe, and to preserve Second Temple traditions by building around them a scaffolding of oral traditions.

Religious historian Jacob Neusner explains how the project of establishing a normative Jewish legal framework, which later came to be called the Mishnah, fit into the larger picture of the trauma the Jewish community had experienced:

> In the age beyond catastrophe, the problem was to reorder a world off course and adrift, to gain reorientation for an age in which the sun has come out after the night and the fog. The Mishnah is a document of imagination and fantasy, describing how things ought to be, as reconstructed out of the shards and remnants of reality, but, in larger measure, building social being out of beams of hope. The Mishnah tells us something about how things were, but everything about how a small group of rabbinic sages wanted things to be. The document is orderly, repetitious, careful in both language and message. It is small-minded, picayune, obvious, dull, routine — everything its age was not. Mishnah stands in contrast with the world to which it speaks. Its message is one of small achievements and modest hope. It means to defy a world of large disorders and immodest demands. The heirs of heroes build an unheroic folk in the new and ordinary age.[1]

The Mishnah was set down in writing at the end of the second century CE at the behest of R. Yehudah ha-Nasi, who feared that the oral traditions that had been growing and circulating for more than two centuries were in danger of being lost to history. Mishnah is a terse account of the practices within, and beyond, the Second Temple when it stood. It records the foundational rituals, practices, and ethical laws that the Sages of the time understood Torah to promulgate, many of which would carry the Jewish community through the tumult and trauma of loss and dislocation engendered by the Temple's destruction.

The *amora'im* who followed the *tanna'im* comprised subsequent generations of Rabbis who studied the Mishnah and authored the Gemara, an elaborate discussion of, and far-reaching commentary on, the Mishnah. Gemara extended Mishnah's reach no doubt far beyond what the *tanna'im* could have imagined—into the lives of Jews in the Land of Israel and the Diaspora. Unlike the *tanna'im*, who looked back wistfully and longingly to a time when the Temple stood, the *amora'im* often looked forward to envision how their people would survive "exile" in a world without the Temple. In so doing, they also often looked back to imagine how their predecessors operated.

In the course of pursuing their mission, the Rabbis (both the *tanna'im* and, after them, the *amora'im*) also created a new layer of Jewish mythology on top of Torah's foundational myths of Creation, Redemption, and Revelation—a rich and elaborate set of narratives that continue to inspire Jews today.[2]

Storytelling of all kinds has long contributed to the development of human society, conveying foundational beliefs and cherished values. Long before the itinerant minister and bookseller Mason Locke Weems penned the iconic cherry tree legend about young George Washington, people constructed stories about famous and consequential figures of history—often, as Weems's creation did, to bolster a heroic image and promote desirable character attributes and behaviors.[3]

More generally, storytelling affords a means to explore the thorny ideas that underlie the complexity of human reality. What noted religious anthropologist Clifford Geertz has written about religious rites and symbols, indeed about religion as a whole, applies to religious storytelling in particular: "[Religion is] a system of symbols which acts to establish powerful, pervasive, and long-lasting moods and motivations in men by formulating conceptions of a general order of existence and clothing these conceptions with such an aura of factuality that the moods and motivations seem uniquely realistic."[4]

Geertz goes on to quote the philosopher Susanne K. Langer, who was among the first to point to the role of symbols in fulfilling the human need to invest one's world with meaning. Human beings, she explains, adroitly marshal the tools of religion (symbols, rites, art, and myths) to combat chaos, the most disruptive and distressing element of human existence, because "our most important assets are always the symbols of our general *orientation* in nature, on the earth, in society, and in what we are doing: The symbols of our *Weltanschauung* [world outlook] and *Lebensanschauung* [life outlook]."[5] In other words, we create rituals, appoint symbols, and tell stories to impose a sense of order on the world around us and the lives we live.

Neil Gillman, scholar of Jewish philosophy, provides this helpful definition of myth:

> A myth is a set of symbols extended and systematized into one coherent structure of meaning. A myth can articulate or describe that structure (a structural myth), or narrate how that structure came into being (a narrative myth). It is a device through which an individual or a community organizes its experience of the world, or of one part of the world . . . so that it forms a coherent whole. . . . [A] myth is a selective, interpretive reading of "the real," designed to introduce or reveal an underlying, hidden structure or order that we can now see.[6]

Gillman further explains the connection between religion and myth-making:

> There is no totally objective, human experience of the world. We construct reality from our simple perception of an apple to our most complex scientific theories. . . . We perceive the world not through our eyes but through our brain, which applies interpretive structures to what is transmitted to us through our senses. Those structures are analogous to myths. Structural myths are often accompanied by narrative myths; the former describes the structure, while the latter tells how it came to be.[7]

Psychologist and author Rollo May explains myth this way: "A myth is a way of making sense in a senseless world. Myths are narrative patterns that give significance to our existence. . . . [M]yths are our way of finding this meaning and significance."[8] May likened myths to "the beams in a house: not exposed to outside view, they are the structure which holds the house together so people can live in it." In other words, myths help us make sense, structure, and meaning in a chaotic world.

Gillman cites as examples the stories of Creation (Genesis 1 and 2) and Revelation (Exodus 19), the two most seminal myths in Jewish tradition. He also provides other helpful metaphors:

> Myths are the connective tissues that knit together the data of experience, thereby enabling these data to form a coherent pattern and acquire meaning. . . . To use another metaphor from our childhood, myths are the lines that connect the dots on the page so that we can see the bunny rabbit, except that now the dots are not pre-numbered. We have to choose the dots that we want to connect (i.e. the "facts"), then assign the numbers, then draw the lines.[9]

Stories often function like classical religious myths—we might say mini-myths—communicating anxiety and the longing for stability and hope; conveying how certain values or behaviors promote coherence and meaning; or reflecting an understanding of the underlying structure of the universe. The stories told by the Rabbis in the Talmud function in these ways as well.

The long story in this chapter begins with the Mishnah, the compilation of oral traditions set down by R. Yehudah ha-Nasi around 200 CE. In the Mishnah, recounting such an extended story is highly unusual: The Mishnah tends to be terse and consist of descriptions of Second Temple practices and early Rabbinic legal decisions. On only a handful of occasions does it deviate into storytelling or midrash. This story, famous in Rabbinic literature, and a few others in the Mishnah like it provide a keyhole view into the world of the *tanna'im*, but, possibly more significantly, they serve as the beginning of Rabbinic mythmaking about the Rabbinic enterprise of preserving Jewish practice (some would say, creating Judaism) in the wake of the catastrophe of 70 CE.

In broad terms the story concerns the formal process for declaring the new moon (the first day of the Hebrew month) on the basis of the testimony of witnesses who appear before the *bet din* (Rabbinic court). Declaration of the new moon then fixes the calendar for the month, and hence when the festivals and holy days fall that month. Therefore, the story touches on three levels of reality: the physical reality of the heavenly orbs whose movements determine years, months, and days (cosmos); the nation and peoplehood of Israel, whose holy days are determined by a calendar that is, in turn, determined by the movement of the heavenly orbs (nation); and the procedures of the *bet midrash*, where authority for interpreting and implementing Torah's instructions resides (halakhah). Establishing the calendar for the nation on the basis of human testimony wove together all three strands: cosmos, nation, and halakhah. And the glue that made it all cohere—or threatened to tear it apart—was the personal relationships between the scholars in the *bet midrash*.

A Broad View to Begin

The authority to set a society's calendar is tantamount to controlling power. Social anthropologist Jack Goody has written, "Whoever controls the calendar, the mode of reckoning time—whether the priesthood in Egypt or the court in central America—acquires a power that extends throughout the social system, reaching into each of the domains of politics, religion, law and the economy."[10] The Roman historian Livy wrote that in 304 BCE Cneius Flavius, a commoner and son of a freedman, "made public the rules of proceeding in judicial causes, hitherto shut up in the closets of the pontiffs; and hung up to public view, round the forum, the calendar on white tablets, that all might know when business could be transacted in the courts."[11] In other words, Cneius Flavius stole the Roman calendar sequestered by the aristocracy and posted it in the Roman Forum for all to see. Until Cneius Flavius's brash move, the

Roman calendar was the secret province of the priests and aristocrats who controlled the society.

In the Jewish calendar lunar months are balanced with solar years. In the first and second centuries, a *bet din* determined Rosh Chodesh (the new month) from reports by credible witnesses who testified that they had sighted the new moon. This was an important function for the *bet din* and its witnesses to fulfill because declaring the new month determined when the festivals of that month would be celebrated. Once Rosh Chodesh was declared, messengers were sent to inform outlying communities, and bonfires were lit on mountaintops to publicize the news quickly to communities farther away. In fact, a chain of bonfires led all the way to Babylonia.

At the time, Rabban Gamliel of Yavne was serving as *nasi* (president) of the Sanhedrin. In this capacity Rabban Gamliel had the authority to declare the new moon, but, notably, he did not do so on his own recognizance. Month after month he relied on the testimony of witnesses, in order to involve the community in the vital process of establishing the calendar. This brief description from Mishnah gives a sense of how seriously the procedure of hearing witnesses was taken: "There was a large courtyard in Jerusalem, and it was called Bet Ya'azek; it was there that all the witnesses gathered, and the court would examine them there. Large meals were made for them, in order that they be accustomed to come [to testify]."[12]

Given the necessity to get the date right, safeguards were in place to ensure that only credible evidence was accepted, but it was not a failsafe system. Faulty—even blatantly incorrect—testimony could be offered and accepted as valid. So the Rabbis had to determine how the integrity of Torah and the Sanhedrin could be maintained when human witnesses gave testimony that conflicted with the physical reality of the universe on which Jewish practice is based. Moreover, they needed to resolve conflicts between Rabbinic authorities when one determined that the testimony was unreliable and another chose to accept it. At stake was Israel's capacity to obey God's will as manifest in the integrity of the calendar and in the celebration of festivals on their proper days.

In this story Rabban Gamliel accepts testimony concerning the new moon of the Hebrew month of Tishrei, thereby fixing the days of Rosh Hashanah, Yom Kippur, and Sukkot. R. Yehoshua b. Chananiah finds fault with the testimony offered and calculates Yom Kippur to fall on a different day. Both Sages seek to do God's will and serve the community's needs. How they respond to the situation—and to one another—can speak to the way we approach valid disagreements in fact, philosophy, and proper procedure in our own lives. How they resolve their conflict can also inform how we weave together the strands of our experience, from the personal to the cosmic, into a coherent whole.

The story is set in the middle of the first century CE. Rabban Gamliel, presiding over the community, is renowned for his piety and learning.[13] His tenure as *nasi* arises during a tumultuous and divisive period in Jewish history. Rome is ruling with an iron fist and Jewish rebellion is in the air. Roman repression has also spawned Jewish unrest in exceptionally broad political realms, threatening to splinter the community.[14]

In this environment the Sages recognize the need to forge Jewish unity and consolidate Jewish law—both goals inextricably intertwined. Clear and coherent decisions concerning Jewish practice are needed to hold the community together. The story reveals the struggle of the *tanna'im* to establish a consistent and cogent understanding of how Torah applied to Jewish life in order for Judaism and the Jewish people to survive.

When Rabban Gamliel and R. Yehoshua b. Chananiah calculate Yom Kippur to fall on different days based on when they believe the new moon has arrived, Rabban Gamliel orders R. Yehoshua to appear before him in the *bet din* (Rabbinic court) on the very day R. Yehoshua considers to be Yom Kippur, to publicly signify his acquiescence to Rabban Gamliel's authority to accept testimony—even faulty evidence—and declare the new month. R. Akiva intervenes as the peacemaker, a role Talmud describes him playing on numerous occasions.

The story is extended and fleshed out by an accompanying discussion in the Gemara that elaborates on R. Akiva's reasoning and provides additional details concerning the two Sages' reconciliation.

Exploring the Nooks and Crannies of Our Passage

The Mishnah, in a series of *mishnayot*, details the lengths to which Rabban Gamliel the Elder and his colleagues went to encourage ordinary people to come before the *bet din* to testify concerning the new moon so that Rosh Chodesh could be declared.

> There was a large courtyard in Jerusalem, and it was called Bet Ya'azek; it was there that all the witnesses gathered and the court would examine them there. They would prepare large meals for them to accustom them to come [and testify]. Originally, [if they arrived on Shabbat] they did not move from [that courtyard] all day.[15] [Later,] Rabban Gamliel the Elder ordained that they [be permitted to] go two thousand *amot* ['cubits'] in every direction. (M Rosh Hashanah 2:5)

Rabban Gamliel thereby enticed people to serve as witnesses by easing the restrictions concerning their movement on Shabbat and providing them with a generous feast.

Declaration of the new moon required the testimony of two credible witnesses. According to M Rosh Hashanah 2:6, the *bet din* would then convene and question the witnesses in pairs, examining first one and then the other. The Mishnah recounts a sampling of the questions the Rabbis of the *bet din* asked to ascertain precisely what the witnesses saw and thereby judge the validity of their testimony: Did the moon follow the sun across the sky, or did the sun follow the moon? Was the moon north or south of the sun? How high was it? How wide was it?

Even when two witnesses were found to be reliable and their testimony acceptable, the next pair would be brought in and questioned, and the pair after that. Indeed, everyone who had made the effort to come give testimony was heard, not because they were needed, "but in order that they not be disappointed, so that they would be accustomed to come [again in the future]."

M Rosh Hashanah 2:7 reports that finally, after sufficient testimony had been offered, the head of the *bet din* would declare, "It [i.e., the moon] is sanctified!" and everyone would repeat after him, "It is sanctified! It is sanctified!" (If no one had seen the moon by the thirtieth day, perhaps because the sky was overcast, the following day was considered Rosh Chodesh nonetheless.)[16]

The Mishnah further tells us that Rabban Gamliel's procedure for declaring the new moon enabled uneducated people to participate in this important function. To ensure that the testimony they offered was clear and accurate, Rabban Gamliel provided drawings on his walls to which people could refer when describing what they had seen.

Most of the time this worked well. As with all carefully contrived procedures, it works until it doesn't. M Rosh Hashanah 2:8 recounts two occasions when the diagrams were not sufficient to elicit valid testimony, but Rabban Gamliel accepted it nonetheless.

Rabban Gamliel used to have a diagram of the phases of the moon on a tablet [hung] on the wall of his upper chamber, and he used to show them to the unlearned and say: Did it look like this or this?

On one occasion, two witnesses came and said, "We saw [the moon] in the morning in the east, and in the evening in the west." R. Yochanan b. Nuri said, "They are false witnesses." When, however, they came to Yavneh, Rabban Gamliel accepted them.

On another occasion, two witnesses came and said, "We saw it at its proper time [the night of the thirtieth day of the month], but on the following intercalary night it was not seen." But Rabban Gamliel [had already] accepted them. R. Dosa b. Horkinas said, "They are false witnesses. How can they testify that a woman gave birth and then the next day [we see] her belly between her teeth?" R. Yehoshua [b. Chananiah] said to him, "I see [the truth of] your argument."

The first pair of witnesses claim to have seen the "old moon" in the morning and the "new moon" the very same evening; this is not possible because there is always a period of twenty-four hours between the disappearance of the old moon the appearance of the new moon. The second pair of witnesses claim to have seen the new moon at its proper time, but no moon the following night; barring complete cloud cover (which makes it impossible to testify that the new moon had disappeared), this too is impossible. R. Dosa B. Horkinas's metaphor is apt: Can a woman give birth one day (the new moon), but be nine months' pregnant (a moonless sky) on the following day? If the sliver of a new moon had truly appeared the previous night, it could not be absent from the sky on the subsequent night.

Rabban Gamliel, we are told, accepted patently faulty evidence in both cases. Why did he accept false testimony? In the first case, perhaps Rabban Gamliel had sighted the new moon, and even though the testimony offered was faulty, the timing was accurate. In the second and seemingly more egregious case, he may have decided that the truth of the testimony didn't ultimately matter: Even if the witnesses gave faulty evidence on the thirtieth day of the month, the following day would have to be declared Rosh Chodesh nonetheless. It was well understood that a lunation (the cycle of the moon) repeats every twenty-nine and a quarter days and therefore a lunar month cannot extend beyond the thirtieth day. Thus, even if the sky were completely overcast and no testimony could be given, the thirty-first day would be Rosh Chodesh. As M Rosh Hashanah 2:7 says, "R. Elazar bar Tzaddok said, 'If [the new moon] had not been seen at its [proper] time [i.e. by the thirtieth day], it was not sanctified because it had already been sanctified by Heaven.'"

Rabban Gamliel was eager to keep the Jewish people involved and invested in the processes of the *bet din* (Rabbinic court). Offering testimony was a way they could participate and make a contribution. Conversely, he was loath to demoralize people who had expended effort, and perhaps time and expense, to travel some distance and testify before the *bet din*. Others might be similarly discouraged.

At the same time, Rabban Gamliel and his colleagues were eager to establish the authority of the Sanhedrin as the legitimate leadership counsel of the Jewish people during this period of turmoil. Having people participate as witnesses served to bolster the legitimacy of the *tanna'im* as interpreters of Torah and leaders of the community. Leaders can only lead if the community recognizes and accepts their authority. And so, at least in principle, the more the people became involved in the practices the Rabbis were instituting, the more likely it was that they would accept the Rabbis' new roles as well.

People do not always provide quality evidence. Sometimes their memories are confused; at times their enthusiasm to participate may overcome their sense of the importance of telling the truth.

R. Yochanan b. Nuri and R. Dosa B. Horkinas are disturbed that Rabban Gamliel accepted patently false testimony. In their eyes, doing so pollutes the legal system: their own courts will be tainted, and Rabbinic colleagues might well refuse to adhere to the calendar declared by the *bet din* on the basis of faulty evidence. Yet to function as a community everyone must celebrate the holy days at the same time. What is more, if non-Rabbis believe that the *bet din* is accepting undeniably false evidence, the integrity of the process and thereby the authority of the Rabbis may be called into question. This, in turn, could threaten the Rabbis' broader claim to authority in the community.

R. Yehoshua, revered and admired by all, agrees with his colleagues; he recognizes the inherent danger in the situation. What we are not told, but can easily conjecture, is that he has calculated the day of Yom Kippur accurately on his own, not wishing to rely on faulty testimony.

From his computation Yom Kippur will fall on a different day than the *bet din* has declared.

The Mishnah continues the story in M Rosh Hashanah 2:9:

> Rabban Gamliel sent [a message] to [R. Yehoshua]: "I order you to appear before me with your walking stick and your money belt on Yom Kippur as it falls according to your calculation."
>
> R. Akiva went and found [R. Yehoshua] in great distress. [R. Akiba] said to [R. Yehoshua], "I can demonstrate that whatever Rabban Gamliel has done is valid, because it says, *These are the festivals of Adonai, holy convocations, which you shall proclaim* (Leviticus 23:4), [which means] whether they are proclaimed at their proper time or not at their proper time, I have no appointed seasons save these."
>
> [R. Yehoshua] then came to R. Dosa b. Horkinas, who said to him, "If we call into question the decisions of the *bet din* of Rabban Gamliel, we must call into question the decisions of every *bet din* that has existed since the days of Moses up to the present time, as it says, *Moses and Aaron, Nadav and Abihu and seventy of the elders of Israel went up* (Exodus 24:9). Why were the names of the elders not [specifically] mentioned? To show that every group of three that has acted as a *bet din* over Israel is equivalent to the *bet din* of Moses."
>
> [R. Yehoshua] took his walking stick and his money belt in his hand and walked to Yavneh to Rabban Gamliel on the day that Yom Kippur fell according to his calculation. Rabban Gamliel arose and kissed [R. Yehoshua] on his head. He said to him, "Come in peace, my teacher and my disciple! My teacher in wisdom and my disciple in that you accepted my words."

R. Akiva takes it on himself to speak with R. Yehoshua.[17] By the logic of the story, we might presume that R. Yehoshua is the one who is distressed, but the Hebrew is ambiguous, leaving open the possibility that R. Akiva is the distressed one. (Gemara will take up this question.) R. Akiva offers R. Yehoshua an argument, grounded in a Torah text, that justifies Rabban Gamliel's acts: Torah itself authorizes the community to declare Rosh Chodesh. Leviticus 23:4, speaking of the sacred festivals in Israel's calendar, contains a peculiar phrase: "you shall appoint them." R. Akiva interprets this to mean that while the festivals are to be determined by the moon, their declaration, in the last analysis, depends on the *bet din*. Even more, if the community does not actively make the declaration—even a faulty declaration—then there can be no festival days, because God has delegated that job to Israel. (Perhaps R. Akiva is also thinking that the mistake cannot be propagated: in one month, there will be another opportunity to bring in witnesses and declare the next Rosh Chodesh properly.) This authorizes Rabban Gamliel to accept testimony he chooses to accept—even if it is erroneous.

We cannot tell whether R. Yehoshua accepts R. Akiva's argument. Most likely, he does not, because he next goes to R. Dosa b. Horkinas. Recall that R. Dosa had declared the witnesses to be false, offering the colorful metaphor of a woman who gives birth one day and is found to be nine months' pregnant the following day. Now, however, R. Dosa supports Rabban Gamliel's decision, citing a verse from Exodus that recounts Moses, Aaron, Aaron's two eldest sons, and the seventy elders of Egypt ascending Mount Sinai in preparation for the Revelation of Torah. The Torah does not list the names of the seventy elders, R. Dosa notes, lest future generations claim that only the judges specified by name in the Torah are to be trusted with full authority and thereby claim that the judges in their day do not rise to the level of those in Moses's time. If it were possible to question the judgment of a *bet din* on that basis, one could call into doubt the judgment of each *bet din* ever constituted, going all the way back to Moses, thereby calling into question all halakhah as interpreted by the Rabbis. Doing that, R. Dosa implies, would be far more undermining than accepting faulty evidence now and then.

R. Yehoshua does not respond, but it is clear that he has accepted at least this second argument in support of Rabban Gamliel's decree. He publicly demonstrates his acceptance of Rabban Gamliel's authority by violating the strictures of Yom Kippur on the day he believes is correct in deference to observing the holy day Rabban Gamliel's *bet din* has declared to be Yom Kippur. Otherwise, perhaps R. Yehoshua might have observed Yom Kippur privately on the day he reckoned as correct. Had his colleagues found out about this, consider how the observance of Yom Kippur on two different days might have affected the broader Jewish community. Could the community have followed two disparate sources of authority and remained unified while various enclaves operated by conflicting calendars?

Rabban Gamliel receives R. Yehoshua with affection and respect, addressing him as "my teacher and my disciple," praising his erudition as well as his cooperation.

This story paints a portrait of the *tanna'im* likely based more on their ideal and ideology than history. There is no evidence to support the picture the Rabbis paint of a large and thriving class of scholars in the first or even second century that all Jews at the time widely acknowledged to be scholars, religious authorities, and communal leaders.[18] David C. Kraemer, scholar of Talmud and Rabbinics, writes:

> The rabbis began as a small group of scholars in master-disciple circles sometime in the first century. By the late second century, the rabbis themselves still amounted to a small number of individuals, certainly no more than a few hundred. They surely had followers, other Jews who were attracted by rabbinic discipline or reputation. But altogether, the rabbis can have served as authorities for a small percentage of the local population—and for almost no one beyond the Galilee itself. Thus, when we consider the Mishnah [the source of our story thus far], we must understand that it was, in its own context, little more than a sectarian movement.[19]

Similarly, religious historian Catherine Hezser writes:

> The rabbinic movement of Roman Palestine seems to have neither been centralized nor institutionalized. . . . While certain renowned rabbis seem to have lived in Yavneh and later in Usha, they do not seem to have exerted control over the rabbinic movement as a whole. The rabbinic movement rather seems to have consisted of individual rabbis and small clusters of rabbis at various locales. . . . No central rabbinic court of "sanhedrin" seems to have existed in Roman Palestine. Some rabbis seem to have had private "courts" and some may have been appointed as judges at local courts, but the majority of rabbis are likely to have functioned as unofficial legal advisors who were approached by all those who acknowledged their scholarship. Besides private study houses or rooms in the houses or apartments of rabbis which were customarily used for Torah study, local study houses are mentioned for a number of towns and villages. There is no reason to assume, however, that these local study houses were "rabbinic academies."[20]

Hezser concludes that the Rabbinic movement "may best be described as an informal network of relationships which constituted a personal alliance system" of Rabbis who maintained intimate friendships and gathered in one another's homes for meals, ceremonies, and study.[21] Even more shockingly, Hezser claims, "It seems that references to the *halakhah* in the sense of commonly accepted opinions were wishful thinking on the part of these [later] editors."[22]

This view stands in stark contrast to the way the Mishnah presents the world of the early Rabbinic community, their endeavors, and their relationship with the larger Jewish society—as populous, vigorous, and robustly authoritative.[23] Perhaps this is why the mishnaic story itself challenges the intrinsic authority of the Rabbis but then resoundingly confirms it, going so far as to claim that God says, "I have only the festivals that the *bet din* declares"—God thus investing the *bet din* with full authority.[24] The telling of the story—and the later redaction—contribute to the Rabbinic myth of robust authority.

Gemara explores and discusses the Mishnah's story. Living several centuries later in Babylonia, the *amora'im* bring a different perspective and set of concerns to the table.

We pick up the Gemara's discussion with "R. Akiva went and found him in great distress." As mentioned above, an element of ambiguity remains in the original Hebrew. Who is in distress? Is it R. Yehoshua, because Rabban Gamliel has ordered him to violate Yom Kippur? Or is it R. Akiva, because he recognizes the potential for this situation to snowball out of control, dividing the community of scholars and possibly the larger Jewish community as well?

The Gemara tells us that R. Yehoshua was distressed and fleshes out a conversation the Rabbis imagine took place between him and R. Akiva. (In this account, R. Yehoshua refers to himself in the third person.)

> Gemara [25a]: *R. Akiva went and found [R. Yehoshua] in great distress.* They [Sages who are listening to and discussing this account] asked: Who was in distress? Was R. Akiva in distress or was R. Yehoshua in distress? Come and hear, for it has been taught [in a *baraita*]: R. Akiva went and found R. Yehoshua in distress. He said to him, "Master, why are you in distress?"
>
> [R. Yehoshua] replied, "Akiva, it were better for a man [i.e., me] to be on a sickbed for twelve months than that such a decree should be issued against him [i.e., against me]."
>
> [R. Akiva] said to [R. Yehoshua], "Master, allow me to tell you something that you taught me."
>
> [R. Yehoshua] said to [R. Akiva], "Speak."
>
> [R. Akiva] said to [R. Yehoshua], "Torah says, *you . . . you . . . you* three times to indicate that *you* [may fix the date of the festivals] even if you err inadvertently, *you*, even if you err deliberately, *you*, even if you are misled [by witnesses]."[25]

[R. Yehoshua] replied to him in these words, "Akiva, you have comforted me, you have comforted me."

Gemara resolves any residual ambiguity by telling us that R. Yehoshua is distressed. What is more, Gemara zeroes in on the nature of his distress: Rabban Gamliel's decree would force him to violate Yom Kippur, to abrogate God's will.

R. Akiva cleverly resolves R. Yehoshua's discomfort. Treating his elder colleague with deference and sensitivity, R. Akiva reminds R. Yehoshua that it was he himself who taught that Torah empowers Israel to declare the new moon for themselves. R. Yehoshua had based this teaching on the three iterations of the word *otam* (an object pronoun meaning "them") in Leviticus 23:2, 4, and 37, passages in which God instructs the Israelites to formally proclaim the festivals as sacred occasions. Since Torah consists only of consonants (vowels were added later), R. Yehoshua reads *otam* as *atem* ("you" in the plural), meaning that the community of Israel, through its *bet din*, has the authority to declare the new moon *even* if they do so in error. The three iterations of *otam* connote even when the error is (1) inadvertent, (2) deliberate, or (3) based on faulty testimony. The community's empowerment *is* God's will.

R. Akiva thus provides R. Yehoshua with a rationale in support of Rabban Gamliel that he can accept—because it rests on his own teaching. R. Yehoshua can now see that Rabban Gamliel's methodology, the cause of so much distress, is in fact the proper enactment of Torah.

The Rabbis next turn their attention to the consideration of what constitutes a valid *bet din*—the substance of R. Dosa's comment, in which he referenced the seventy elders of Israel who accompanied Moses halfway up Mount Sinai (Exodus 24).

> [R. Yehoshua] then came to R. Dosa b. Horkinas. Our Rabbis taught [in a *baraita*]: Why were the names of these elders not mentioned [specifically]? So that a person should not say: "Is So-and-so like Moses and

Aaron? Is So-and-so like Nadab and Abihu? Is So-and-so like Eldad and Medad?" [Scripture] also says, *Samuel said to the people: It is Adonai, who appointed Moses and Aaron* (1 Samuel 12:6), and it says, *And Adonai sent Jerubbaal and Bedan and Jephthah and Samuel* (1 Samuel 12:11). Jerubbaal is Gideon. Why is he called Jerubbaal? Because he quarreled with Baal. Bedan is Samson. Why is he called Bedan? Because he came from [the tribe of] Dan. Jephthah is Jephthah. [25b] [Scripture also] says: *Moses and Aaron were among [God's] priests, Samuel among they who call on [God's] name [when they called, Adonai, God answered them]* (Psalm 99:6). [Therefore] Scripture places three of the least significant [leaders] on the same level as three of the most significant [leaders] to show that Jerubbaal in his generation is like Moses in his generation; Bedan in his generation is like Aaron in his generation; Jephthah in his generation is like Samuel in his generation—to teach you that even the most insignificant among the insignificant, once appointed a leader of the community, is like the most significant among the significant. [Scripture also] says: *You shall appear before the levitical priests, or the judge in those days* (Deuteronomy 17:9). Would it enter your mind that a person would go to a judge who is not [alive] in his days? This shows that you need not go to a judge other than one who is in your days. [Scripture also] says: *Do not say: How has it happened that former days were better than these? [For it is not wise of you to ask that question]* (Ecclesiastes 7:10).

In M Rosh Hashanah 2:9, R. Dosa b. Horkinas invoked the Torah's account of the Revelation at Mount Sinai in Exodus 24 to persuade R. Yehoshua to relent in his opposition to Rabban Gamliel's setting Rosh Chodesh on the basis of faulty witnesses. The Rabbis now summon a *baraita* concerning this same episode in Torah. When Torah says, *Then Moses and Aaron, Nadab, and Abihu, and seventy of the elders of Israel ascended* (Exodus 24:9), why are "the elders" not named? The *baraita* teaches that this is to prevent people from making direct comparisons between the leaders of their generation and those who came before. A strong current in Jewish thinking contends that those who stood at Mount Sinai and experienced the Revelation of Torah directly enjoyed superior spirituality, insight, and understanding of Torah. Every successive generation has a diminished and more attenuated connection, and accordingly less wisdom and insight. One problem with this thinking is that it invites comparison to earlier generations; present leaders may at any time be deemed inadequate because previous authorities (including those long deceased) were inherently superior.

Gemara then provides two more examples. Numbers 11:24–26 describes how God endows the seventy elders with the gift of prophecy when the sole prophet, Moses, is overwhelmed by the taxing burden of caring for all Israel. Of the seventy elders, only two are named: Eldad and Medad. The others remain anonymous, but no less gifted with prophecy. Similarly, in 1 Samuel 12:11, the prophet cites only four of the generals and warriors whom God sends to fight for Israel; the rest are unnamed.

Gemara next digresses to explain the leaders named in 1 Samuel 12:11, identifying Jerubbaal as the charismatic Gideon and Bedan as the maniacal Samson on the basis of the supposed "meaning" of their names. Jephthah is not known by any other name in the Bible.

Finally, the Gemara cites Psalm 99:6, which mentions Moses, Aaron, and the prophet Samuel in a similar fashion to the mention of Jerubbaal/ Gideon, Bedan/Samson, and Jephthah.

Scripture has thus identified six leaders by name, but they are not all equal in caliber. Three—Moses, Aaron, and Samuel—are unquestionably superb. The other three—Gideon, Samson, and Jephthah—are rash and violent warriors with unsavory reputations.

Juxtaposing these scriptural citations paves the way for Gemara to make its point: One should not compare the leaders in one's own generation unfavorably with the fabled leaders of yore. After all, Gideon, Samson, and Jephthah are named, but they are hardly role models to admire. Nonetheless, this teaches us to respect the leaders of each generation *as if* they were on par with the great leaders of the past. The Rabbis are keenly aware that if we question the legitimacy and authority of the courts in our day, the entire system of authority that holds the community together may unravel. What is more, each generation of Rabbis is "the end of the line" and could be deemed inferior to all who came before.

The last section of our passage describes the Babylonian Rabbis' reflection on the Mishnah's resolution of the conflict between Gamliel and Yehoshua.

> [25b] [*R. Yehoshua*] *took his walking stick and his money belt in his hand.* Our Rabbis taught [in a *baraita*]: When [Rabban Gamliel] saw [R. Yehoshua], he rose from his seat and kissed him on the head, saying, "Peace to you, my teacher and my disciple—my teacher because you have taught me Torah publicly, my disciple because I lay an injunction on you and you fulfill it like a disciple. Happy is the generation in which the greater defer to the [authority of] the lesser, and all the more so when the lesser [defer] to [the authority of] the greater."
>
> All the more so? It is their duty. Rather, it means that because the greater defer to [the authority of] the lesser, the lesser [apply the principle of "all the more so"] to themselves all the more so.

In the Mishnah's version of the reconciliation, the *nasi* graciously expresses unabashed admiration for R. Yehoshua's intellect and gratitude for accepting his authority. The Gemara's version of their reconciliation, while similar, is different in tone and capped with a substantive claim about leadership and authority that reflects the agenda of the Babylonian academies. If R. Yehoshua, beloved, revered, and admired—and technically correct in his assessment of the poor evidence accepted by Rabban Gamliel's *bet din*—nonetheless defers to Rabban Gamliel's authority, the message is clear: a Sage should respect the authority of the *nasi*.

The question of who is a "greater" or "lesser" authority runs throughout this passage. The tradition in which greatness is correlated with temporal proximity to Sinai (such that each subsequent generation of teachers and judges falls further and further from the lofty heights of Revelation) is functional in the *bet midrash*, where people look back, but less so in the community, where people look forward. To hold to that line is to say to the community: We are inferior to all who came before us. Hence Torah is interpreted to declare instead: Torah teaches us that current leaders are no less authoritative than past leaders and direct comparisons should not be made.

Meanwhile, within the community of scholars, there is an effort to level the playing field for the sake of peace. Rabban Gamliel terms R. Yehoshua both his "teacher and disciple."

We might draw several conclusions. First, there are times when those with superior intellect (R. Yehoshua) must defer to those with greater authority (Rabban Gamliel) in order to promote community cohesion and continuity in the short term and survival in the long term. Second, this story may well be a window on the period of transition from aristocracy (Rabban Gamliel, wealthy and a direct descendant of Hillel) to meritocracy (R. Yehoshua, an exceptional, but impoverished, Sage [26]). Third, wielding authority requires sensitivity and finesse more than perfection and consistency. Rabban Gamliel recognizes the value of engaging ordinary Jews in the processes of the *bet din*, even to the point of accepting blatantly errant testimony, yet at the same time does not brook condescension from other Sages. The extent to which he succeeds remains an open question.

Overall, the story evinces an early stage of Rabbinic mythmaking. The *tanna'im* are not the stuff of fairy tales, which Langer describes as tales of "personal gratification, the expression of desires and of their imaginary fulfillment, a compensation for the shortcomings of real life, an escape from actual frustration and conflict."[27] Rather, she explains, "[t]he great step from fairytale to myth is taken when not only social forces — persons, customs, laws, traditions — but also cosmic forces surrounding mankind, are expressed in the story; when not only relationships of an individual to society, but of mankind to nature, are conceived through the spontaneous metaphor of poetic fantasy."[28]

The early Rabbis are larger-than-life characters standing on a cosmic stage, wielding the weapons of Torah study and interpretation to save Israel and thereby redeem the world for the Messiah. They flirt with hero legends (about R. Eliezer and R. Akiva, in particular), but it is the institution of the *bet midrash* that is ultimately idealized, apostheosized, and immortalized.

While Hezser points out, "The rabbinic movement of Roman Palestine seems to have neither been centralized nor institutionalized," Lapin notes that stories such as this contributed to the Rabbis' efforts to consolidate and expand their authority over the Jewish community. Tannaitic literature does not hide the Rabbis' struggle to assert their authority in marital, calendrical, and purity matters, which are hardly minor concerns. Lapin observes that the Sages' claims to authority in these arenas took time and wrangling to work it all out:

> The claims [to authority] themselves are important . . . because they indicate the ideological or mythologizing dimensions of a struggle for a kind of institutionalization among the members of the rabbinic movement and the parties within it in the second to the fifth centuries. . . . In a significant way, the formation of literary conventions such as halakhic dicta and midrashic comments, the redaction of corpora themselves, and the emergence of the Mishnah as a foundational text for later corpora are all part of the developing coherence, even institutionalization, of the rabbinic movement.[29]

In other words, the Mishnah did not so much arise from the institution imagined in stories such as this one, but rather gave rise to an institution modeled on this image. Such is the power of myth, which evokes eternal truths and bids us to actualize them in our lives.

Continuing the Conversation

1. Leadership: Top Down or Bottom Up?

Today's management styles generally fall into one of two broad categories: top down or bottom up. As historian and professor of business ethics James Hoopes reports, in America, the earliest management style was exceedingly top down: Southern plantation owners owned their labor force and overseers exerted unmitigated power over them. Northern factory owners in the mid-nineteenth century operated much the same way until labor unions emerged in response to the horrors of extreme top-down management. In the twentieth century, democracy and egalitarian ideals gave rise to an alternate, collaborative, participatory approach: bottom-up management that invites people to see themselves as team members empowered to share in decision-making. Bottom-up management has tended to engender greater morale but the decision-making process can become encumbered and impede efficiency—and even merely project the appearance of bottom up without genuinely welcoming input.

Business consultant Mark Lukens writes that management need not be either-or, because "leaders can—and probably should—have it both ways. Neither top-down nor bottom-up leadership work well consistently if they're seen as absolutes. There's usually room for both within a single organization at the same time. The reason is simple: The usefulness of either approach depends on what you're trying to achieve."[30]

As *nasi*, Rabban Gamliel's position was political, religious, and managerial, all rolled into one. In the story he comes across as a top-down authoritarian manager in his treatment of R. Yehoshua, against the background of his decidedly bottom-up approach to witnesses who sought to attest to the new moon. In general, halakhah is a top-down system: experts in halakhah examine questions and promulgate decisions that are binding on the one who posed the question and, indeed, come to be binding on segments of the community that acknowledge their authority.

What do you think are the benefits and drawbacks, advantages and risks, of the traditional top-down approach of halakhah? What was gained by Rabban Gamliel's acceptance of faulty testimony, and what was lost? Would you have done as he did?

Conversely, what do you think of the trend found in many parts of the Jewish world today toward a bottom-up approach—favoring individual choice in Jewish practice?

Which approach is best for you?

2. Keeping the Peace between the People in Power

R. Akiva places a premium on maintaining peace among the Sages because the community's well-being depends on leaders who can work together amicably. In another talmudic story, R. Eliezer b. Hyrcanus refuses to abide by a majority decision in the *bet midrash*.[31] His colleagues attempt to convince him to side with the majority, but he steadfastly holds to his dissenting halakhic view. The other Sages then vote to expel him from the *bet midrash*. R. Akiva, however, fears that R. Eliezer will retaliate by exerting magical powers against Rabban Gamliel, whom R. Eliezer holds responsible for his expulsion, and harm the *nasi*. R. Akiva takes it upon himself to visit R. Eliezer and attempt to persuade him not to act vindictively. While he is not successful, the story nevertheless testifies to R. Akiva's keen inclination to be a peacemaker.

In our story as well, R. Akiva exhibits exemplary sensitivity to R. Yehoshua, creating the psychological and intellectual space for R. Yehoshua to compromise his high standards in favor of peace in the Sanhedrin and cohesion in the community. All three leaders—Rabban Gamliel, R. Akiva, and R. Yehoshua—understand that they must look at the Big Picture.

Have you ever held a leadership position in which balancing your power, authority, reputation, and relationships with peer leaders was a tricky business? How did you decide when to hold fast, when to concede, when to compromise, and when to turn the reins over to another? How would R. Akiva's approach play out in your community, workplace, and family?

3. Rational Judgment and Moral Judgment

Rabbi David Hartman writes: "The eternal significance of the Torah is that it constitutes a God-given challenge that must be met in every generation by a covenantal community that trusts its own autonomous rational and moral judgment in applying the Torah to life."[32] The leaders in our passage are challenged to balance objective *rational* judgment with subjective *moral* judgment. In this instance Rabban Gamliel privileges subjective moral judgment, while R. Yehoshua (so often the champion of subjective moral judgment) privileges objective rational judgment.

When facing heart/mind conflicts, do you tend to favor objective rational decisions or subjective moral ones? Are rational and moral judgments necessarily separate and competing assessments? Have you ever found a way to bridge the two, as R. Akiva cleverly does in the story?

4. R. Akiva of the Mishnah and R. Akiva of the Gemara

The Mishnah and the Gemara present two versions of R. Akiva's effort to persuade R. Yehoshua to support Rabban Gamliel's handling of the Rosh Chodesh witnesses. Here again are both versions:

> **Mishnah:** R. Akiva went and found [R. Yehoshua] in great distress. He said to him, "I can demonstrate that whatever Rabban Gamliel has done is valid, because it says, *These are the festivals of Adonai, holy convocations, which you shall proclaim* (Leviticus 23:4), [which means] whether they are proclaimed at their proper time, or not at their proper time, I have no appointed seasons save these."

> **Gemara:** R. Akiva went and found R. Yehoshua in distress. He said to him, "Master, why are you in distress?"
>
> [R. Yehoshua] replied, "Akiva, it were better for a man [i.e., me] to be on a sickbed for twelve months than that such an decree should be issued against him [i.e., against me]."

[R. Akiva] said to [R. Yehoshua], "Master, allow me to tell you something that you taught me."

[R. Yehoshua] said to [R. Akiva], "Speak."

[R. Akiva] said to [R. Yehoshua], "Torah says, *you . . . you . . . you* three times to indicate that *you* [may fix the date of the festivals] even if you err inadvertently, *you*, even if you err deliberately, *you*, even if you are misled [by witnesses]."[33]

[R. Yehoshua] replied to him in these words, "Akiva, you have comforted me, you have comforted me."

In the mishnah's telling, R. Akiva expounds "these" in Leviticus 23:4 to argue that God places the authority to declare when festivals will occur in the hands of people, knowing that sometimes people will get it right and sometimes they will not. In the Gemara's telling, R. Akiva supplies a different, but similar, argument: the word *otam* (them), written without the letter *vav*, can be vocalized *atem* ("you" pl.), conveying that "you" (the Jewish people) have the authority to declare the festival times—even if doing so entails three types of errors (mirroring the three iterations of *otam/atem*). In both cases, R. Akiva's argument relies on interpreting verses in Leviticus.

Which of R. Akiva's arguments do you believe is more effective and why?

R. Akiva helps R. Yehoshua see the situation differently by referring to a teaching he attributes to R. Yehoshua. What do you think of this approach to peacemaking? Have you ever tried to resolve a dispute this way?

5. Exegesis vs Eisegesis

In the world of academic biblical study, a distinction is made between exegesis and eisegesis. Exegesis, "drawing out from the text," means to interpret the text in accord with its context. Motivated by the essential question "What does the text say and mean in its own words and context?" biblical interpreters use hermeneutical tools such as philology, history, archaeology, and biblical criticism to seek out answers.

In contrast, eisegesis, "reading into the text," occurs when interpreters impose their own meanings onto the text—usually meanings they wish to find there. In other words, through eisegesis, the text conforms to what an interpreter wants it to say.[34]

Do you believe R. Akiva's interpretations are exegesis or eisegesis? How would you support your perspective?

Summing Things Up

Myths, unlike fairy tales, reflect the reality of the world we experience and depict the meaning and hopes we ascribe to this world and to our lives. The Rabbis engaged in mythmaking, telling stories about their lives and endeavors in the *bet midrash* and their relationships with one another. Scholars had long presumed that the stories of the *tanna'im* in the *bet midrash* and *bet din* reflected the historical reality of a strong and vibrant Rabbinic class that served as halakhic decisors, ideologues, and leaders of the Jewish people. The Rabbis' portrayal of themselves as flawed human beings and the transcripts of seemingly real conversations added to the sense that these were actual accounts. Recent scholarship, however, has taught us that these stories are the creations of masterful storytellers and mythmakers who sought to place Judaism on a solid footing in a post-Temple world. In fact, these narratives guided the construction of actual institutions modeled on the myth. What is more, the stories serve to help us weigh how we as leaders—and other leaders in our midst—should treat one another.

4 Clashing Titans

Babylonian Talmud, Tractate Horayot 13b–14a

> Rabbi taught: Which is the path of virtue a person should
> follow? That which brings honor to one's Maker as well as
> respect from one's fellow human beings.
>
> —Pirkei Avot 2:1

Why Study This Passage?

How important is it for the movers and shakers of an institution to get
along? Does the well-being of an institution or society depend on leaders
trusting and treating with respect one another, as opposed to jockeying
viciously for power and authority?

When thorny issues of hierarchy, status, legitimacy in office, intellectual superiority, and ego among community leaders all converge, the
result can be a hundred-car pileup on the interstate, jamming up the
traffic of community affairs and progress. Alternatively, if the personal-
ities involved remain focused on goals higher than their own egos and
self-interest, placing the needs of the institution or society they lead
above their own, the outcome may be entirely different.

Writing in the *Harvard Business Review*, Christine Porath and Christine
Pearson document the surprisingly severe damage wrought by "mere

rudeness" in the workplace: "The costs chip away at the bottom line. Nearly everybody who experiences workplace incivility responds in a negative way, in some cases overtly retaliating. Employees are less creative when they feel disrespected, and many get fed up and leave. About half deliberately decrease their effort or lower the quality of their work."[1]

What is true for the workplace holds as well for other communal institutions; incivility and power struggles can interfere with and even thwart the overriding mission, with disastrous consequences. For this reason, keeping a lid on such behavior — even if it appears to serve short-term, individual needs — supports long-term institutional welfare.

Choosing between the two is the dilemma we encounter in a talmudic story that involves a cornucopia of raw human emotions around competition and ego. The story comes from Tractate Horayot (Decisions), in the talmudic Order Nezikim (Damages). Horayot discusses errors in judgment made by a *kohen* (priest) offering sacrifices or by the *bet din* (Rabbinical court) rulings on such errors that might lead others to commit sins *bi-sh'gagah* (unwittingly). One might wonder why the Rabbis would expend time and energy discussing, debating, and delineating the laws of sacrifices brought to the Temple — no longer standing — and, even more, potential errors made by a Rabbinic court concerning sacrifices that could no longer be made. For the Rabbis, sacrificial offerings were a fulfillment of divine will as expressed in Torah, and hence the hope of rebuilding the Temple was ever present and fervent, even if it had to be postponed to some later time in history. Beyond this deeply felt religious hope, the Rabbis were keenly aware that their own errors of judgment could lead the community astray. The story describes an incident when that danger was keenly felt.

How the Sages grapple with challenging relationships with one another and remain focused on the larger picture of their roles as communal leaders, given the intense emotions and egos at play, provides both a window into the world of the early Rabbis and a valuable lesson for all who undertake leadership.

A Broad View to Begin

In the story we meet Rabban Shimon b. Gamliel II, a third-generation *tanna* (mishnaic Sage and *nasi*) who is patriarch and president of the Sanhedrin.[2] In his youth he was present at R. Shimon bar Kokhba's stronghold, Betar, in 132 CE, when Bar Kokhba led a rebellion against Rome. Initially successful, Bar Kokhba established himself as *nasi* for several years.[3] The Yerushalmi reports that in 135 CE the Romans overran the Betar fortress and put all its defenders to the sword except R. Shimon b. Gamliel, who escaped.[4] The Sanhedrin then moved to Usha, in the western Galilee near Shefar'am, Tiberias, and Tzippori.[5] Rabbi Shimon b. Gamliel became the *nasi* and took on the title "Rabban."

The *nasi*—patriarch—in *Eretz Yisrael* (parallel to the *resh galuta*—exilarch—in Babylonia) was a civil, political position whose officeholders claimed descent from the ancient Davidic monarchy. Stuart A. Cohen, scholar of Jewish political theory and practice, explains: "As wealthy landowners and magnates, [the patriarchs] deliberately cultivated their eminence at the economic pinnacle of Jewish society; in political matters, they similarly operated from a constitutional power-base which they unreservedly regarded to be theirs alone."[6] In other words, they claimed biblical authority to lead the Jewish community as descendants of the Davidic line through Hillel.[7]

The patriarchate, Cohen says, constituted one leg of a three-legged stool of Jewish governance articulated in a statement attributed to R. Shimon bar Yochai, a *tanna* of the mid-second century: "There are three crowns: the crown of Torah, the crown of Priesthood, and the crown of Royalty. But the crown of a good name surpasses them all."[8] The patriarchate (the crown of Royalty) operated in cooperation with the Rabbis (the crown of Torah), but each was a separate instrument in the Jewish governance matrix.[9]

The two branches did find it politic to co-operate, most obviously at various Galilean locations in [the Land of Israel], where rabbis and patriarchs regularly joined council for administrative and judicial purposes in the conclaves sometimes (perhaps erroneously) designated a 'sanhedrin'. Nevertheless, as the records appertaining to those meetings themselves show, the relationship was often tense and occasionally stormy.... [Nonetheless] [e]ach franchise appreciated that it needed the other in order to further its own theological and political ends, and that their collusion was essential for the survival of their people and the preservation of its faith. Yet, at the same time, each was also determined, wherever possible, to deny the other an overriding advantage. Thus it was that several of the recorded dialogues of the period came to be characterised by tension, with champions of the two sides defending with some intensity the interests of the estates which they claimed to represent.[10]

The story makes the tension and struggle for power between two legs of the stool—the "crown of Royalty" and the "crown of Torah"—explicitly clear.

Writing about the rise of the patriarchate, the inherited ruling Rabbinic office that, according to Jewish tradition, comprised the direct descendants of Hillel, Shaye Cohen, scholar of Hebrew literature and philosophy, notes that while the patriarchs were Rabbis, their position and political authority lent them authority, responsibilities, goals, and a viewpoint that set them apart from their colleagues:

The patriarchate began as a rabbinic office. Its most enduring product is the first rabbinic document, the Mishnah, which was edited in about 200 CE by Rabbi Judah the Patriarch, often called simply "Rabbi." However, as the office expanded its power and prestige, it became less rabbinic. The goals of the patriarch were no longer identical to those of the rabbis. Most of the rabbis of the second century, if we may trust the evidence of the Mishnah and related corpora, were well-to-do landowners who lived in villages and small towns. The civil legislation of the Mishnah (and some of its religious legislation as well) treats questions that interested this economic class. In the third century, however, the rabbinic estate came to include the poor, who depended on charity or public employment for their survival, and became increasingly urban, with centers in Caesarea, Tiberias, and Sepphoris. In other words, the patriarchate was becoming the leader not just for the rabbis but also for the Jewry of the land of Israel as a whole, and the office of rabbi was becoming a profession as much as the affectation of a social elite. This transition was largely the work of Judah the Patriarch and his immediate successors. The urban elites who originally opposed rabbinic hegemony were gradually brought into the patriarchal government. Many rabbis resisted these changes, and the two Talmudim preserve many stories of great tension between the rabbis and the patriarch in the third century. But these changes were essential to the ultimate triumph of rabbinic Judaism, because they broadened the rabbis' reach and placed them at the center of communal life.[11]

The tension between the patriarchs and the Rabbis is in evidence throughout the Talmud, encoded in many of its stories. An illustrative example appears in the Yerushalmi. According to JT Chagigah 3:1; 78d, R. Yonah in the name of R. Chiyya bar Ba recounts an incident in the immediate aftermath of the failed Bar Kokhba rebellion. Assembling in the Rimmon Valley to intercalate the calendar are seven elders, among them R. Meir, featured in this chapter's story. The Sages initially disagree, but ultimately succeed in intercalating the year. They part in mutual respect and affection, sharing their cloaks with one another. As they leave, they participate in a "sign" of their achievement: each sinks a nail into a slab of marble found at that spot.

Prior to the Temple's destruction, the priests set the calendar; after 70 CE, the patriarch had that responsibility, which attested to his authority. Therefore, the first noticeable feature of the account is that the patriarch—Rabban Shimon b. Gamliel—is *not* present at Rimmon Valley; rather, seven Rabbis who are prominent disciples of R. Akiva intercalate the calendar. Midrash Genesis Rabbah lists these same seven Rabbis as the disciples who replaced "twelve thousand pairs of disciples [of R. Akiva] from Gevat to Antipatris" who died in a plague.[12] The number seven is significant, symbolizing Creation (the world having been created in seven days according to Genesis 1). Hence, the seven disciples of R. Akiva represent a new beginning, a fresh creation, following the cataclysm of the Bar Kokhba rebellion.[13] The patriarch's absence is not explained; it is ignored. The story thereby asserts the authority of R. Akiva over that of the patriarch.

There is a second notable feature to the tale. While the recounted events have the ring of historical authenticity—certainly they could have happened—the story ends with a miracle, signaling that something religiously important is at stake. As Albert Baumgarten, scholar of religion, notes:

> The presence of a miracle story in a rabbinic source is . . . grounds for inquiring into the reasons for invoking divine witness. A miracle story is a clue that matters of authority *may* be at stake. God Himself is being represented as intervening in nature and history; this should be our hint that the point *may have been* so significant and sensitive that no lesser testimony would do.[14]

For Baumgarten, the story is "a political document with a polemical meaning and purpose."[15] As Stuart A. Cohen, with a nod to the extensive work of Jewish religious historian Jacob Neusner, explains about Rabbinic writings, "Even when they do claim to recount historical events, the materials tend to deploy their data in a way more likely to create Rabbinic myths and/or confirm Rabbinic dogma than to transmit verifiable and objective information."[16] The miracle of nails in marble drives home the Akivans' authority over that of the patriarchate.

Driving in nails is a symbol of legitimate possession of the place into which the nails are driven; in our case, as suggested by Klein, the Land of Israel. The Akibans are thus the agents of the Jewish people as a whole in reasserting Jewish title to the land. If this meeting took place after the Bar Kochba revolt, the need to reassert Jewish claims after the loss to Rome was apparent. The miracle, of course, has another significance: it is a sign of divine approval and sanction for everything that has taken place.[17]

Historian David Goodblatt offers another view. Given the fact that many scholars have long viewed the story as reflecting the reconstruction of Jewish autonomy in *Eretz Yisrael* following the rebellion, he notes that the account could easily be accepted as historical, or at least as preserving what he calls a "historical kernel."[18] However, there is warrant to view the story through a literary lens, and not merely because the story is attributed to R. Chiyya bar Ba, who lived in the early fourth century, 150 years after the events it purports to recount. Goodblatt quotes the sage advice of Shamma Friedman, scholar of Talmud and Rabbinics: "Before you search for the historical kernel, you must search for the literary kernel and base your historical research on it."[19]

In line with Friedman's counsel Goodblatt suggests a non-supernatural meaning to the nailed rock, given that marble is not indigenous to Israel and the rock was probably limestone, which is far softer.[20] Marble certainly points to the message the story comes to convey, but it is symbolic rather than miraculous; marble connotes strength and endurance in contrast to the far more fragile limestone. The story, as a literary artifact from the early fourth century, may or may not recall actual events, but certainly appears to reflect a challenge to the patriarch's authority mounted by R. Akiva's followers in the aftermath of the Bar Kokhba rebellion.

With that background, this chapter's story recounts another—and far more direct—challenge to Rabban Shimon b. Gamliel's authority brought by R. Meir and R. Natan. Again, the conflict between intellectual leadership and political authority runs throughout the account.

No doubt, Rabban Shimon was an intelligent man and a scholar in his own right. However, his colleagues R. Meir and R. Natan outshone him intellectually. Rabban Shimon established the office of *chakham* (Teacher, lit. "wise one"), the third-highest position in the Sanhedrin, and appointed R. Meir to the new position.[21]

R. Natan, the son of a Babylonian exilarch, occupied the position of *av bet din* (Head of Court), the second-in-command in the Sanhedrin, and the highest-ranking scholar of the institution. When the *nasi* was not present, the *av bet din* presided. Talmud tells us that R. Natan assisted R. Yehudah ha-Nasi in compiling the Mishnah[22] and attributes many halakhic teachings to him. The authorship of *Avot de-Rabbi Natan* (a midrashic interpretation of Pirkei Avot that functions much like a Gemara on the treatise) is ascribed to him as well.

R. Meir, a student of R. Akiva and Elisha b. Abuyah and a *sofer* (scribe) who wrote *sifrei Torah* (Torah scrolls) and *megillot* (other biblical texts) to support his family, was renowned as a brilliant Sage. "Meir," meaning "illuminate," may well be a sobriquet conveying that his teachings illuminated the eyes of the Sages; his real name was Nahorai or Misha. His teachings are found in all but five tractates of the Bavli, and tradition attributes a wealth of Talmud's teachings to him—but anonymously, as this story will explain.[23]

Together, Rabban Shimon b. Gamliel, R. Natan, and R. Meir were the officers of the Rabbinic community that coalesced in the first century, produced the Mishnah at the end of the second century, and grew into a thriving scholarly class in the third and fourth centuries. They dubbed their growing scholarly institution the "Sanhedrin," harkening back to the assembly that ruled Israel during the Second Temple period.

The term Sanhedrin conjures an image of a large, powerful, and impressive body. The Rabbis themselves promoted such an image, even referring to themselves as *ba'alei trisim* ("shield bearers" or "warriors")—

Rabbinic titans—on one occasion.[24] In the sense that they reconstituted Judaism in the wake of the devastating destruction of the Second Temple and the failed revolt against Rome, and against all odds shaped a Judaism that could transcend time and space thanks to the oral tradition they crafted, they deserve that title. Yet consider for a moment just how transitory the Sanhedrin itself was—how it too struggled to survive: Following the Second Temple's destruction in 70 CE, the school that had assembled around Rabban Yochanan b. Zakkai was reconstituted in Yavneh. The Roman government ruling over the Land of Israel recognized the patriarchate—the familial line of leaders claiming descent from Hillel (and, through Hillel, from King David)—as the religious authority of the Jewish people. Nonetheless, this self-proclaimed seat of Jewish authority moved seven times in the ensuing 113 years.[25] A politically strong and vibrant institution would not have been compelled to move with such frequency. This testifies to the precarious footing of the "Sanhedrin" from 70 CE until the latter half of the third century, when, during the reign of Rabban Gamliel b. Yehudah (also known as Gamliel IV) and under Roman pressure, it became the *bet midrash*.

Rabban Shimon b. Gamliel presided at a precarious time of national instability. The Romans were persecuting and oppressing the Jews. They had destroyed the Second Temple, leaving the Jewish people without an altar on which to fulfill their obligations to God in the form of sacrifices. On top of this, the Bar Kokhba rebellion had been an unmitigated disaster resulting in the deaths of tens of thousands. The land had been decimated and much of the population impoverished. The Jewish people were religiously traumatized and spiritually demoralized. They no longer lived independently. They were also bereft of a political and social center. The Babylonian Talmud reports Rabban Shimon b. Gamliel's reflection, "Were we, as of old, to inscribe on a memorial scroll our sufferings and our occasional deliverances from them, we should not find room for it all."[26] Song of Songs Rabbah 3:3, a midrash on the Song of Songs, ascribes these words to him: "Our ancestors knew suffering only from a distance, but we have been surrounded by it for so many days, years, and cycles that we are more justified than they in becoming impatient." At this deeply challenging time, Rabban Shimon b. Gamliel believed it was his personal responsibility as *nasi* to rebuild the community and restore its morale, if not its political and economic power.

Yet Rabban Shimon would soon encounter formidable internal challenges, as his personal power and position would become entangled with communal issues of status and authority. In institutional life, when the extent and limits of leaders' authority are poorly defined, second-tier leaders may seek to boost their position and authority, challenging the legitimacy of those above them, as Korach and his followers challenged Moses and Aaron (Numbers 16–17).

Leaders also need to monitor their own internal conflicts and be cognizant of their ego needs and motivations. As Shimon b. Zoma taught: "Who is mighty? Those who conquer their evil impulse. . . . Who is honored? Those who honor all people."[27]

Ultimately, Rabban Shimon and the other Rabbinic titans will have to decide this question: How do we place the Jewish community's needs above our own narrow self-interests?

Exploring the Nooks and Crannies of Our Passage

In many societies, when a head of state or judge enters the room, people are expected to stand. This tradition also applied to the Sanhedrin, Israel's "supreme court," where the Rabbinic leaders of the nation gathered. Our passage opens with a description of the formal Sanhedrin protocol concerning the entrances of the *nasi* (Patriarch, or President), *av bet din* (Head of Court), and *chakham* (Teacher, or Sage).

> Our Rabbis taught: When the *nasi* ['Patriarch,' or 'President'] enters, all the people rise and do not resume their seats until he says, "Sit." When the *av bet din* ['Head of Court'] enters, one row rises on one side and another row on the other [and they remain standing] until he sits down

in his place. When the *chakham* ['Teacher,' or 'Sage'] enters, every one rises [as he passes] and sits down [as soon as he passes] until he sits down in his place.

A clear hierarchy of honors is accorded to the Sanhedrin's three top officers. According to the protocol: Everyone present rises when the *nasi* enters from the rear of the chamber. He walks to the front, sits in his place, and only then tells the others to take their seats. Next, the *av bet din* enters. As he walks from the rear of the chamber to the front, people stand as he passes by their row; they remain standing until he takes his place at the front of the room beside the *nasi*. As the *chakham* walks to the front of the chamber, people rise as he passes their row and take their seats again after he has passed. The protocol makes clear to even the most casual observer that the *nasi* holds the highest position of authority, the *av bet din* the second-highest position, and the *chakham* the third in the troika.

The passage then detours to consider various issues of proper behavior, priority, and hierarchy in the Sanhedrin before returning to the topic of the protocol for the *nasi*, *av bet din*, and *chakham* to enter the chamber. R. Yochanan informs us that Rabban Shimon b. Gamliel innovated this protocol.

R. Yochanan said: "That instruction was issued in the days of Rabban Shimon b. Gamliel [II], when Rabban Shimon b. Gamliel was the *nasi*, R. Meir was the *chakham*, and R. Natan was the *av bet din*. Whenever Rabban Shimon b. Gamliel entered, everyone stood for him; when R. Meir and R. Natan entered, everyone stood for them [as well]."

Rabban Shimon b. Gamliel said, "Should there not be a distinction between my honor and theirs?" And so he enacted that ordinance. R. Meir and R. Natan were not present on that day.

Under the previous protocol, R. Yochanan tells us, the three leaders were accorded equal honor; no distinctions were made for rank. Why, then, did Rabban Shimon b. Gamliel institute a new protocol, clearly designed to demonstrate the primacy of the *nasi*? Perhaps Rabban Shimon seeks publicly expressed, ego-gratifying deference from his colleagues. Or the enactment of hierarchy is intended to reinforce (or increase) his power and authority.

Alternatively, we might conjecture that at a fragile time in Israel's history, when the nation is fractured and weak, Rabban Shimon b. Gamliel seeks to bolster the *position* of *nasi* (not necessarily the person occupying the position) for its historic and symbolic value. Since the *nasi*, by tradition, is a direct descendant of Hillel and King David, those who serve as patriarch are tantamount to Jewish royalty, possessing a distinguished pedigree and the authority of Scripture to serve as the civil leaders of the Jewish people. Lacking independence and power, the people need a visible and symbolic rallying point for the sake of communal cohesion; the *nasi* fulfills that function.

There are other reasons why Rabban Shimon b. Gamliel might seek change at this particular time. As a child he witnessed the disaster of the Bar Kokhba rebellion. He knows firsthand the danger and folly of placing trust and hope in a charismatic military leader. He fervently believes that Judaism's future lies in the hands of its Rabbis, who must shape a new way of being Jewish in a post-temple world. R. Yochanan's assertion that Rabban Shimon ben Gamliel said, "Should there be no distinction between my [office] and theirs?" supports this theory. Perhaps Rabban Shimon b. Gamliel's scheme is meant to strengthen the community and the emerging Rabbinic tradition through its connection to, and cooperation with, the *nasi*.

It is also possible that Rabban Shimon b. Gamliel's plan was informed by a combination of honorable motives and all-too-human (but less noble) impulses. Is he concerned with his *office*, the respect that ought to be accorded anyone occupying the *nasi* seat, and/or does he seek to increase and consolidate his power above and beyond that of the *av bet din* and the *chakham*? To better understand his motives, we need to look for clues throughout the narrative.

The first clue jumps out at us: Rabban Shimon b. Gamliel enacts the new protocol that affects R. Meir and R. Natan most of all at a time when both are out of town. What is more, he does not discuss, consult, or even inform them ahead of time. Upon their return, they are caught off guard to find that people are not treating them with the accustomed deference.

> Coming on the following day and seeing that the people did not rise for them as usual, they said, "What happened?"
>
> They said to them, "This is what Rabban Shimon b. Gamliel enacted."
>
> R. Meir said to R. Natan, "I am the *chakham* and you are the *av bet din*. Let us enact something like [he did] to us."
>
> [R. Natan asked R. Meir,] "What shall we do to him?"
>
> [R. Meir replied,] "Let us say to him, 'Expound [Tractate] Uktzin,' which he does not know. And since he has not learned it, we shall [then] say to him: *Who can express the mighty acts of Adonai; make all God's praise heard* (Psalm 106:2)—For *whom* is it becoming to express *the mighty acts of Adonai*? For the one who can *make all God's praise heard*. We shall then depose him, and I shall become *av bet din* and you the *nasi*."

The scene, as the Gemara describes it, raises many questions: Does Rabban Shimon institute the new protocol surreptitiously—while R. Meir and R. Natan are away—because he thinks they will object and undermine his plan? Could it be that he himself is not fully comfortable with the new protocol and unsure it is the best course of action? If he is fully comfortable with the changes, why not smooth the transition by informing his colleagues? It appears that he fears their response. Is he operating under the presumption that it is better to implement the changes when those who would most vociferously object are not present and, if necessary, request forgiveness later? Perhaps he believes that changes, once implemented, will be accepted with fewer objections.

As readers, we may naturally question whether the *nasi* made the right decisions. From our understandings of politics, are the *nasi's* actions likely to cultivate trust, cooperation, and goodwill, or undermine them? Are his actions likely to consolidate or threaten his power? Might it have been politically prudent to have informed the *av bet din* and *chakham*, discussed it with them, and sought their support ahead of enacting the new protocol? And, from the perspective of *derekh eretz* (kindness, courtesy), is the *nasi* morally obligated to consult or inform the *av bet din* and *chakham* prior to enacting the new procedure?

For their part, R. Meir and R. Natan may feel blindsided, insulted, and possibly humiliated. R. Meir's response suggests that this is precisely what he feels. Consider his tone of voice when he says, "Let us enact something like [he did] to us." The narrative suggests that R. Meir is plotting political revenge rather than a diplomatic response.

R. Natan's concise and immediate response to R. Meir's suggestion—"What shall we do to him?"—is revealing. Without hesitation or objection, R. Natan becomes R. Meir's coconspirator. The interchange is reminiscent of Rebekah's plot to deceive Isaac into bestowing the blessing intended for Esau on Jacob instead (Genesis 27). While Esau is conveniently occupied outside the camp hunting game to prepare a special repast for Isaac, Rebekah instructs Jacob to fetch from the herd two goats; she will cook these for Jacob to bring to his nearly blind father so as to secure the blessing intended for Esau—before Esau returns with the game. Jacob might have responded, "But Mom, that would be dishonest! I can't be involved in a scheme to deceive my own father." But no, his immediate response is complicity: *Jacob answered his mother Rebekah, "But my brother Esau is a hairy man and I am smooth-skinned. If my father touches me, I shall appear to him as a trickster and bring upon myself a curse, not a blessing"* (Genesis 27:11–12). Jacob expresses no concern for any inherent immorality in the plot, only pragmatic doubts concerning its likelihood of success. In a similar vein, R. Natan voices no objection to R. Meir's plot for revenge; he asks only how they will proceed: "I'm with you; what's the plan?"

R. Meir's plan is based on his superior intellect; he knows more Oral Torah than Rabban Shimon b. Gamliel. In the academy that carries great weight. R. Meir and R. Natan will publicly request that Rabban Shimon b. Gamliel teach the obscure talmudic tractate Uktzin (Stalks), which discusses issues surrounding *tum'ah* (ritual impurity) conveyed by various parts of plants. The Written Torah does not touch on this subject; the Rabbis developed it themselves from general principles of ritual purity. The material in Uktzin is not only arcane, but also esoteric.

It is not necessarily a stain on Rabban Shimon's integrity as a scholar that he has not mastered this material. It could be argued that the *nasi's* limited time is better spent negotiating the complex relationship between the Jewish community and the Roman government, managing issues of community unity, and running the Sanhedrin. He has considerable command of more common halakhic questions, but not the bandwidth for the minutia of how and when roots, stalks, and hulls convey impurity to other objects.

Nonetheless R. Meir plans to engineer a situation whereby the *nasi's* lapse in knowledge will be publicly revealed by asking the *nasi* to discourse on a passage he is unqualified to teach. When his incomplete knowledge is evident to all, R. Meir plans to quote Psalm 106:2, interpreting its two parallel phrases not as poetic repetition through parallel phrases,[28] but rather as a question and its response. Notwithstanding that the phrase *Who can express the mighty acts of Adonai* means much the same thing as [*who can*] *make all God's praise heard*, R. Meir plans to interpret the verse as follows:

Question: *Who can express the mighty acts of Adonai?*
Answer: [*Only one who can*] *make **all** God's praise heard.*

The implication of R. Meir's interpretation of the verse is to declare Rabban Shimon b. Gamliel unfit to hold the position of *nasi*:

Question: Who is fit to sit in the seat of the *nasi*, who by dint of this position expresses the mighty acts of God to the Jewish people?

Answer: Only one who is capable of making all God's praise heard—and "all" includes the obscure tractate Uktzin."

R. Meir presumes that when Rabban Shimon b. Gamliel fails to provide an impressive discourse on Uktzin he will be revealed as unfit for his post, at which point R. Meir and R. Natan can rally the Sanhedrin to depose him. Following the coup d'état, R. Meir and R. Natan will each climb one rung higher on the ladder: R. Natan will become the new *nasi*, and R. Meir the *av bet din*.

Unfortunately for R. Meir and R. Natan, but fortunately for Rabban Shimon, R. Yaakov b. Karshi, assistant to the *nasi*, overhears their clandestine conversation.

> R. Yaakov b. Karshi overheard them. He said [to himself,] "The matter might, heaven forbid, lead to [the *nasi*'s] disgrace." So he went and sat behind the upper story of R. Shimon b. Gamliel's upper chamber, expounding [Tractate Uktzin] and reciting and reviewing, reciting and reviewing.
>
> [R. Shimon] said [to himself]: "Why is this [happening]? Did anything, heaven forbid, happen at the *bet midrash*?" [R. Shimon] concentrated his attention and repeated it.

R. Yaakov b. Karshi recognizes that the plot is not only politically dangerous, but also immoral by Rabbinic standards, because it will cause the *nasi* public embarrassment. Talmud expressly forbids causing the public humiliation of another. On the basis of the verse, *You shall not, therefore, wrong one another* (Leviticus 25:17), the Talmud teaches: "One who publicly shames a neighbor is like one who has shed blood," as well as the even more dramatic teaching: "It is better that a man throw himself into a fiery furnace than publicly shame a neighbor."[29] While these statements are clearly hyperbolic—causing someone's public humiliation is not equivalent to murder, nor does it warrant suicide—through them the Rabbis convey their extreme disapprobation of inflicting such humiliation.

R. Yaakov b. Karshi therefore devises a plan to thwart R. Meir and R. Natan's scheme. He spends the entire night teaching his master Uktzin. For the *tanna'im*, this meant memorizing it.[30] Uktzin consists of twenty-eight *mishnayot* in three short chapters; for Rabban Shimon one night is sufficient to learn it all.

That R. Yaakov seeks to protect his master seems natural. How he goes about it and how the *nasi* responds, however, are surprising. Strikingly, R. Yaakov does not inform the *nasi* that he seeks to protect him from the plot afoot to depose him. Doing so would afford Rabban Shimon greater freedom to choose a proper course of action. What is more, although the *nasi* senses that something is awry and even wonders, "Why is this [happening]? Did anything, heaven forbid, happen at the *bet midrash*?" he does not explicitly ask his assistant why he keeps him up all night studying this esoteric material.

We are reading a carefully constructed story, not history, so some literary analysis is warranted. The storyteller relays that R. Meir's learning surpasses that of Rabban Gamliel, but also that Rabban Gamliel has admirable intellectual qualities; after all, without even being told he needs to memorize Uktzin to protect his position, he stays up all night and masters the material. Moreover, in minimizing the exchange between R. Yaakov and the *nasi*, the story's focus remains on the *nasi*'s relationship with R. Meir and R. Natan—and the action is almost entirely in the public realm of the *bet midrash*, not behind closed doors. In addition, it is worth noting how thoroughly the *nasi* trusts R. Yaakov b. Karshi.

> On the following day [R. Meir and R. Natan] said to [Rabban Shimon], "Let the Master come and teach us Uktzin."
>
> He began and discoursed upon it. After he had finished, he said to them, "Had I not learned it, you would have disgraced me!" He gave the order that they be expelled from the *bet midrash*.

Rabban Shimon's confidence in his assistant is well placed. Come morning, he rises to the challenge to discourse on Uktzin and, in fact, handles it like a champion, foiling the plot to depose him. We cannot know precisely when the *nasi* realized the depth and intent of R. Meir and R. Natan's challenge, given that we have no evidence that R. Yaakov informed him directly, but his comment, "Had I not learned it, you would have disgraced me!" makes it clear that he knew what was at stake when he recited Uktzin that day. If the underlying concern is truly scholarship, Rabban Shimon has proven himself worthy. If it is a political challenge to the patriarchate's authority, then the *nasi*'s public teaching and punitive response serve to assert his power. The remedy—tossing R. Meir and R. Natan out of the academy—succeeds in firmly establishing the *nasi*'s position in the *bet midrash*, but it is not the most severe option available to Rabban Shimon. He might have used his considerable political heft to insist that his two challengers be placed in *cherem* (complete excommunication from the community) or *nidui* (a temporary ban). Instead, Rabban Shimon evicts them from the *bet midrash* for an unspecified period of time, suggesting that his purpose is a public demonstration of his power rather than a genuine ban. The story, as it proceeds, confirms this.

One might expect R. Meir and R. Natan to go home, or attempt to start a rival academy, or concoct yet another stratagem to undermine Rabban Shimon. Yet they do none of these.

> [Thereupon R. Meir and R. Natan] wrote down halakhic questions and threw them into [the *bet midrash*]. That which he [R. Shimon] resolved was resolved, and for that which he did not resolve, they wrote down the answers and threw them in.

R. Meir and R. Natan sit just outside the academy, probably under a window, scribbling halakhic questions onto scraps of paper and tossing them inside. You might picture them folding the papers into paper airplanes and sending them soaring through the window into the *bet midrash*. If they lived today, they would be tweeting, texting, or emailing their questions to the *nasi*. It is extremely significant that they neither distance themselves from their colleagues and the proceedings inside the *bet midrash* nor rebel against the institution. It is equally significant that Rabban Shimon, knowing they are sitting right outside the *bet midrash* and interacting with those inside, makes no effort to interfere. Not only do R. Meir and R. Natan continue their participation with their colleagues in the *bet midrash*, but, as we will soon learn, the *nasi* himself facilitates their engagement.

Although their projectile missives seem intended to challenge and possibly trip up Rabban Shimon b. Gamliel, he permits them to reach the floor and have a hearing. And far more: he answers those he can, but when he is unable to supply an answer R. Meir and R. Natan fly in epistles containing the answers, which Rabban Shimon b. Gamliel himself accepts and teaches. In so doing, he endorses their value to the academy and to the Jewish people.

This is astounding. R. Meir and R. Natan have attempted to depose Rabban Shimon, yet he appreciates their erudition and wisdom, engages with them, and teaches their interpretations of halakhah. Clearly, his intent was never to expel them permanently; they are in a very public "time-out for bad behavior" that serves to demonstrate his authority over them. His tactic affords time and space for everyone involved to cool down.

> Yose said to [the Rabbis in the *bet midrash*,] "The Torah is outside and we are inside!"
> R. Shimon b. Gamliel to them, "We shall readmit them, but impose on them the penalty that no teaching shall be reported in their names."
> R. Meir was designated "others" and R. Natan "some say."

Finally, R. Yose gives voice to what many in the academy—and those reading the story—are undoubtedly thinking: "This situation has gone on long enough! The greatest Torah minds of our age are sitting outside the *bet midrash*. We need them inside with us, teaching us directly." The *nasi* accedes, perhaps recognizing that his unilateral action in changing the protocols and thereby diminishing the honor publicly accorded the *av bet din* and *chakham* set the plot to depose him in motion. The swift timing of the readmittance may also have to do with the murmurings of discontent in the *bet midrash*. The Rabbis are annoyed, or dismayed, or angry—we cannot tell for sure—but this poses a danger to Rabban Shimon: what if those remaining in the *bet midrash* consummate the effort initiated by their two colleagues?

What is more, as hurt and insulted as the *nasi* may personally still be, or as much as he feels the need to bolster the position of the patriarchate in the *bet midrash*, R. Yose is correct. If his purpose in expelling them was personal and punitive, he has accomplished that—but now, in light of R. Yose's comment, this seems a trivial and unworthy goal. If his purpose was related to political power and professional authority, he has unquestionably succeeded in demonstrating this as well. And so the *nasi* rises above whatever private thoughts and feelings may still be flowing through him to place the needs of the academy and the community over his own. Political bridges must be mended for the sake of Torah learning and the nation's larger concerns.

Rabban Shimon b. Gamliel readmits R. Meir and R. Natan, accompanied by a devastating punishment: their halakhic teachings will no longer be conveyed in their own names, but by the ambiguous prefaces, "Others say . . ." and "Some say . . ." This is a shocking pronouncement in a tradition that places enormous value on quoting *b'shem omro* (in the name of the one who taught it).

As an example, earlier we considered a talmudic teaching concerning the emotional violence done to one who is publicly humiliated. The Talmud goes to great lengths to identify the source of the teaching, citing three possibilities:

Mar Zutra b. Toviyah said in Rav's name—others state, R. Chana b. Bizna said in the name of R. Shimon the Pious—others again state,

R. Yochanan said on the authority of R. Shimon b. Yochai: "Better that a man throw himself into a fiery furnace than publicly shame a neighbor."

Consider how much effort was expended to provide full attribution for this teaching, which itself is merely a hyperbolic statement reinforcing a ruling. In the minds of the Sages, every teaching or ruling has a lineage that legitimates it and is transmitted with the teaching. The lineage testifies to its authenticity and value. It must have been a devastating blow to R. Meir and R. Natan to be denied credit for their teachings. Even more, R. Shimon's ruling would punish the generations to come, who would be denied the source of these teachings, a significant part of the heritage of Oral Torah.

R. Meir and R. Natan are repatriated to the house of study, but reconciliation has not yet been achieved. We have seen no attempt at *teshuvah* (repentance) or *kapparah* (atonement).

In their dreams, they received [a message] to go and appease R. Shimon b. Gamliel. R. Natan went. R. Meir did not go, for he said, "Dreams neither raise nor lower [i.e., dreams are of no consequence]."

When R. Natan went, R. Shimon b. Gamliel said to him, "Granted, the belt of your father benefited you in becoming the *av bet din*. Shall it also make you *nasi*?"

In the Torah dreams are considered messages from the divine realm.[31] Talmud's understanding of the realm of the unconscious is more equivocal. In their dreams, both R. Meir and R. Natan are instructed to apologize to Rabban Shimon b. Gamliel. R. Meir dismisses the dream as meaningless, but R. Natan understands it as a message from heaven and therefore visits the *nasi*.

Rabban Shimon tells R. Natan that he should realize — lest he contemplate another coup d'état — that he could never become *nasi* because he lacks the proper lineage (this is the meaning of "the belt of your father"). Although R. Natan's father, the *resh galuta* (exilarch) in Babylonia, occupied a political position of power parallel to that of the *nasi*, and the line of the *resh galuta* also made the atavistic claim of descent from King David,[32] R. Natan is now living in *Eretz Yisrael*, where the patriarchate is in the hands of the family of Gamliel the Elder. R. Natan is not a descendant of Gamliel and therefore cannot be promoted to *nasi*. The plot to depose Rabban Shimon b. Gamliel was for naught.

The story now jumps ahead one generation to the study of R. Yehudah ha-Nasi, compiler of the Mishnah, and the son of Rabban Shimon b. Gamliel. The Gemara generally refers to him simply as "Rabbi." Rabbi is teaching his son Shimon (named for his grandfather, Rabban Shimon b. Gamliel). The text of the Talmud that has come down to us refers here to Shimon as "Rabban," but R. Yehudah ha-Nasi was succeeded by his son Gamliel, so I have amended the text to reflect that Shimon was a Rabbi, but not a *nasi*.

To clarify who these people are and how they are related, here are the presidents of the Sanhedrin from the time of Hillel. Our story concerns the last three generations (the dates are their terms in office):

Hillel (see "Continuing the Conversation," #3), c. 31 BCE–9 CE
Shimon b. Hillel, 9 CE
Rabban Gamliel ha-Zaken (Gamliel the Elder, Gamliel I,), 30–50 CE
Rabban Shimon b. Gamliel I, 50–70 CE
(Rabban Yochanan b. Zakkai, not a descendant of Hillel, 70–80 CE)
Rabban Gamliel of Yavneh (Gamliel II) (see chapters 2 and 3 of this volume), 80–118 CE
(R. Elazar b. Azariah, not a descendant of Hillel, 118–120 CE)
Interregnum — Bar Kokhba rebellion
Rabban Shimon b. Gamliel II, 142–165 CE
Rabbi Yehudah ha-Nasi, 165–220 CE
Gamliel III, 220–230 CE
Judah II, 230–270 CE

Rabbi [Yehudah ha-Nasi] taught his son R. Shimon, "Others say: If it were a substitute, it would not have been sacrificed."[33]

[R. Shimon] said to him, "Who are those whose waters we drink but whose names we do not mention?"

[Rabbi] answered him, "These are people who sought to uproot your honor and the honor of your ancestral house."

[R. Shimon] said to him, "*Their love, their hatred, and their envy have long since perished! (Ecclesiastes 9:6).*"

[Rabbi] said to him, "*The enemy is no more, but the ruins are everlasting (Psalm 9:7).*"

[R. Shimon] said to him, "Those words apply when [the enemies'] deeds remain in effect but these Rabbis' deeds are no longer in effect."

[Rabbi] subsequently taught him: "They said in the name of R. Meir: if it were a substitute, it would not have been sacrificed."

Rava said, "Even Rabbi, who was a humble person, taught: "They said in the name of R. Meir." He did not say: "R. Meir said.""

Rabbi Yehudah ha-Nasi had two sons. Rabbi planned for his elder son, Gamliel III, to succeed him as *nasi*, and his younger son, Shimon, to become the *chakham*.[34] On this particular day R. Yehudah ha-Nasi is teaching his younger son a mishnah from Tractate Bekhorot, which concerns the designation of animals from one's flocks and herds for the biblically required tithe of the firstborn. Given that when this conversation takes place the Temple has not stood for more than a century, it is an esoteric teaching. Nonetheless, R. Shimon asks his father the source of the teaching. His father responds, in essence: "We don't mention their names because long ago they attempted to depose your grandfather and had they succeeded they would have brought dishonor to our family and quite possibly neither you nor I would have become *nasi*."

Shades of the Hatfields and the McCoys? R. Shimon understands that insult can act like a temporal contagion, carried through several generations. He also understands that Torah itself is healing and redemptive in each generation. He quotes Ecclesiastes 9:6 to his father to say: "The hatred and envy you speak about occurred long ago. It's over. Let it go. The enterprise of learning and teaching Torah must take priority over the wounds of the past." Rabbi relents in the face of his son's compelling moral argument.

If we consider the mishnah Rabbi and his son are studying, we see that R. Meir's name *is* encoded in it. After explaining how herd and flock animals are to be counted for the purposes of paying tithes and redeeming the firstborn, M Bekhorot 9:8 (60a) ends: "They said in the name of R. Meir: If it were a substitute, it would not have been sacrificed."

The unusual phrasing—"They said in the name of R. Meir" rather than "R. Meir said"— provides Rava with an opening to make a subtle point: as humble and self-effacing as R. Yehudah ha-Nasi was, he nonetheless had a difficult time restoring R. Meir's name completely. Hence the mishnah (attributed to R. Yehudah ha-Nasi) does not give R. Meir direct credit for the teaching. Perhaps this is Rava's acknowledgement that even R. Yehudah ha-Nasi struggled to forgive.

Restoring R. Meir's name to his teachings is a sign that the rift that occurred in the generation of Rabban Shimon b. Gamliel is healed. His grandson and namesake, Shimon, accomplishes this through compassionately and nonjudgmentally listening to his father's pain and addressing his concerns with the wisdom of Scripture.[35] In this way, he has carved out space for R. Yehudah ha-Nasi to forgive and let go.

Stepping back and considering the story in its Babylonian context— recall it was composed by *amora'im* in Babylonia several centuries after the *tanna'im* named in the story lived—it is noteworthy that the author considered R. Meir, R. Natan, and R. Yaakov b. Karshi far more learned yet under the thumb of the powerful patriarch, Rabban Shimon b. Gamliel. Perhaps the story reveals the struggles between the patriarchate and the early generations of Rabbis in *Eretz Yisrael*. Yet it is equally possible that the story reflects the contemporary struggles between the *amora'im* and the exilarch in Babylonia, a familiar communal-political conflict projected onto an earlier time and distant place.

Continuing the Conversation

1. Derekh Eretz *in the Political Arena*

When the Sages look back on the Temple's destruction from their temporally and spatially distant perch in Babylonia of several centuries later and a thousand miles away, they tell us that *sinat chinam* (gratuitous hatred) so frayed the fabric of Jewish society in the first century that Rome was able to destroy the Second Temple and conquer the Jewish nation (BT Gittin 55–57). In another story recounting the devastation during the final revolt against Rome in the second century CE, the Sages also cast the blame inward: "R. Akiva had twelve thousand pairs of students from Gevat to Antipatris. All of them died [over thirty-two days between Passover and Lag Ba'Omer] because they did not honor one another, and the world was left barren of Torah" (BT Yevamot 62b). Few of us would ascribe the vicissitudes of history or pandemic disease to the moral failings of the victims, but Talmud does not hesitate to draw a straight line between the behavior of leaders and the well-being of the nation, and counsel *derekh eretz* (kindness, courtesy, and consideration) as the antidote.

Have you encountered a situation in which people's failure to respect and honor one another had devastating consequences for an institution, community, or nation?

How important is it for community leaders—whether in a synagogue, community organization, town committee, Congress, or the world stage—to treat one another with civility and respect?

2. *The Ego Agenda*

The Sage Ben Zoma taught, "Who is honored? The one who honors others."[36]

In our passage leaders and Sages struggle with issues of honor. Like us, they sometimes find it difficult to honor others when personal agendas and egos intervene. What role do you believe the egos of Rabban Shimon b. Gamliel, R. Natan, and R. Meir played in their interactions?

If our Sages struggled so much to contain their egos, how can we keep ours at bay? According to Sigmund Freud, the rational ego works to balance the hedonistic tendencies of the id with the moralistic superego. He likened the relationship between ego and id to a charioteer and his horses: the horses provide the energy and momentum, but the charioteer must provide the direction. Our egos must engage with our instinctual needs and desires and steer them in a proper direction.

Today, when we find our negative egos encroaching into dangerous terrain, some of us try to concentrate instead on the bigger picture, as Rabban Shimon b. Gamliel, R. Meir, and R. Natan eventually do. To calm and control ourselves, some of us use prayer, others Torah study, and still others meditation and mantras. To redirect our thoughts, some of us may prioritize family, professionalism, and community in the forefront of our minds.

What role does ego play in your life and relationships? What methods of directing your ego work for you?

3. Staying Connected

The existential psychologist Rollo May taught: "Communication leads to community—that is, to understanding, intimacy, and the mutual valuing that was previously lacking."[37]

Both communication and its opposite run throughout this story. Imagine how differently the situation might have unfolded had R. Shimon b. Gamliel taken R. Meir and R. Natan out for coffee to explain his plan and the purpose behind it, asked their opinions, and enlisted their support. At the same time, the story portrays Rabbis who model appropriate communication as means of reconciliation. Even when Rabban Shimon b. Gamliel tosses R. Meir and R. Natan out of the house of study following the failed coup, alternative channels of communication open up to maintain connection until the Sages can reestablish a working relationship.

Joseph Priestley, the eighteenth-century chemist, theologian, natural philosopher, and political theorist, is attributed with this prescient warning: "The more elaborate our means of communication, the less we communicate." At the same time, the words of business consultant and author Peter Drucker are equally true: "The most important thing in communication is hearing what isn't said." Priestly and Drucker remind us that communication is never simple, but direct communication from the heart is the most effective. And, as the poet, philosopher, and theologian Samuel Taylor Coleridge said, "What comes from the heart, goes to the heart."

How do Rollo May's words apply to the Sages in this story? How do they apply to your life?

Do you believe the three Sages ultimately fulfill the three principles articulated by Priestly, Drucker, and Coleridge? Why or why not?

How do you relate to these three principles? Do you agree that elaborate communication translates into less communication? Have you experienced the wisdom of working to hear what isn't being said? Can you recall an instance when someone's words communicated one idea, but the way it was said communicated something entirely different?

What unintended "messages" have people received about you? Can you recall a time when someone significantly mistook what you thought you had communicated?

4. Aristocracy or Meritocracy?
Should positions of authority and power be filled on the basis of heredity or talent and ability?

The patriarchs—in Stuart A. Cohen's words, "wealthy landowners and magnates"—passed the inherited position of *nasi* from father to son and claimed (however unlikely this was to be true) descent from King David through Hillel. In contrast, while the Rabbis supplanted the priests as the religious leaders of Israel, they made no claim to familial qualification. Rather, they built a scholar class based on a meritocracy of intellectual acumen and scholarship. In the section of the *sugya* we did not examine, Talmud states:

> Sons of a scholar whose father holds the office of *parnas* ['paid communal employee'] may, if they possess the capability of understanding [the discourses], enter and sit down before their father with their backs to the people. When, however, they do not possess the capability of understanding [the discourses], they enter and sit down before their father with their faces toward the public.

Rabban Shimon b. Gamliel and R. Natan had family "pedigrees," but even R. Natan's lineage was not sufficient for the patriarchate of *Eretz Yisrael*. R. Meir lacked a "pedigree" but was considered the finest mind of his generation. Similarly his teacher R. Akiva grew up in obscurity and extreme poverty and rose to be the greatest Sage of his time.

Why do you believe R. Meir and R. Natan even attempted to depose Rabban Shimon b. Gamliel, given that neither qualified to serve as *nasi*? Is the story suggesting that inheriting leadership and authority by dint of lineage is no longer appropriate?

Questions of hierarchy pervade Tractate Horayot. The very last mishnah in Horayot (3:8), to which our story is attached, tells us: "If a scholar is illegitimate and the High Priest is an ignoramus, the illegitimate ['mamzer'] scholar takes precedence over the ignorant High Priest." How might our story and Mishnah 3:8 be addressing a shift in the culture of the *bet midrash* from inheritance to meritocracy?

5. The Benefit of the Doubt

Have you noticed how quickly people judge one another and draw negative conclusions about their motives and actions, even before they have all the pertinent information at hand? Yehoshua b. Perakhya taught

(Pirkei Avot 1:6): *Ve-hevei dan et kol ha-adam l'khaf zekhut* (Judge others favorably, or for merit). Alfred, Lord Tennyson expressed it rather more poetically: "Cleave ever to the sunnier side of doubt." Had Rabban Shimon b. Gamliel, R. Meir, and R. Natan all operated according to this principle, how do you believe the story would have been different? Imagine too that we all operated by this principle. How would our lives be different?

The anonymous author of *Orchot Tzaddikim* (Paths of the righteous),[38] a work of *musar* (Jewish ethics) from fifteenth-century Germany, offers practical advice to avoid falling into a pattern of judging others' morality, wisdom, piety, wealth, deeds, and spirituality:

> The humble person judges everyone favorably. As an example: When they asked one of the pious, "How is it that you deserved to become a master among your contemporaries?" he responded, "Because everyone whom I saw I assumed to be better than I am. If he were wiser than me, I told myself, 'He is also more reverent of God than I am because of his great wisdom.' If he were lesser in wisdom than me, I told myself, 'He [sins] unknowingly, but I [sin] knowingly.' If he were more advanced in years than I am, I told myself, 'His merits exceed my merits.' If I were older than he, I told myself, 'His transgressions are fewer than my transgressions.' If he were my equal in wisdom and years, I told myself 'His conscience is clearer before God than my conscience, since I know the sins I have committed, but I do not know the sins he has committed.' If he were richer than me, I told myself that he does more charitable deeds than I do. If he were poorer than me, I told myself that he is more contrite and more subdued in spirit than I, and he is better than me. And through this thinking, I would honor all people and I would defer to them."[39]

Does this sound like an unreachably high standard of moral behavior or a desirable way to train one's mind? What are the obvious and hidden benefits?

Summing Things Up

In the aftermath of the Temple's destruction and the failure of the Bar Kokhba rebellion to reestablish Jewish sovereignty in *Eretz Yisrael*, a leadership void came to be filled by a growing contingent of Rabbis pursuing an oral tradition that sought both to preserve the traditions of the Second Temple and to pursue interpretations of Torah for the new conditions in which Jews found themselves. In addition, a patriarchate arose from the family of Gamliel the Elder, claiming descent from King David through Hillel the Elder and hence the patina of royalty. Allying itself with the *tanna'im*, the early Rabbis, the patriarchs nonetheless also struggled with them for communal authority. Many stories in the Talmud reflect this struggle, and those found in the Gemara, written much later in Babylonia, may also reflect the tension between the Babylonian *amora'im* and the exilarchs, the civil leaders of the Jewish community in the Babylonian Diaspora.

In this story, the high-ranking scholars R. Meir and R. Natan take offense at the unilateral decision of the patriarch Rabban Shimon b. Gamliel to publicly display his higher (and thereby their lower) rank in the Sanhedrin, and they scheme to co-opt his authority and power. Their coup is unsuccessful, in large measure because the *nasi* prevents the situation from boiling over and causing an irreparable breach. His measured response, and their willingness to remain engaged with him, provides a stunning model of leaders in conflict who, even after making personal and political mistakes, nonetheless remain focused on the larger goal: serving the greater good.

PART 2 THIRD SPHERE

Relationships in the Larger World

5 Moving to the Land of Israel

Babylonian Talmud, Tractate Ketubot 110b–111a

R. Elazar said, "Whoever lives in the Land of Israel lives without sin, for it says, *And none who lives there shall say, 'I am sick'; it shall be inhabited by folk whose sin has been forgiven* (Isaiah 33:24). Rava said to R. Ashi, "We apply [this verse] to those who suffer from disease." R. Anan said, "Whoever is buried in the Land of Israel it is as if they are buried under the altar since here it is written, *Make for Me an altar of earth* (Exodus 20:21), and there it is written, *And [God's] land atones for [God's] people* (Deuteronomy 32:43). . . . Rav Yehudah said in the name of Shmuel, "As it is forbidden to leave the Land of Israel for Babylon, so it is forbidden to leave Babylon for other countries." . . . Rav Yehudah said, "Whoever lives in Babylon is accounted as though they lived in the Land of Israel, for it is said, *Away, escape, O Zion, you who dwell in Fair Babylon!* (Zechariah 2:11).

—BT Ketubot 111a

Why Study This Passage?

Once, Jewish religious ethos revolved around sovereignty in the Land of Israel, which Jews understood to be their inheritance from God. The pages of Hebrew Scripture are populated with powerhouse heroes like Joshua, Deborah, Samson, and David, who, empowered by God, wrest the land from intruders and secure it for the People of Israel. History, however, proved that the divinely bestowed patrimony was difficult to maintain. Since the Romans seized control of the Land of Israel in the first century BCE, until 1948—and therefore for most of Jewish history— Jews had little or no political sovereignty or power (and certainly no military power). Over the centuries they became acclimated to powerlessness and shaped a religious culture that addressed their political and military impotence.

A revealing joke: A Jewish man who lives in England sits reading an Arab newspaper while riding the London Underground. A friend approaches. "Moishe," the friend says, "have you lost your mind? Why are you reading an Arab newspaper?" Moishe replies, "I used to read the Jewish newspaper, but what did I find? Jews are being persecuted, Israel is being attacked, Jews are living in poverty and disappearing through assimilation and intermarriage. Very depressing. So I switched to the Arab newspaper. Now what do I find? Jews own all the banks and control the media, all Jews are rich and powerful, and Jews rule the world. The news here is so much better!"

This joke reveals our ambivalence about power and its conundrums. Do we have as much power as others believe we do? Should we seek power? If we have it, how do we use it and how ought we to use it? We can trace this ambivalence not only to a long history pockmarked by persecution, oppression, expulsions, pogroms, and worse, but also to conversations held by the Rabbis and preserved in the pages of Talmud.

It is instructive to view Jewish history through the lens of Jews' perceptions of and relations to the idea of Jewish power, in both legal formulations and legends. Whereas Torah describes a people newly released from Egyptian bondage, reticent to engage in military maneuvers, yet seeking sovereignty over their land and ultimately rising to the challenge — conquering the Land of Israel — later Rabbinic commentaries, written from the post-70 CE standpoint of powerlessness, portray a people waiting for God to fight their battles and redeem their suffering.

In the hands of the Rabbis, the book of Exodus makes clear that God is Israel's redeemer; Israel is the passive, powerless, and often ambivalent recipient of God's salvation. The book of Numbers goes further, as the Rabbis read it, recounting stories of the Israelites' futile rebellions against Moses and Aaron that all have one common denominator: the people's refusal to take constructive responsibility for the power their freedom has bestowed on them. In other words, they are fulfilling Alice Walker's adage, "The most common way people give up their power is by thinking they don't have any."

Here is a telling example: Shortly after leaving Egypt, the Israelites cry out to Moses, *"Was it for want of graves in Egypt that you brought us to die in the wilderness? What have you done to us, taking us out of Egypt? Is this not the very thing we told you in Egypt, saying, 'Let us be, and we will serve the Egyptians, for it is better for us to serve the Egyptians than to die in the wilderness'?"* (Exodus 14:11–12). Moses assures the people that God will come to their rescue and battle the Egyptians on their behalf, but when Moses pleads with God, God issues this empowering response:

> "Why do you cry out to Me? [You] tell the Israelites to go forward. And you lift up your rod and hold out your arm over the sea and split it, so that the Israelites may march into the sea on dry ground. And I will stiffen the hearts of the Egyptians so that they go in after them." . . . Then Moses held out his arm over the sea and Adonai drove back the sea with a strong east wind all that night, and turned the sea into dry ground. The waters split. (Exodus 14:15–17,21)

When the Rabbis read these verses, they zero in on Moses's passivity and God's demand for action, a view quite different from what we read in the Torah:

> Moses was engaged for a long while in prayer, so the Holy Blessed One said to him, "My beloved ones are drowning in the sea and you prolong prayer before Me?!" Moses replied to God, "Lord of the Universe, what else is there in my power to do?" God replied to him, *Tell the Israelites to go forward. And you lift up your rod and hold out your arm, etc.*[1]

The Rabbis attributed to Moses a measure of courage, strength, and power that is sorely lacking among the biblical Hebrews and also the Jews of their own time. To the extent that Moses was a synecdoche for Israel, this painted a poignant account of a people raised from degradation to freedom whose self-image did not rise along with their condition. The Jewish people were imbued with a sense of strength from their covenantal connection to God and accompanying national story (told in Hebrew Scripture) but also with a sense of fragility imparted by the vicissitudes of history.

In essence, as the talmudic Rabbis and their descendants shaped traditional Jewish liturgy, they wove passivity into the Jewish foundational myth of the Exodus: Israel had come into being as a nation through God's power and direction, with no substantive physical assist by the people, and despite their fear and reticence to leave slavery in Egypt. And when this staple text of the Jews was recited daily, weekly, year in and year out, it reinforced their sense of Jewish passivity, powerlessness, and dependence on God for substantive change in their conditions of life.

Ironically, Jewish history replicated this foundational myth. After the wars with Rome, Jews "wandered the wilderness" for nearly two thousand years before regaining sovereignty in their ancestral homeland in 1948. During the intervening centuries of exile Jewish culture developed in a context in which power was, at best, theoretical. Emphasis was placed, therefore, on other matters: the importance of learning, ritual, and ethics, as well as having a family and making a living. With the advent of the Enlightenment, and in the context of Christian Protestantism, Judaism came under new scrutiny and reassessment: How should Judaism be characterized and categorized? Was Judaism a nationality? A religion? Something else?

For the Jews of Western Europe much was at stake. When civil emancipation came knocking on Jewish doors in the eighteenth century, many were eager to immerse themselves in the cosmopolitan world of modernity. The implicit "deal" was perhaps best expressed by Count Stanislas de Clermont-Tonnere of Paris, who told the French National Assembly in 1798: "We must refuse everything to the Jews as a nation and accord everything to Jews as individuals." After living as a nation in exile, scattered throughout the world for nearly eighteen hundred years, Jews in Western Europe were redefined from "nation" to "religion," and the dream of Jews communally exerting power seemed to have been set to rest.[2]

For assimilated Jews, defining Judaism as a "religion" was a relief; they eagerly shed many vestiges of Jewishness in order to enter the mainstream of European society. But this reconceptualization did not rest well with everyone. The nineteenth-century Jewish historian Heinrich Graetz argued vehemently against the claim that Judaism was a religion—a set of theological claims and ritual acts—as his contemporary, the German reformer Abraham Geiger, had sought to establish. For Graetz, Judaism was far more than a "mere" religion. Leora Batnitzky, scholar of Jewish religion, explains:

> In arguing for the creative vitality of Jewish history, Graetz argues not only against Geiger but also against Georg Wilhelm Friedrich Hegel (1770–1831), who in his philosophy of history declares Judaism a religion of transcendence arrested at the adolescent stage of historical development. Hegel contends that Judaism posits an absolute dichotomy between humanity and God that is then overcome by Christianity's notion of the unity of the human and divine in Christ's incarnation.

Noting that Hegel treats "Judaism with crude prejudice," Graetz seeks to show that Hegel's conception is wrong—and results from a particularly Christian view: "The Christian conception of history, as is well-known, fully denies to Judaism any history, in the higher sense of the word, since the loss of its national independence, an event which coincided with another of great importance for the Christian world. . . . [A]ll the more urgent is the demand on us to vindicate the right of Jewish history, to present its tenacious and indestructible character."

But . . . Graetz adopts Hegel's idealist conception of history as the unfolding of ideas, or what Hegel calls "spirit" through time. . . . Against both Geiger and Hegel, Graetz maintains that the germ of Judaism is something "infinitely richer, infinitely deeper" than the idea of monotheism. Judaism's essence consists of the interplay between the idea of a transcendent God and the political reality into which this idea is always rendered concurrently. According to Graetz, this constant dialectical relationship between theology and politics means that "Judaism is not a religion of the individual but of the community. That actually means that Judaism, in the strict sense of the word, is not even a religion—if one understands thereby the relationship of man to his creator and his hopes for his earthly existence—but rather a constitution for a body politic."[3]

Many hoped that once Judaism was no longer what Graetz termed "a constitution for the body politic" but an ordinary religion, entirely distinct from one's national citizenship, Jews could live comfortably in Europe. But anti-Semitism did not abate, and the nineteenth-century pogroms of Eastern Europe kindled a new fire under the ancient dream of Jewish nationalism, giving rise to the first sparks of modern Zionism.

Today, with a strong and well-established State of Israel, the spectrum of views on Jewish nationalism within the Jewish community is exceptionally broad. Zionists, whether religious or secular, occupy the middle terrain. On one end of the spectrum are Jews who prefer to regard Judaism as a "religion" and feel no need for a Jewish country or attachment to Israel. On the opposite end are Jews who reject Zionism precisely because it promotes Jewish political nationhood and claims that the State of Israel is the third Jewish commonwealth in the ancient ancestral homeland.

The passage in this chapter has surprising echoes to this day. A small, extremely anti-Zionist, ultra-Orthodox Jewish group known as Naturei Karta (Guardians of the City), established in 1938 in Jerusalem, views the State of Israel as a halakhically illegitimate "heresy." Ever since Israel declared independence on May 14, 1948, Naturei Karta's adherents have refused to recognize Israel as a legitimate Jewish state because we live in a pre-Messianic era.[4] They believe that only after God brings the Messiah can there be a legitimate third Jewish commonwealth—and only at God's instigation. Therefore, reestablishing Jewish sovereignty prematurely in the ancient ancestral homeland is a violation of God's will. On their website they profess:

> The only time that the People of Israel were permitted to have a state was two thousand years ago when the glory of the creator was upon us, and likewise in the future when the glory of the creator will once more be revealed, and the whole world will serve Him, then He Himself (without any human effort or force of arms) will grant us a kingdom founded on Divine Service. However, a worldly state, like those possessed by other peoples, is contradictory to the true essence of the People of Israel.
>
> [Furthermore] the Torah forbids us to end the exile and establish a state and army until the Holy One, blessed be He, in His Glory and Essence, will redeem us. This is forbidden even if the state is conducted according to the law of the Torah because arising from the exile itself is forbidden, and we are required to remain under the rule of the nations of the world. . . . If we transgress this injunction, He will bring upon us (may we be spared) terrible punishment.[5]

In addition to the Naturei Karta, and of far greater concern within the modern State of Israel, are the *haredim* (those who tremble before God) or, as they are otherwise known, "ultra-Orthodox" Jews.[6] Their ideological and religious forebears are Rabbi Chaim of Volozhin (1749–1821), founder of the famed Volozhin Yeshiva in Lithuania, and Rabbi Yisrael Meir Kagan (also known as the Chofetz Chaim, 1838–1933), founder of a yeshivah in Radin, Poland, both of whom rejected the nascent Zionist movement, and others who responded to the sweeping changes in Europe following the Enlightenment by rejecting modernity and advising their followers to live in self-segregating silos of intense religious observance. *Haredi* Jews reject most everything deemed "secular," oppose efforts at religious reform, and live on the margins of Israeli society.

While not all *haredim* today reject the State of Israel, they have a complicated relationship with both the state and Zionism. They benefit from generous financial endowments to their families and communities—in essence taxpayer handouts. The 2016 survey of Israel's *haredi* community conducted by the Israel Democratic Institute and the Jerusalem Institute for Israel Studies points to "profound differences between the haredi, overall Israeli, and non-haredi Jewish populations when it comes to workforce participation, employment rates, and income levels of individuals and households."[7] Employment levels, particularly among men, lag far behind those of other Israelis.[8] Due to the priority placed on study over work, 52 percent of the *haredim* (and 67 percent of their children) live below the poverty level.

The community is also growing at a staggering rate. The same 2016 study revealed that while the current birth rate among secular Jews in Israel is the replacement rate of 2.1 children per woman, and among non-*haredi* religious Jews it is 4.2 (with both figures expected to remain stable for the foreseeable future), the birth rate among the *haredim* is 6.9 and staying robust. At this rate, the *haredim*, currently approximately 10 percent of the population, would triple from approximately one million to three million by 2050.

Meanwhile, the *haredi* vote is a bloc aimed at turning Israel into a the-
ocracy that functions according to halakhah. They find their justification
to do so in the Talmud—and, in particular, the passage in this chapter
describing a conversation between R. Zeira and his teacher, Rav Yehudah.

A Broad View to Begin

In *The Gifts of the Jews: How a Tribe of Desert Nomads Changed the Way
Everyone Thinks and Feels*, Thomas Cahill enumerates Jewish contributions
to civilization in broad and glowing terms. He credits Jews and Judaism
with revolutionary ideas: monotheism, a personal relationship with God,
new conceptions of time and purpose. While the peoples of ancient
Egypt, Greek, and India viewed time as an ever-turning, never-changing
wheel and approached life with resignation to "fate," Jews, who viewed
the world and their lives as purposeful creations of God, understood time
as a progression. Cahill contends that the idea of progress and the sense
that history follows a purposeful trajectory began when Abram broke
away from the ever-changing wheel, leaving his home in Ur Kasdim at
God's behest: *Go forth from your native land and from your birthplace to a
land that I will show you!* (Genesis 12:1).

From the beginning, the Jewish narrative of divine plan and purpose
has affirmed the momentous and inseparable connection of the Jewish
people to *Eretz Yisrael*. Indeed it is impossible to exaggerate the centrality
of the Land of Israel to Jewish thinking and identity. From the moment
God called out to the first Jew, Abram, his trajectory was toward *Eretz
Yisrael*, through both divine command and promise.[9] The book of Genesis
catalogs the trials and travails of four generations of Patriarchs and
Matriarchs who emigrate and return, time and again, always coming
home to the land that is their destiny. The master story of the Jewish
people, the Exodus from Egypt and Revelation at Mount Sinai, describes
their redemption from a foreign land where they experienced servitude
and suffering, in order to enter into a covenant with God to be fulfilled
in the Land of Israel.

The Torah describes the Land of Israel as fertile, beautiful, and possessed of abundant natural resources—a paradise outside the Garden of Eden.

For Adonai your God is bringing you into a good land, a land with streams and springs and fountains issuing from plain and hill; a land of wheat and barley, of vines, figs, and pomegranates, a land of olive trees and honey; a land where you may eat food without stint, where you will lack nothing; a land whose rocks are iron and from whose hills you can mine copper. When you have eaten your fill, give thanks to Adonai your God for the good land which God has given you. (Deuteronomy 8:7–10)

Torah explains that the land will be the venue for Israel to serve God. As Moses explains to the Israelites:

And this is the Instruction—the laws and the rules—that Adonai your God has commanded [me] to impart to you, to be observed in the land that you are about to cross into and occupy, so that you, your children, and your children's children may revere Adonai your God and follow, as long as you live, all God's laws and commandments that I enjoin upon you, to the end that you may long endure. Obey, O Israel, willingly and faithfully, that it may go well with you and that you may increase greatly [in] a land flowing with milk and honey,[10] as Adonai, the God of your ancestors, spoke to you. (Deuteronomy 6:1–3; see also 12:1)

Although the Torah foresees a time when the Jewish people will so offend God that they will be exiled from their land, it also forecasts their return:

When all these things befall you—the blessing and the curse that I have set before you—and you take them to heart amidst the various nations to which Adonai your God has banished you, and you return to Adonai your God, and you and your children heed God's command with all your heart and soul, just as I enjoin upon you this day, then Adonai your God will restore your fortunes and take you back in love. God will bring you together again from all the peoples where Adonai your God has scattered you. Even if your outcasts are at the ends of the world, from there Adonai your God will gather you, from there God will fetch you. And Adonai your God will bring you to the land that your ancestors possessed, and you shall possess it; and God will make you more prosperous and more numerous than your ancestors. (Deuteronomy 30:1–5)

The classical Hebrew prophets, from Isaiah to Malachi, spoke extensively about the people's relationship with the Land of Israel: their endurance in, exile from, and return to the land of their ancestors as consequences of their keeping, violating, and returning to their covenant with God. The prophet Zechariah was the first to term the land *admat kodesh* (holy land), though his precise meaning remains unclear.

Abram's route to the Promised Land and his descendants' route out of Egypt toward the same goal were no straighter than the Rabbis' conceptual route to understanding the Jewish place and purpose in history. Similarly, when viewed from above, the Judge Harry Pregerson Interchange in Los Angeles looks like a messy bowl of spaghetti, with five stacked, mazelike roadways soaring and curving, merging and diverging.[11] It provides a fine visual model of tannaitic and amoraic Jewish ideas concerning the Land of Israel, Jewish sovereignty over the land, the Davidic dynasty, the meaning of history, Jewish power, and our relationships with both power and the Land of Israel: roadways stacking, merging, and diverging.

At the symbolic center of this Jewish interchange of ideas stands King David (~1,000 BCE). During David's long reign Israel enjoyed relative peace, security, and prosperity. Upon David's death, civil war ensued, splitting the nation into two small, weak kingdoms, each with its own monarchy, army, and religious cult: the Northern Kingdom with a capital in Samaria, and the Southern Kingdom whose capital was Jerusalem. In the eighth century BCE, the Assyrians defeated the Northern Kingdom; its ten tribes were scattered and lost to history. In the sixth century BCE, the Babylonians defeated the Southern Kingdom and destroyed the Temple in Jerusalem; many died and a large swath of the surviving population was sent into exile in Babylonia. National and religious hopes for reunification coalesced around the belief that God would send a descendant of David, the anointed king of Israel, to reunify the nation.

The fervent belief that God would deliver a savior from the line of David came into sharp focus when Alexander the Great conquered the Land of Israel in the late fourth century BCE, and this belief grew following the Maccabean war with Alexander's Hellenistic successors in the second century BCE. The figure of David became the paradigm for the future king God had promised the people: a leader who would reinstate Jewish sovereignty over the Land of Israel. But in 70 CE, the Romans destroyed the Second Temple, appropriated Judea, and permitted the Jews sovereignty only in a limited religious arena, dashing Jewish hopes that Jewish political sovereignty over the land would be restored in history. Full and genuine sovereignty, the Rabbis concluded, would come only when the Messiah, God's anointed one, redeemed Israel from Roman straits.

The idea of the Messianic Age was now mythologized and shifted to the eschaton, the consummation of history. Looking back on Jewish history, the Rabbis viewed the Land of Israel as the Jewish people's eternal inheritance from God and the reign of King David as its historical apex. Looking into the future, they professed that God would send a Messiah—a descendant of David—who would overthrow the Roman overlords and gather the exiles from Babylonia into *Eretz Yisrael*. They conceived the Messianic Age to be the consummation of history: an eternal era marked by peace and prosperity. This messianic vision lent purpose to the painful Jewish historical trajectory.

The precise role of the Land of Israel in this configuration, and an individual Jew's obligation to live in the land, were never precisely defined. After the temporally distant 586 BCE destruction of the First Temple and the consequent exile to Babylonia and the far more proximate—and spiritually crushing—70 CE destruction of the Second Temple and the Roman exile that followed, the Rabbis explored and expanded Zechariah's notion of "holy land" and its implications, not always arriving at a unanimous conclusion.

A mishnah in Tractate Kelim understands holiness to derive from the mitzvot fulfilled in the land: the performance of mitzvot lends holiness to the land.

> There are ten degrees of holiness. The Land of Israel is holier than all other lands. And wherein lies its holiness? That from it are brought the *omer* [barley offering brought from the second day of Pesach through Shavuot—Leviticus 23:9-14], the *bikkurim* [first fruits—Leviticus 2:14], and the two loaves [offered on Shavuot—Leviticus 23:17], none of which may be brought from any other land.[12]

Midrash Leviticus Rabbah, however, claims that the land is inherently superior, the outcome of God's choosing it for the People of Israel, whom Torah terms an *am kadosh* ("holy people"—Deuteronomy 7:6).

> R. Shimon b. Yochai opened a discourse with, *[God] rose and measured the earth* (Habakkuk 3:3). The Holy Blessed One measured [i.e., considered] every generation and found no generation fitting to receive the Torah other than the generation of the wilderness. The Holy Blessed One measured every mountain and found no mountain fitting to give the Torah other than Sinai. The Holy Blessed One measured every city and found no city where the Temple might be built other than Jerusalem. The Holy Blessed One measured every land and found no land fitting to give to Israel other than the Land of Israel. This is indicated by what is written, *[God] rose and measured the earth ... and released the nations.*[13]

It is not challenging to account for this difference of viewpoint. After the compilation of the Mishnah at the end of the second century, the center of Jewish life and learning shifted from *Eretz Yisrael*, where living conditions were challenging, to Babylonia, where Jews had lived since the first exile in the sixth century BCE and numerous thriving communities had taken root and blossomed.

With this shift came widely divergent opinions concerning where a Jew should reside. Tosefta, a mishnaic-era text written in *Eretz Yisrael*, roundly declares that those who live in the Diaspora are at risk of committing idolatry. Quoting 1 Samuel 26:19, in which David pleads with King Saul for his life, the Tosefta explains that those who go abroad, leaving the land at a time of peace, are susceptible to idol worship. Contact with the land keeps one close to God; separation from the land is tantamount to separation from God.

> And so Scripture says, *For they have driven me out this day, that I should have no share in the heritage of Adonai, saying, "Go and worship other gods"* (1 Samuel 26:19). Now would it ever enter your mind that David would go and worship idols? But David made the following exegesis: Whoever leaves the land in time of peace and goes abroad is as if he worships idols, as it is said, *I will plant them in this land in faithfulness, with all my heart and all my soul* (Jeremiah 32:41). So long as they are located upon it, it is as if they are planted before me in faithfulness with all my heart and all my soul. Lo, if they are not located upon it, they are not planted before me in faithfulness with all my heart and all my soul.[14]

The view from Babylonia, however, was entirely different. R. Yehudah, whom we meet in this story, asserts: "One who lives in Babylonia is as one who lives in *Eretz Yisrael*." This view may reflect the belief among the Sages of Babylonia that their academies and scholars were superior to those of *Eretz Yisrael*. While the Land of Israel possessed inherent sanctity, exceptional Torah learning was an even higher priority in Babylonia. The only reason to forego the finest learning was to partake in the ultimate ingathering of Israel to welcome the Messiah. In the Babylonian theological climate, it is not surprising that the seemingly simple act of moving from Babylonia to *Eretz Yisrael* carried a messianic valence.

Our story concerns R. Zeira, who longs to make *aliyah* to pursue his personal, spiritual needs. His teacher, Rav Yehudah, however, considers *aliyah* to be an act of defiance against God, who ordained that Jews should continue to live passively in exile in Babylonia until God redeems them. Their combative conversation is part of a larger discussion of Jewish power, which in its many manifestations always circles back to the Land of Israel.

Power is a moral issue; imagined power is a dangerous liability. For much of the past two millennia, Jewish power has been a staple fantasy in the dark minds of anti-Semites who fabricated pernicious tales of political cabals and financial conspiracies engineered by Jews. Only in the early 1880s, with the emergence of Chovevei Tzion, a movement of organizations that were forerunners of Zionism, did anyone seriously consider that long-held dreams of Jewish sovereignty in the Land of Israel might become historical reality. Leaders of the early Zionist organizations promoted immigration and agricultural settlement as preliminary steps toward the reestablishment of the Jewish homeland in the historical Land of Israel. In the decades preceding Israel's establishment, when the Zionist pioneers in *Eretz Yisrael* required defense as much as hoes, seeds, and water, Jews picked up guns to claim, protect, and defend the land. Particularly in the years since Israel declared independence in 1948, Jewish political, economic, and military power has become reality.

A prayer for the State of Israel, composed by the Israeli rabbinate to be recited when Torah is read publicly in synagogues, speaks of the state as *reshit tzemichat ge'ulatenu* (the first flowering of redemption). Israel's rise as a powerful nation and this characterization of its redemptive significance raise many questions concerning God's role in the birth of a Jewish state in the modern era, the proper relationship of a Jew with both the Land of Israel and the State of Israel, and how specifically *Jewish* power should be exercised.

Exploring the Nooks and Crannies of Our Passage

Torah avers that God brought the Israelites out of slavery in Egypt in order to give them the Land of Israel where they could live and worship Adonai: *I Adonai am your God, who brought you out of the land of Egypt, to give you the land of Canaan, to be your God* (Leviticus 25:38). Torah further recounts that when the Israelites passed through Jericho toward the end of their forty-year journey through the wilderness, God instructed Moses to tell the people, *And you shall take possession of the land and settle in it, for I have assigned the land to you to possess* (Numbers 33:53). These verses (and others like them) strongly suggest that living in the Land of Israel is a positive commandment. Yet Torah does not explicitly state this. The Rabbis of the Talmud are divided on the question. Ultimately Talmud does not declare it to be a religious obligation, but acknowledges it to be a worthy goal and a righteous act.

The Rabbis' view of the world encompasses both the physical geography of the ancient Near East and their understanding of its metaphysical structure. For the Sages, as we saw, the universe is constructed of concentric circles of holiness, from the highest level of holiness at the center to decreasing levels as one moves further from the core. At the center and pinnacle of the universe sits the Holy of Holies, the nexus of heaven and earth; the Holy of Holies is contained within the Jerusalem Temple; beyond that, the holy city of Jerusalem; after Jerusalem, the Land of Israel; and, finally, the world beyond the Land of Israel.[15] Anthropologist and theologian Seth Daniel Kunin writes of what he terms this Rabbinic "structure of sacred geography":

> This text presents a model for organizing space into a coherent pattern. The model works from the outside in. Israel is contrasted with the

rest of the world, Jerusalem is contrasted with the other cities of the land, the Temple is contrasted with Jerusalem, and the Holy of Holies is contrasted with the Temple. The text combines two levels of geography. It presents the relationships within macro-space, that is, the world, Israel, Jerusalem, and finally the Temple. It then presents micro-space, which is a recapitulation of the structure of macro-space, that is, the various areas within the Temple. The micro-level focuses an association of space with humanity. All people can enter Temple Mount; yet as we move inward, the groups of people who are allowed to enter are progressively reduced.[16]

Kunin portrays the Rabbinic view in five collapsed concentric circles. From the outside in (increasing in holiness): the world, the Land of Israel, Jerusalem, the Temple, the Holy of Holies.

Far from being an artifact of an ancient viewpoint, this perspective is encoded in Jewish thought and the Hebrew language to this day. When one travels from the Diaspora to Israel, one "ascends to Israel." Similarly, when one travels to Jerusalem from any location within Israel, one "ascends to Jerusalem."

The schematic of concentric circles of holiness ultimately conveys that living in the Land of Israel is spiritually superior to living in the Diaspora, thereby raising numerous questions. Is a Jew required to live in the Land of Israel? If so, should Jews born outside the land move to *Eretz Yisrael*? If Jews wish to make *aliyah*, should their families be compelled to move as well?

With these questions in mind, we turn to the first part of the mishnah.

We begin with M Ketubot 13:11; 110b, the last mishnah in the tractate, which discusses the consequence of moving from one's birthplace in *Eretz Yisrael* to the Diaspora, or making *aliyah* from one's birthplace outside the land. Well before the second century, Jewish communities were established outside the Land of Israel throughout Asia Minor, Babylonia, and Egypt. Jews often traveled between these communities and the Land of Israel to trade, visit family, or study with a particular Rabbi or circle of Sages. Sometimes, in the process, the family also relocated, but there were times when the spouse refused to move.

Mishnah: One [who lives outside the Land of Israel] can compel all [members of their family] to go up [i.e., move] to the Land of Israel, but can compel none to leave the Land of Israel. One [who lives outside Jerusalem, but within the Land of Israel] can compel all [members of their family] to go up to Jerusalem, but can compel none to leave Jerusalem. This applies to both men and women.

If [a man] married a woman in the Land of Israel and divorced her in the Land of Israel, he pays [her ketubah][17] with the currency of the Land of Israel.

If [a man] married a woman in the Land of Israel and divorced her in Cappadocia,[18] he pays [her ketubah] with the currency of the Land of Israel.

If [a man] married a woman in Cappadocia and divorced her in the Land of Israel, he pays [her ketubah] with the currency of the Land of Israel. But Rabban Shimon b. Gamliel says [concerning the last of the three rulings], "He pays her with the currency of Cappadocia."

If [a man] married a woman in Cappadocia and divorced her in Cappadocia, he pays [her ketubah] with the currency of Cappadocia.

Mishnah rules it permissible to compel one's family to move up the ladder of holiness—from the Diaspora to *Eretz Yisrael*, and from *Eretz Yisrael* to Jerusalem—but impermissible to force one's family to move down the ladder.[19] The depth of the Rabbis' support for people moving up to *Eretz Yisrael* and Jerusalem is reflected in the Rabbis' ruling that not only may husbands compel their wives, but wives may compel their husbands to do so.

On this basis, the mishnah permits a modicum of financial—though not physical—coercion to reach the goal of settling in the Land of Israel and Jerusalem.[20] How so? The Rabbis require that every married woman be given a ketubah, a marriage document that delineates her legal lien on her husband's property: what she will receive should the marriage end through divorce or her husband's death. The mishnah promulgates four rulings that define the financial consequences of a marriage that ends in divorce, as a function of where the marriage was initiated and where it ended — either in or outside the Land of Israel.

Generally, in Jewish contract law, payments are made in the currency of the location where the obligation is incurred. We see, however, that while the marriage ends outside the Land of Israel in half the hypothetical cases, the wife's ketubah must be paid in the currency of the Land of Israel in 75 percent of these cases. Holding currency of the Land of Israel is a strong incentive to live where the currency can be spent.

In short:

MARRIED IN . . . DIVORCED IN . . .	CURRENCY FOR PAYING KETUBAH
Land of Israel — Land of Israel	Land of Israel
Land of Israel — Diaspora	Land of Israel
Diaspora — Land of Israel	Land of Israel (Rabban Gamliel: Diaspora)
Diaspora — Diaspora	Diaspora

In three of the four cases, the ketubah is paid in the currency of the Land of Israel, facilitating and/or encouraging Jews to live there. Rabban Shimon b. Gamliel's objection to the third case likely derives from his assumption that the wife will likely return to live with her family outside the Land of Israel following the divorce.

In the Gemara that directly follows this mishnah and precedes our passage, the Rabbis discuss whether "all" in the first part of the mishnah includes servants, and whether "none" would include those who want to leave Jerusalem to live in a superior-quality dwelling outside the holy city. Next, they present a *baraita* saying that while a man may compel his wife to move from the Diaspora to *Eretz Yisrael*, or from within *Eretz Yisrael* to Jerusalem, if she refuses, he may divorce her without her ketubah; however, if a woman compels her husband to an analogous move and he refuses, he must divorce her and pay her ketubah. Conversely, if the wife wants to leave *Eretz Yisrael* or Jerusalem, her husband may compel her to remain, and if she refuses, he may divorce her without paying her ketubah. However, if he wants to leave, she may compel him to remain, and if he refuses, he must divorce her and pay her ketubah. A brief discussion of the currency in which the ketubah is to be paid follows—again prioritizing currency in use in the Land of Israel. In all, the Rabbis express a clear preference for living in *Eretz Yisrael*.

We pick up the Gemara's discussion on *daf* 110b. Indulging in purple prose on the spiritual value of living in *Eretz Yisrael*, the Rabbis cite a *baraita* that interprets Leviticus 25:38 to suggest that not only is living in the Land of Israel a positive obligation, but God's original purpose when bringing the nation of Israel out of Egypt was to settle them in the land where God could be their God:

> **Gemara:** (110b) The Rabbis taught [in a *baraita*]: A person should always live in *Eretz Yisrael*, even in a city the majority of whose inhabitants are idolaters, and should not live outside the Land even in a city whose majority is Jews, because whoever lives in the Land of Israel is like one who has a God, and whoever lives outside the Land is like one who is without a God, as it says, [*I, Adonai, am your God, who brought you out of the land of Egypt] to give you the land of Canaan, to be your God* (Leviticus 25:38).
>
> And whoever does not live in the Land is godless? Rather, it teaches you that whoever lives outside the Land is like one who worships idols. And similarly, concerning David, it says, *For they have driven me out today so that I cannot have a share in Adonai's possession, saying, "Go and*

worship other gods" (1 Samuel 26:19). Who told David, "Go and worship others gods!"? Rather, [the verse] teaches you that whoever lives outside the Land is as if he worships idols.

The *baraita* understands *to be your God* as dependent on *to give you the land of Canaan*; that is, living in the Land of Israel was a prerequisite for God to fully function as Israel's God. Put another way, the *baraita* reads the Leviticus verse to say that living in the Land of Israel is necessary for Jews to have a fully committed connection with God. In the wilderness Israel received the Torah and obeyed many of its laws, but only in the Land of Israel could the people observe all the mitzvot, many of which relate to agricultural practice in *Eretz Yisrael*.

Gemara responds with surprise and consternation to the *baraita*'s claim that living outside *Eretz Yisrael* is tantamount to godlessness. After all, God's domain is the entire universe. How, then, could the *baraita* suggest that one can be committed to, and connected with, God only in the Land of Israel? The Gemara therefore offers an alternative interpretation of the *baraita*'s provocative statement: one who lives outside the Land of Israel is not, in fact, an outright idolater, but is considered *like* an idol worshiper. This hardly solves the problem, since it is not clear what "like an idolater" means, but the Talmud continues, drawing on the biblical story of David's emotional experience when fleeing from King Saul. David left *Eretz Yisrael* and sought refuge with the kings of Moab and Akish, both of whom were idolaters. Saul caught up with David in Chakhilah, in the vicinity of Ein Gedi. David pled his innocence directly to the king, saying that Saul was driven to pursue David not at God's behest, but rather incited by David's jealous enemies, *For they have driven me out today so that I cannot have a share in Adonai's possession* — the Rabbis read this as meaning outside the Land of Israel — *saying, "Go and worship other gods"* (1 Samuel 26:19). Gemara concludes that living outside the Land of Israel exposes one to the influence of pagan society, a cultural setting that conveys the message, *"Go worship other gods!"* Hence, living outside *Eretz Yisrael* is *like* idolatry because it poses the temptation and risk of engaging in idolatry.

Given the passionate preference expressed thus far for living in the Land of Israel, the story of R. Zeira and Rav Yehudah that follows is surprising. R. Zeira, a third-century *amora* born and raised in "the east," in Babylonia, is intent on moving to the Land of Israel. He would have appreciated a famous verse by the eleventh-century Spanish poet Yehudah ha-Levi, "My heart is in the east, and I in the uttermost west—How can I find savour in food? How can it be sweet to me?"[21] R. Zeira might have put it this way: "My heart is in the West (*Eretz Yisrael*), but I am in the East (Babylonia). Life, and even food, would be so much sweeter there."

R. Zeira's teacher, Rav Yehudah b. Yechezkel, however, does not approve of Jews leaving Babylonia to make *aliyah*. Therefore, R. Zeira is avoiding Rav Yehudah.

> R. Zeira was evading Rav Yehudah because [R. Zeira] wanted to go up to the Land of Israel, but Rav Yehudah had expressed [the opinion]: Whoever goes up from Babylon to the Land of Israel transgresses a positive commandment, [111a] as it is said, *They shall be brought to Babylon, and there they shall remain, until I take note of them, declares Adonai, [and bring them up and restore them to this place]* (Jeremiah 27:22).

In the Rabbinic era, the master-disciple relationship was exceptionally close. A student often lived in his teacher's home. It would have been extraordinarily difficult for R. Zeira to withhold from Rav Yehudah his passionate desire to make *aliyah*—let alone his plans to move there—but he feels compelled to do so because Rav Yehudah is on record as opposing such a move on the basis of Jeremiah 27:22.

Note that often the Rabbis quote only part of a verse, presuming the reader knows the entire verse and its context, as well as the verses before and after it. Rav Yehudah understands the Jeremiah verse to say that when the Babylonians destroyed the First Temple in 586 BCE and exiled the Jews to Babylonia, God decreed that Israel remain there until God would *take note of them*, meaning until God would initiate action to end the exile and return the Jews living in Babylonia to the Land of Israel (*bring them up and restore them to this place* — the part of the verse Gemara does not include, but presumes the reader knows). Accordingly, Rav Yehudah considers it an outright violation of God's will for Jews to leave Babylonia of their own accord.

Note, as well, that books of the Prophets, such as Jeremiah, are not the source of mitzvot — mitzvot derive from the Torah.[22]

Our text now follows an argument that ensues between R. Zeira and Rav Yehudah, a duel with weaponized verses and each Rabbi's interpretation of them.

> And R. Zeira [how does he explain Jeremiah 27:22]?
> [He says:] That text refers to the service vessels [for the Temple in Jerusalem].

Gemara asks how R. Zeira responds to Rav Yehudah's claim that, on the basis of Jeremiah 27:22, God has decreed that Jews may not leave Babylonia, because if Rav Yehudah has drawn an indisputable conclusion from it, then R. Zeira must adhere to Rav Yehudah's dictum to remain in Babylonia. R. Zeira considers the context of the verse; he explains that Jeremiah 27:22 does not refer to the Jewish people but rather to the vessels and utensils that the Babylonians looted from the Temple in 586 BCE and brought to Babylonia.[23] The *vessels* were carried to Babylon (the Jews walked there) and God intends *the vessels* — not the Jews living in Babylonia — to remain in exile until God ordains that they be brought back to the Land of Israel. The basis for R. Zeira's claim is the preceding verses, which speak not about the Jewish people, but about the vessels used in the Temple.

> For thus said Adonai Tzeva'ot concerning the columns, the tank, the stands, and the rest of the vessels remaining in this city, which King

Nebuchadnezzar of Babylon did not take when he exiled King Jeconiah son of Jehoiakim of Judah from Jerusalem; for thus said Adonai Tzeva'ot, the God of Israel, concerning the vessels remaining in the House of Adonai, in the royal palace of Judah, and in Jerusalem (Jeremiah 27:19–21).

R. Zeira concedes that the return of the temple vessels will happen only when the Temple is rebuilt in the Messianic Era. However, according to his reading, Jeremiah 27:22 does not constrain Jews to remain in Babylonia, as R. Yehudah has argued. Hence, he is free to make *aliyah*.

Although it appears that R. Zeira has undermined Rav Yehudah's argument, the debate continues.

> And Rav Yehudah [what is his response]?
> [He says:] Another text is written: *I adjure you, O maidens of Jerusalem, by gazelles or by hinds of the field: [do not wake or rouse love until it please!]* (Song of Songs 2:7).
> And R. Zeira [what is his response]?
> [He says:] That [verse, i.e., Song of Songs 2:7] implies that Israel shall not go up by a wall [i.e., en masse].

Rav Yehudah introduces a second biblical verse to bolster his argument. Note that the Rabbis interpret Song of Songs, poetry that celebrates love and sexual intimacy, as speaking not of the passionate love between a man and a woman, but metaphorically describing the love relationship between God and Israel.[24] Rav Yehudah understands Song of Songs 2:7 to say that God obligates Jews (*O maidens of Jerusalem*) by oath (*I adjure you*) not to emigrate from Babylonia in an attempt to rebuild the Temple (*do not wake or rouse love*) until *it please* God to end their exile in Babylonia. *Do not wake or rouse love*, for Rav Yehudah, means that Jews should not act to hasten the coming of the Messiah—even by relocating in *Eretz Yisrael*.

R. Zeira does not fully reject his teacher's interpretation, but rather its application. He acknowledges that Song of Songs 2:7 disallows Jews from making *aliyah* en masse. Such a corporate entity would connote the use of force and carry clear messianic implications. If indeed this verse solely prohibits *aliyah* by the community as part of a messianic movement, then individuals such as he himself may go up to the Land of Israel for personal, spiritual reasons. Hence, he reasons, private *aliyah* is not covered by this prohibition and is permissible.

R. Zeira's concession does not satisfy Rav Yehudah, however, since he objected to individuals resettling in *Eretz Yisrael*.

> Rav Yehudah [how does he respond]?
> [He says that there is] another [instance of] *I adjure you* written in Scripture [i.e., Song of Songs 3:5].

Rav Yehudah responds to R. Zeira's challenge by pointing out that *I adjure you* is found a second time in Song of Songs 3:5 (verses 2:7 and 3:5 are identical). Therefore, if R. Zeira's interpretation of the first iteration of *I adjure you* is accepted as forbidding Jews from organizing a corporate messianic immigration to the Land of Israel, then 3:5 prohibits individuals from making *aliyah* as well.

Following the established pattern of this passage, the Gemara now asks R. Zeira to respond to Rav Yehudah's declaration that even if the first *I adjure you* pertains to a corporate, messianic effort to settle in the Holy Land, the second *I adjure you* prohibits individuals from making *aliyah*. R. Zeira notes that, in fact, three such adjurations appear in Song of Songs: 2:7, 3:5, and 8:4.[25] He asserts that all three are needed to uphold the teaching of another Sage.

> And R. Zeira [how does he respond]?
> [He says:] That text is required for [an explanation] like that of R. Yose b. R. Chanina, who said: What was the purpose of the three adjurations? One—that Israel shall not go up like a wall [i.e., en masse]. Two—by

it the Holy Blessed One adjured Israel not to rebel against the nations of the world. Three—by it the Holy Blessed One adjured the idolaters not to oppress Israel overmuch.

R. Zeira comments that, in fact, the verse *I adjure you, O maidens of Jerusalem, by gazelles or by hinds of the field: Do not wake or rouse love until it please!* occurs a third time in Song of Songs 8:4. Although this third verse is not precisely identical to the previous two, it conveys the same idea. All three instances of *I adjure you*, he asserts, are needed as prooftexts of R. Yose b. R. Chanina's teaching that God promulgated three rules pertaining to Israel's experience in exile: (1) Jews may not organize a national movement to settle in the Land of Israel in expectation of the coming of the Messiah or in order to hasten the coming; (2) Jews are forbidden to rebel against gentile rulers in the lands in which they live, which also means they cannot recapture *Eretz Yisrael* by force; and (3) gentiles are forbidden from persecuting Jews excessively.

R. Yose's three rules sound disturbing to the modern ear. Why would the Rabbis, in the voice of R. Zeira, have preserved this teaching? Perhaps because it follows logically (if not happily) from their theological understanding that Jews must accept God's "punishment" of *galut* (exile) until God—and God alone—sends the Messiah, who will bring them back to the Land of Israel. Persecution was already a fact of life in exile, but R. Yose's teaching affords a measure of hope that it will not grow more intense.

By this time, R. Zeira has claimed that while Jeremiah 27:22 prohibits the return of the temple vessels, it says nothing about Jews returning to the Land of Israel. He has also avowed that the three adjurations in Song of Songs, taken together, mitigate against the formation of a national, messianic movement to move to, reclaim, or attempt to forcefully retake the Holy Land—but, again, they say nothing concerning an individual Jew's wish to make *aliyah*.

Having dismantled Rav Yehudah's objection through exegesis, the Gemara looks now to his teacher's response.

And Rav Yehudah [how does he respond]?

[He says:] It is written: *That you neither awaken nor stir up [love until it please]*.

Rav Yehudah does not object to R. Yose b. R. Chanina's application of *I adjure you* to formulate the three rules prohibiting Israel's rebellion against the nations. Instead, he argues that the latter part of each verse in the troika from Song of Songs—*that you neither awaken nor stir up love until it please*—introduces another verb, suggesting that it conveys another limitation. Rav Yehudah says that while the first half of the verses (*I adjure you*) applies to groups who seek to relocate to *Eretz Yisrael*, the second half of the verses (*that you neither awaken nor stir up love until it please*) imposes the same prohibitions on individuals. Rav Yehudah is effectively saying that there are *six* adjurations, not three: all three of R. Yose b. R. Chanina's rules apply to the People of Israel as a whole, but also to Jews as individuals, for a total of six.

R. Zeira is now afforded an opportunity to defend his position against Rav Yehudah's claim that the latter half of the three Song of Songs verses forbids individual Jews from making *aliyah*.

And R. Zeira [how does he respond]?

[He says:] That text is required for [an explanation] like that of R. Levi, who said: Why those six adjurations? Three [are] those we articulated. The others are: [4] that they not reveal the end; [5] that they not distance the end; and [6] that they not reveal the secrets to the gentiles.

R. Zeira's attempt to dismantle Rav Yehudah's claim about the latter half of the three Song of Songs verses leads him to R. Levi's alternative explanation that they allude to three additional rules.

While the language in the Gemara is terse, its meaning uncertain and open to debate, later commentators generally understand "that they not reveal the end" to forbid prophets of the Jewish people from revealing when the messianic redemption will take place. This, in itself, affirms that exile will end and the redemption will arrive.

The classical commentators also debate the meaning of "that they not distance the end." Rashi (Rabbi Shlomo Yitzhak, 1040–1105, France) holds that it may mean that Jews should not impede the end-time by sinning and thereby causing God to delay sending the Messiah. He also offers an alternative understanding: Jews should not excessively implore God to bring the final redemption. The Maharsha (Rabbi Shmuel Eidels, 1555–1631, Poland) suggests a perhaps more motivating meaning: Jews should not despair of being redeemed and consign themselves to the Messianic Age being far away; as difficult and drawn out as *galut* feels, Jews should retain hope for redemption.

Even more obscure is the meaning of "that they not reveal the secrets to the gentiles." According to Rabbi Chananel b. Chushiel (990–1053, Tunisia) and Rashi (in his first of two explanations), this concerns the secrets of calendrical intercalation.[26] Rashi's second, and perhaps more relatable, explanation is that Jews should not reveal to gentiles secrets concerning interpretations of the Torah. Possibly the injunction was also rooted in political anxiety. Messianic political movements were recognized as dangerous, and Jewish leaders might have feared the potential consequences: upheaval, violence, and death.

However uncertain the meaning of R. Levi's three additional rules, it is clear that while R. Yose b. R. Chanina's three adjurations focus on the continuing exile of the Jewish people, R. Levi's three adjurations elevate the hope of redemption by affirming that it will come one day. R. Zeira effectively won the argument: he moved from Babylonia to *Eretz Yisrael*, where he lived out his life.

R. Yose b. R. Chanina's three rules turned out to be far more than an interesting footnote to talmudic thinking about the *galut* and *aliyah*. In the late-eighteenth and early-nineteenth centuries, they fueled a fierce anti-Zionist reaction to the Haskalah (the Central and Eastern European Jewish intellectual enlightenment movement). Rejecting wholesale everything he deemed to be secular as threatening Jewish tradition and survival, the Chatam Sofer (Rabbi Moses Schreiber, 1762–1839, Hungary) promoted a secessionist Orthodoxy that isolated itself from Jews "tainted" by modernity and secular culture. To his followers and successors in the *haredi* movement, his rallying cry, *Chadash asur min ha-torah b'khol makom u'v'khol z'man* (Anything new is forbidden by Torah in any place and at any time),[27] became the broad, overarching principle for all Jewish life. To this day, anti-Zionist Jews, and particularly Neturei Karta, hold that R. Yose's rules, articulated in the third century CE, apply to Zionism and the modern State of Israel in the twentieth and twenty-first centuries. They claim that all acts of building a Jewish state are in essence efforts to hasten the coming of the Messiah. These acts violate God's will and are tantamount to rebellion against God.

Continuing the Conversation

1. The Messianic Dream and the Power of Hope

What happens when a sacred myth springs a leak? Rav Yehudah claims that halakhah forbids Jews from leaving Babylonia on their own initiative to resettle in the Land of Israel, because doing so violates God's will for the Jewish people. Might he have been afraid that if moving to *Eretz Yisrael* did not hasten the Messianic Age, that would deflate the spiritual power of the messianic myth, depleting Jews' longing for redemption and draining the Jewish community of hope for the future?

How do you relate to Jewish ideas about the end of days, redemption, and the Messiah?

2. Looking in the Mirror of Power

What does this passage say about how Jews in Babylonia viewed themselves vis-à-vis power? Does the passage betray a sense of powerlessness? Does it inculcate a self-image of powerlessness?

As a measure of how Jewish self-government led to a change in communal self-image, consider this popular joke that circulated in Israel following the 1967 Six Day War:

At a Russian military academy, a general delivers a lecture entitled "Potential Problems and Military Strategy" and then asks if there are any questions.

An officer stands up: "Will there be a third world war? Will Russia take part in it?"

The general answers both questions in the affirmative.

"Who will be our enemy?" the officer queries.

The general replies, "All indications point to China," to the shock of the audience.

"General," the officer asks, "we are only 150 million. There are more than 750 million Chinese. Is there any chance we can win?"

"In modern warfare," the general explains, "it is not the quantity but rather the quality that matters. For example, in a few recent wars in the Middle East, 5 million Jews fought 50 million Arabs and won."

"Sir," the officer asks, "do we have enough Jews?"

What does this joke say about how the Jewish self-image changed after 1967? Do you believe that this transformed self-image still prevails today?

3. The Power and Meaning of Words: Israel and Egypt

Ruth Wisse, scholar of Yiddish and comparative literature, asserts in *Jews and Power*: "The loss of Jewish sovereignty was the defining political event in the life of the Jewish people."[28] While Jews have reason to be proud of their survival, she notes, "this pride in sheer survival demonstrates how the tolerance of political weakness could cross the moral line into veneration of political weakness."[29] In other words, powerlessness can be a disease that afflicts the spirit. For Wisse, Zionism, the movement to reclaim sovereignty and build an independent Jewish state in the Jews' ancestral homeland is the antidote.

Wisse recounts an oft-told story concerning the historic 1977 visit of Egyptian president Anwar Sadat to Jerusalem. Israel's prime minister Golda Meir reportedly said to him, "We can forgive you for killing our sons, but we will never forgive you for making us kill yours." Wisse appreciates the deep Jewish humanism underlying this statement, but warns of the danger of "moral solipsism," by which she means extreme preoccupation with one's own moral performance to the exclusion of everyone else's. Jews, she says, tend to focus on and value their own moral conduct more than the necessities of survival. Attributing this proclivity to many centuries of Jewish powerlessness that begot a deep ambivalence concerning power, she writes:

> Golda expressed more concern with Israeli children's decency than with her enemies' designs on them. She would have demonstrated greater understanding of her Egyptian counterpart and greater appreciation of political reality had she asked Sadat to convey to his people the message, "We Jews are here to stay," requiring decency, tolerance, and realism of *them*.

Rabbi, author, and speaker Daniel Gordis says of Meir's observation: "There is something almost perverse about Golda's possibly apocryphal remark, and something even more disturbing about the fact that it has been lauded and cited thousands of times across the Jewish world. [Try googling it.] For how can Jews not understand how wrong—and how dangerous—her sentiment was?"For Gordis, the source of the problem is that modern Jews worldwide "have internalized an incorrect reading of the role of war and self-defense in Jewish tradition. They have been taught, explicitly or not, that Judaism is a virtually pacifist tradition. And they thus incorrectly believe that being required to use military force has pushed Israel into an 'un-Jewish' posture."[30]

Another way to read Meir's words might be to see them as deriving from a foundation of confidence in Israel's military prowess—that Israel's power to protect herself was great enough to shift the focus to issues of morality rather than power.

How do you understand Meir's purported words to Sadat? What do you think of Wisse's and Gordis's interpretations of her statement? Can you relate to the alternative explanation? Might Meir's words be understood in yet another way?

Do you wrestle with the idea of Jewish power, especially as it is deployed by the State of Israel?

4. Power and Character

Abraham Lincoln purportedly said: "Nearly all men can stand adversity, but if you want to test a man's character, give him power."

Do you agree or disagree? Why or why not? What are the risks of having power? Where in your life have you seen this play out?

The psychologists Renee Garfinkel and Hannah Rothstein, both Orthodox Jews, contend that the Rabbis and their successors, who lacked political or military power, developed the art of discourse as a tool of communal authority and power. Weakness begot strength. Today, they assert, Orthodox rabbinical institutions have shed the art of discourse and adopted authoritarian ways—abusing their power as a result.

> Differentiating between legitimate and abusive uses of power and authority by rabbis and (other Jewish leaders) has been a concern for the Jewish community ever since the advent of Rabbinic Judaism following the destruction of the second temple. The great rabbinic authorities of the Mishna and Talmud were aware of the potential for abuse of power, and even while establishing their authority, they established ways of limiting this authority, for example, the traditions of debate and of the (respectful) acknowledgement and careful setting down of minority opinions. Even those whose views or behavior were considered heretical were not written out of our tradition. Despite, or perhaps because of, the need to govern the Jewish people without the usual political and military tools, discourse was privileged over dictatorship. Despite, or perhaps because the Jewish people lived as a minority among powerful others, Jewish tradition emphasized

restraint in the exercise of power, and developed narrow legal rulings that were sensitive to local and even individual conditions.

Today, however, most rabbinic institutions actually oppose presenting or examining the merits of points of view other than their own. In place of careful consideration of the merits of different opinions before offering a halakhic ruling, these points of view are ignored, ridiculed, or besmirched, and their owners are vilified as evil enemies of Torah. Instead of seeking to understand the social, religious, and economic realities of specific communities, they presume to know what is best for everyone without bothering to consult them. Our knowledge and experience as psychologists (one clinical, one organizational) leads us to assert that the growth of rabbinical authoritarianism, the abuse of rabbinic power, and other pressures for conformity—not the voices they are attempting to censor—are the biggest threats to the future of Judaism and to the nature of the Jewish State.[31]

What do you think of Garfinkel and Rothstein's contentions? Do you agree that the growth of rabbinical authoritarianism threatens the Jewish future and the nature of the Jewish state? Do you distinguish between how the Rabbis of the Talmud and contemporary rabbis approach issues of power, and if so, how?

5. Power and Morality

In *My Promised Land*, Israeli journalist Ari Shavit describes morally questionable acts Israel undertook to secure victory in the War of Independence. "If need be, I'll stand by the damned," he writes. "Because I know that if it wasn't for them, the State of Israel would not have been born. If it wasn't for them, I would not have been born. They did the dirty, filthy work that enables my people, myself, my daughter and my sons to live."[32]

Consider these two views of the conflict between Israel and Gaza in the summer of 2014. Both were published by British media outlets approximately one month apart, one year after the conflict.

#1—Israel has claimed the Israel Defence Forces' operation in Gaza last summer was a moral, defensive war conducted in accordance with international law. . . .

Israel's report highlights efforts by the IDF to avoid harm to civilians and presents the operation as an "imperative necessity" in response to incessant rocket fire from Gaza and the threat of Hamas infiltrating through its tunnels.

It states that the goals were "restoring security to Israeli civilians living under Hamas rocket fire" and "dismantling the Hamas tunnel network used to infiltrate Israel."

The majority of the 250-page report is dedicated to showing Hamas's human rights violations and war crimes. It holds Hamas responsible for many of the Palestinian civilian casualties caused by the IDF, arguing that they were unavoidable due to Hamas's tactics of embedding militants among civilian populations, whether in homes, schools, mosques or UN buildings.[33]

#2—A collection of harrowing testimonies published on Monday by Breaking the Silence, an NGO run by former Israeli soldiers, describes lax rules of engagement that allowed troops wide discretion to open fire in built-up areas—leading to mass non-combatant casualties and devastating damage to homes and civilian infrastructure.

Forces operated under the assumption that they were entering areas that had been cleared of inhabitants after the Israeli army launched its military offensive, Operation Protective Edge, last July. Soldiers were told to target any Palestinian encountered as a "terrorist" and to shoot to kill.

In reality, many residents had remained behind in neighbourhoods where military officials had dropped leaflets or made phone calls ordering inhabitants to evacuate—leaving them at the mercy of massive shelling, air attacks or gunfire from troops who identified them as militants.[34]

Should standards of morality change dependent on circumstances? Should they change during wartime? Should they change in order to achieve a larger objective, such as hastening the Messianic Age? Does being perceived as "powerful" or "powerless" change the moral equation?

Summing Things Up

The existential experience of living in exile and the Rabbis' theological explanations for their predicament combined to foster a worldview in which Jews believed they were living in exile as a God-ordained punishment for their sins—and only God would, or could, restore them to *Eretz Yisrael* and the land to their sovereignty. This thinking continued to influence how Jews approached ideas of Jewish power.

Our passage considered whether it is permissible for an individual to move from Babylonia to *Eretz Yisrael*. The ensuing conversation, with all the trappings of a halakhic, legal debate, complete with biblical proof-texts, is ultimately grounded not in scriptural principles and values so much as Rabbinic theological beliefs about why Jews found themselves in exile and, therefore, how they should behave. The ramifications of this debate are still felt today.

6 Straddling Two Worlds

Babylonian Talmud, Tractate Shabbat 33b–34a

R. Elazar b. Azariah taught: If there is no Torah, there is no decency; if there is no decency, there is no Torah. If there is no wisdom, there is no piety; if there is no piety, there is no wisdom. If there is no understanding, there is no knowledge; if there is no knowledge, there is no understanding. If there is no sustenance, there is no Torah; if there is no Torah, there is no sustenance.

—Pirkei Avot 3:21

Why Study This Passage?

In "The Melting Pot," a 1908 play by the British author Israel Zangwill, the protagonist, David, his family's sole survivor of the Kishinev pogrom, emigrates to America, where he falls in love with Vera, a Russian Christian immigrant. In an irony worthy of Shakespeare, her father turns out to be the Russian military officer responsible for annihilating David's family, but in the melting pot of America apologies and forgiveness bridge the chasm, erase the past, and, as the curtain falls, assure the audience that David and Vera will marry and live happily ever after. With the cast's final bows, the term "melting pot" entered the U.S. lexicon, conveying the assumption that minority cultures would assimilate into the American majority host culture and lose their particularity, resulting in a homogeneous society.

That never happened, either on screen or in the street. Alternative colorful metaphors—"the salad bowl" and "cultural mosaic" among them—have arisen to describe the more realistic situation of a person living with a foot in each of two worlds. As Safi Mahmoud Mahfouz, scholar of modern American literature and theater, writes in a study of the portrayal of immigrants on the stage:

> The salad bowl or the cultural mosaic theory has called for the integration of the diverse ethnicities of United States residents, thus combining them like the different ingredients of a salad. This model has challenged the more traditional concept of cultural assimilation in the melting pot. In the salad bowl notion various American cultures remain distinct and do not merge together into a single homogeneous society. Immigrants who favor the salad bowl assimilate into the new world culture, but at the same time keep certain cultural practices of their old world. Some, however, do not assimilate, but choose to live a life on the margins, in ethnic enclaves where they can stick to their old world culture.[1]

Immigrants invariably confront a host of challenges inherent in navigating the complexities of a new society and culture. A myriad of difficult questions arise. What elements of the mainstream host culture should they assimilate? Which customs and traditions integral to their identity should they maintain, and which interfere with their effort to adapt to their new surroundings?

Similarly, Jews living in almost every age and land—recent immigrants or not—have faced this challenge, couched in many ways: How to live with one foot in each of two worlds—the world of Jewish traditions and values and the larger world around them; how to straddle two worlds;

how to dwell within and between two worlds. More recently, a large wave of Jewish immigration in the nineteenth and twentieth centuries brought the ancestors of many contemporary American Jews to the United States. These Jews entered the mainstream of their host cultures, never living completely isolated from the majority culture, and frequently weighing their responses when public institutions, customs, and mores of society conflicted with Jewish values and practices.

The story in this chapter reflects a considerably earlier yet similar struggle: the *tanna'im* — or, perhaps more authentically, the *amora'im* who told the story about their predecessors, the *tanna'im* — had to decide which elements of the dominant and sovereign Greco-Roman culture in the Land of Israel in the first and second centuries were consonant with Jewish life and which were not.

A Broad View to Begin

In 63 BCE, at the close of the Third Mithridatic War, Pompey sacked Jerusalem and created the province of Syria, initiating Rome's incursion into Jewish affairs in the Land of Israel. Sixty-nine years later Judea became a Roman province, marking the end of Jewish sovereignty in the Land of Israel. For the Jews living in their ancestral land, this situation was the inverse of the Jewish immigrant experience in America: the dominant culture came from without and imposed itself on the indigenous people. The Roman administrative agenda included cultural dominance (much like the Hellenists before them) for the purpose of consolidating power and governing efficiently.

Under Roman domination, the urbanization of various towns progressed significantly. Several towns populated by the early Rabbis — Tiberias, Tzippori, and Lydda — developed into Roman-style cities, their public spaces suffused with pagan images of gods and emperors, their economic life fueled by Roman coinage, and their thriving commerce benefiting from Roman roads connected to other urban centers. Historian Seth Schwartz notes:

The rabbis probably gravitated to the cities because their conviction that they constituted the true leadership of Israel made them not sectarian but expansionist. In the cities they had access to networks of trade, communications, patronage and political power. Yet they cannot readily be "normalized." It must finally be admitted that the culture of the Greco-Roman city and the Judaism of the rabbis contradicted each other both essentially and in superficial detail. As far as we can tell from the surviving literature, the rabbis, no less than their Christian counterparts, largely rejected high imperial urban culture and offered their followers a radical and coherent alternative to it.[2]

Mishnah is written against the background of Jews living in overlapping cultures: Jews lived with one foot in the Jewish world of Torah as practiced in their day and the other foot in the Greco-Roman material and cultural world. Jews wore the same clothing, used the same currency,[3] spoke Greek,[4] practiced similar burial customs, and visited the same bathhouses as non-Jews. The early Rabbis were both thoroughly integrated into Greco-Roman culture and simultaneously wary of its incursion into Jewish life and sensibilities. As they shaped a Judaism that could endure and flourish in the absence of the Temple, they faced the unenviable task of determining which aspects of the host culture to accept as benign and which to condemn as threatening and malignant.

A case in point, central to the story in this chapter, concerns idolatry: How are the Rabbis to address the ubiquitous reality of Greco-Roman statuary in Roman bathhouses in the face of the Torah's vehement condemnation of idolatry and unequivocal requirement to destroy idols? There is the classical prohibition — *You shall not make for yourself a sculptured image, or any likeness of what is in the heavens above, or on the earth below, or in the waters under the earth* (Exodus 20:4 and Deuteronomy 5:8) — as well as this stern instruction: *You shall consign the images of their gods to fire; you shall not covet the silver and gold on them and keep it for yourselves, lest you be ensnared thereby; for that is abhorrent to Adonai your God* (Deuteronomy 7:25). Given these fervid statements, it is surprising that in Tractate Avodah Zarah, which itself means "idolatry," only a single mishnah discusses the disposition of idols (they are to be dumped into the Dead Sea). Rather, Mishnah virtually erases the biblical imperative to destroy idols, as Talmud scholar Ephraim Urbach was the first to point out.[5] According to Urbach, the *tanna'im* redefined a pillar of biblical religion—the severe prohibition against idolatry and the commandment to expunge idols and their appurtenances from the Land of Israel—for two reasons. First, they were attempting to adapt to changing economic conditions. Second, they did not take seriously the power ascribed to gods.

We see proof of this in Tractate Avodah Zarah itself, where the Rabbis redefine "destroy" to connote a prohibition to deriving benefit from the idol, and further distinguish between benefit for profit (*b'tovah*), which is not prohibited, and benefit that is not for profit (*she'lo b'tovah*), which is permitted. Going even further, the Rabbis find a way to circumvent the prohibition entirely through *bitul* (nullification).[6] Curiously, the *mishnayot* on *bitul* in chapter 4 of Avodah Zarah, the only text in which *bitul* connotes actual destruction, culminates in a story.

They asked the [Jewish] elders in Rome: "If [God] does not desire idolatry, why does [God] not annul it?" They answered: "If they worshiped things not needed by the world, [God] would annul them. But they worship the sun, the moon, the stars, and the constellations. Shall [God] destroy the world because of fools!" They replied: "If so, let [God] destroy the things not needed by the world and leave the others!" The elders responded: "We would thus strengthen the hands of their worshipers, who would say: 'Know that these [the sun, moon, and stars] are true gods, for they have not been destroyed!'" (M Avodah Zarah 4:7)

The inclusion of this story in the Mishnah demonstrates that the Rabbis, living in a Greco-Roman society permeated with images of pagan deities, struggled to work out how to relate to them.

Until recently, scholars of the tannaitic period tended to analyze the Rabbinic view as either "assimilationist" or "rejectionist," which is to say that the Rabbis were either tacitly assimilating elements of Roman culture or fiercely rejecting that culture as "foreign" and anathema to Judaism. One example: In exploring the tannaitic writings about the Passover meal, the scholar Siegfried Stein famously held that the Rabbis consciously "borrowed" the forms of the Greco-Roman banquet or symposium—particularly the table manners, dietary customs, and philosophical discussions—in describing and prescribing the Passover meal, thereby seamlessly *assimilating* Hellenistic customs that served their purposes, without any concern that doing so would conflict with Jewish identity.[7] In contrast, Talmud scholar Baruch M. Bokser argued that the Rabbis sought to overcome the loss of the Temple through a "reinterpretation of cultic rites and legitimization of extratemple means of religious expression."[8] In other words, the Rabbis purposefully *rejected* various forms of the Hellenistic symposia and imposed their own alternative practices,[9] among them the requirement that everyone present participate, including women and children; the attachment of wine to be drunk to specific moments in the meal; and the ascription of ritual value to dipping hors d'oeuvres.

Today, a new generation of scholars holds that the "cultural strife" model of the encounter between Judaism and Greco-Roman culture—exemplified by Bokser's view—speaks more to the concerns of the scholars espousing the paradigm than to tannaitic reality. Lapin warns of the tendency to read our own situations and sensitivities into the lives of the *tanna'im* and *amora'im*:

Almost inevitably . . . studies of identity often deploy strongly dichotomous models of cultural contact (assimilation, accommodation,

acculturation, resistance) that the best of these studies also then prob-
lematize. Within this broader field, studies focused on Jews within the
Roman Empire are more dichotomous than most. Among the reasons
for this are the fact that Jews and Judaism still exist in the present
day, and often provide an unacknowledged model for what Judaism
ought to have looked like; that scholars who write about them often
have their own stake in the history of Jews in the Roman Empire; and
not least that within the contemporary division of knowledge in the
academy, "ancient historians" and experts on Jews and Judaism often
occupy different professional universes beginning from their graduate
training and extending to departmental appointments, publication
venues, and professional meetings.[10]

As against the "assimilation, accommodation, acculturation, resistance" models Lapin cites, Yaron Z. Eliav, historian of late antiquity
and Rabbinic literature, prefers a view he calls "filtered absorption" or
"controlled incorporation."[11] Roman culture and society were the background of life, Eliav says, much as American culture is the invisible
milieu in which American Jews live: we dress and furnish our homes
much as other Americans without giving it much thought. We don't
consciously choose "American fashions" or "American furniture"—we
simply select garments and furnishings that serve our purposes and
please our aesthetic senses.

Among this new generation of scholars, Lapin, examining Jews
and Judaism in the provincial culture of the eastern Roman Empire
in late antiquity, similarly argues for "the fundamental embeddedness
of Rabbis within a broader world" as "a corrective to the tendency
[among some scholars] to treat Jews as unique in the ancient world."[12]
Lapin reminds us that "Rabbis developed as they did in part because
of when and where they lived and who they were."[13] In other words,
the Rabbis were neither consciously adapting Greco-Roman customs
nor purposefully rejecting them.

The bathhouse, a cultural staple of first- and second-century Greco-Roman cities, provides a particularly interesting example, because it is quintessentially Roman and potentially problematic in a Jewish context. Lapin writes:

> Unlike the Babylonian characterization of second-century rabbinic debate, Palestinian rabbinic texts, and particularly tannaitic legal texts, do not generally treat baths as an artifact of empire imposed upon an admiring or resistant population. Baths and bathing appear instead as an almost entirely naturalized aspect of the material practice of daily life. This tendency is already present in the Mishnah, and attests to the "domestication" of bathing (or, as Tacitus might have it, Rabbis' enslavement through it),[14] even as the diffusion of the institution was still in its relatively early stages. Thus, when the Mishnah considers the implications of vows of prohibition, it includes among "things belonging to the town": [the town square, the bathhouse, the synagogue, the ark, and the scrolls, according to a list in M Nedarim 5:5].... A bath, then, like a synagogue, is a communal appurtenance, in which town inhabitants are deemed to hold a share.[15]

Eliav notes that Roman bathhouses were a feat of Roman design and engineering benefiting from the development of cement and concrete, the use of the arch, and the provision of water (in a desert environment) thanks to the aqueduct. By the second century CE, "thousands of bathhouses dotted the Mediterranean world, in cities, towns, and even small villages."[16]

Bathhouses posed several cultural challenges to Jews. For one, people bathed without clothing in a semipublic setting. More significantly, perhaps, bathhouses were decorated with mosaics and sculptures that represented the imperial power, reflected hedonistic experiences, and depicted gods and goddesses. The Mishnah's restrictions reflect the Rabbis' unease with the setting: One may not pray or wear tefillin in the bathhouse. In a town with a majority Jewish population, heating the bathhouse on Shabbat for use by Jews after Shabbat is prohibited.[17] Bathhouses are to be closed on public fast days.[18] During Pesach, women are not permitted to soak bran (apparently brought to the bath for scrubbing) lest it leaven in the water.[19]

To Lapin, these restrictions reveal just how ingrained and widely accepted bathhouses were in Jewish daily life. Eliav comments, "Early rabbinic legal traditions refer to the bathhouse in the most neutral terms, testifying to the flawless integration of this institution into Jewish life."[20] He concludes:

> A priori, there could have been bathhouses that Jews strongly resented. But despite the interpretations of some scholars, close examination reveals that the sources do not voice such objections, neither during the last century of the Second Temple nor in the centuries thereafter. On the contrary, exhaustive examination of rabbinic texts shows that the bathhouse was an integral and legitimate component of Jewish life in those times.[21]

However, the *tanna'im* did express concern about the potentially idolatrous aspect of bathing culture. Bathhouses were replete with mosaics, friezes, busts, and statuary—what Eliav terms "'plastic language' that communicated political, religious, and social messages."[22] A mishnah in Tractate Avodah Zarah rules that bathhouses are specifically exempted from the urban structures Jews were forbidden to build in partnership with non-Jews. However, although Jews could construct bathhouses with non-Jews, they were prohibited from building the niche where statuary was to be installed, presumably because this space might be used for idolatrous worship. Yet the mishnah assumes that after the building is erected it may be used even though it contains statuary.[23]

A story is told in the Mishnah concerning Rabban Gamliel's use of a bathhouse.[24] The incident centers around a conversation between Rabban

Gamliel and a gentile who challenges the propriety of his use of the bathhouse given Torah's prohibition against idolatry.[25] While on the surface Rabban Gamliel expresses little anxiety over the presence of a statue of Aphrodite in the bathhouse, dismissing any notion of religious conflict, the very presence of the story suggests that the bathhouse is, for some Rabbis, simultaneously socially normative and at least potentially religiously transgressive.[26]

> Proklos son of Plosfos asked Rabban Gamliel in Akko, while bathing in the bathhouse of Aphrodite [a question of halakhah]. [Proklos] said to him, "It is written in your Torah, *Let nothing that has been censured stick to your hand* (Deuteronomy 13:18). Why then are you bathing in the bathhouse of Aphrodite?" [Rabban Gamliel] said to him, "One does not respond [to halakhic questions] in the bathhouse." After he had left, [Rabban Gamliel] said to [Proklos], "I did not come into her territory; she came into my territory. They did not say [at the time the bathhouse was constructed], 'Let us make a beautiful bathhouse for Aphrodite.' Rather, they said: 'Let us make Aphrodite to beautify the bathhouse.' Another reason: If you were given a lot of money, you would not enter into your idolatrous worship naked and defiled and urinating in front of it. Yet she stands on the sewer pipe and the entire nation urinates before her. [Torah] says 'their gods' (Deuteronomy 12:3) to connote: that which one treats like a god is forbidden, but that which is not treated like a god is permitted."[27]

Proklos son of Plosfos questions the propriety of a Jew patronizing a bathhouse containing a statue of Aphrodite.[28] The Rabbis' discomfort is projected onto the gentile who raises the issue. Rabban Gamliel offers four justifications: (1) He refuses to hold the conversation in the bathhouse. BT Berakhot 24b prohibits pondering Torah matters in a bathhouse, and certainly discussing halakhah would fall into that category. (2) He claims that the bathhouse is not intrinsically constituted as sacred space; it was built for bathing, not worship. (3) He asserts that the statue of Aphrodite is a decoration installed to beautify the bathhouse, not to serve as the object of religious worship or adoration. (4) He maintains that those who frequent the bathhouse do not treat the statue as an idol; to the contrary, it sits over, and amid, bodily filth. If it is not treated as a god, it is not a god. Therefore, it is not what the statue *is*, but rather how people think about it, that matters. Presumably, the fourth and final argument proffered is the strongest, relying as it does on a prooftext from Torah—but is it?

Curiously, Proklos cites Deuteronomy 13:18, which concerns a town that is seduced into idolatry. We might have expected him to quote Deuteronomy 12:3: *Tear down their altars, smash their pillars, put their sacred posts to the fire, and cut down the images of **their gods**, obliterating their name from that site.* This latter verse unambiguously requires the physical destruction of all objects and appurtenances of idolatrous worship: altars, pillars, posts, and imagery of any kind. Or perhaps he might have quoted Deuteronomy 7:25, cited above. Yet, in the exegetical hands of the Rabbis, this verse's requirement to burn and destroy idols is instead wholly transformed into a prohibition against using or benefiting from them.[29]

The story of Rabban Gamliel and Proklos undermines even this attenuation of Torah's requirement: it amounts to a leniency on top of a leniency, effectively rendering the bathhouse "neutral space" for the Rabbis and their followers—no doubt reflecting the degree to which the bathhouse was a fixture in the culture of the day and widely patronized by Jews.[30] Yet, at the same time, it reflects Rabbinic anxiety about Greco-Roman society and concern for where Jews should set boundaries on their participation in the culture.

Having reviewed the Rabbis' acceptance of, and limitations on, the use of the bathhouse, we have the context to fully comprehend a story about R. Shimon bar Yochai, a *tanna* of the second century who lived, learned, and taught in the shadow of the Second Temple's destruction. A student of Rabban Gamliel II (the same Sage engaged by Proklos son of Plosfos in conversation at Aphrodite's bathhouse in Akko) and R. Yehoshua b.

Chananiah, he later studied with R. Akiva for thirteen years in B'nai B'rak. Talmud records that during the Hadrianic persecutions that followed the final revolt against Rome (132–135 CE), R. Shimon visited R. Akiva in prison and implored his master to teach him Torah. To understand R. Shimon b. Yochai's antipathy toward the Romans, it helps to know the Talmud's tradition of his ordination as a Rabbi:

> At one time, the wicked government [of Rome] decreed against Israel that whoever confers ordination would be killed, and whoever was ordained would be killed, and any town in which ordination took place would be destroyed, and the boundaries of any town in which ordination took place would be uprooted. What did R. Yehudah b. Bava do? He went and sat between two large mountains and between two large cities, and between two Shabbat boundaries, between Usha and Shefar'am, and he ordained five elders there: R. Meir, R. Yehudah, R. Shimon, R. Yose, and R. Elazar b. Shamua. Rav Avya added: also R. Nechemiah. When their enemies discovered them, [R. Yehudah b. Bava] said to [his students], "My children, run!" They said to him, "Our teacher, what will happen to you?" He said to them, "I will place myself before [the Romans] like a rock that cannot be overturned." They said that [the Roman soldiers] did not leave that place until they had driven three hundred iron spears into him, making him like a sieve.[31]

R. Shimon's life experiences help explain why he considered the Roman Empire to be barbaric and savage, the ruthless enemy of Israel.

Our passage narrates an incident from around 161 CE in which R. Shimon expresses his antipathy toward Rome to a small group of colleagues, leading the Roman governor Varus to sentence him to death. For thirteen years, he hides in a cave with his son, R. Elazar b. Shimon. Numerous versions of this story appear in the Yerushalmi (Jerusalem Talmud) and four works of midrash (*Pesikta Rabbati*, Genesis Rabbah, Ecclesiastes Rabbah, and Esther Rabbah), indicating how strongly it resonated with the Rabbis.

The events take place in and around Tiberias, on the shore of the Sea of Galilee. According to the historian Josephus, Herod Antipas built Tiberias over a site containing numerous tombs. Therefore, the area containing the graves is considered *tame* (ritually unclean), and *kohanim* (priests descended from Aaron) are accordingly banned from entering it.

As our story paints him, R. Shimon b. Yochai is the model of a zealot or a fanatic. He considers the pursuit of Torah as the singular proper endeavor for a Jew. For him, living with a foot in each of two worlds is not only a religious concession, it is a violation. What is more, he even disdains a Jew setting foot in the "real world"; he reviles a Jew's practice of mundane tasks and occupations that sustain life, such as farming, despite the well-known Rabbinic dictum *Im en kemach, en Torah* (If there is no flour, there is no Torah).[32] The Rabbis convey that R. Shimon must learn—through painful experience—how to achieve a proper balance and make allowances for the needs of physical existence by living simultaneously in several overlapping worlds.

Looking beyond the Talmud, a much later tradition holds that during the thirteen years R. Shimon b. Yochai and his son R. Elazar spend hiding from the Romans in a cave, they study not only the Torah but also *Torat haSod* (the Hidden, or Secret, Torah), a term for the (historically later) Jewish mystical tradition of Kabbalah. R. Shimon b. Yochai is later credited with writing the *Zohar* (Splendor), a mystical work actually authored by Moses de Leon in Spain in the thirteenth century. De Leon had ascribed his work to R. Shimon to claim greater credibility and authority for the *Zohar*, and indeed it became wildly popular in many circles. Today it is considered a foundational work of Jewish mysticism.

Exploring the Nooks and Crannies of Our Passage

The scene is the *bet midrash*. R. Shimon b. Yochai, several students, and some others are discussing the Roman Empire's effect on life in the Land of Israel.

R. Yehudah, R. Yose, and R. Shimon were sitting [together], and Yehudah b. Gerim was sitting near them. R. Yehudah commenced [the discussion] by observing, "How fine are the works of this people! They have established marketplaces! They have built bridges! They have erected bathhouses!"

R. Yose was silent.

R. Shimon b. Yochai, however, answered and said, "All that they made they made entirely to serve their own needs. They established marketplaces to lodge harlots in them, bathhouses to rejuvenate themselves, bridges to collect tolls for them."

Yehudah b. Gerim went and recounted their words, and they were heard by the government. [Roman officials] decreed: Yehudah, who exalted [us], shall be exalted. Yose, who was silent, shall be exiled to Tzippori. Shimon, who denigrated [us], shall be executed.

The three opinions expressed about Roman influence lie along a spectrum from pro-Roman to anti-Roman.

R. Yehudah lauds the engineering feats of the empire. He points out that the Romans have built marketplaces, making an array of goods available to people; bridges, facilitating easier travel; and bathhouses, furnishing comfort and pleasure. Taken together, the Romans have improved the quality of life.

R. Yose does not respond. His silence may be interpreted as an expression of neutrality. Perhaps he recognizes both Rome's engineering feats and the horrors Rome has wrought on the Jewish people.

R. Shimon b. Yochai avows that all the Romans have built is essentially an exercise in self-aggrandizement and decadence. Rome is thus corrupted and immoral to the core.

After the Second Temple's destruction and in a world ruled by the Romans, R. Shimon's viewpoint does not come as a surprise, but expressing it aloud is dangerous. Yehudah b. Gerim (whose name means, literally, "Jew, son of proselytes") either recounts this conversation to someone who conveys it to the Roman government or himself informs on R. Shimon to the government. The response is swift and proportionate to the views expressed: the Romans reward their friends—exalting R. Yehudah—and punish those they consider enemies—condemning R. Shimon to execution.

Why are we told that R. Yose, who said nothing, is to be exiled to Tzippori (Sepphoris, in Greek),[33] a bustling center of Jewish life and learning in the upper Galilee? During the first Jewish revolt against Rome, the people of Tzippori refused to join the rebellion. In 67 CE they signed a pact with the Roman government and opened Tzippori to General Vespasian, thereby preventing the city's destruction. After the Temple was destroyed and Jerusalem decimated in 70 CE, many Jews in Jerusalem and Judea moved to Tzippori, home (according to the Jewish Roman historian Josephus) of "the only people in Galilee who desired peace" (*The Jewish War* 3:33). Apparently Tzippori is where the pacifists lived. R. Yose is thus exiled to a place where he is unlikely to incite, or be incited to, rebellion.

Now, with a price on this head, R. Shimon must retreat from society and hide from the Romans.

> [R. Shimon] and his son went and hid in the *bet midrash*. Every day his wife brought him bread and a small jug of water and they ate. [But] when the decree became more severe, [R. Shimon] said to his son, "Women's minds are unstable. Perhaps she may be tortured and reveal us."

R. Shimon's withdrawal progresses in two stages. In the first stage, he withdraws from the broader society and lives in the *bet midrash* as if under house arrest. He never ventures out because he might be seen by the Roman authorities. His wife brings him bread—a subsistence diet that nonetheless reflects the combined benefits of the material world (earth, sun, water, grain); cooperation facilitated by civilized society (many hands—farmer, thresher, grinder, baker—working together to produce it); and considerable manufacturing technology. For this story, bread not only represents the blessings of the material world but, significantly, the benefits of civilization.

The first stage ends when R. Shimon recognizes that the *bet midrash* is too public a venue and therefore not safe. Should the Romans suspect he is nearby, they might torture his wife for information. R. Shimon withdraws further, hiding in a cave, separated now not only from Greco-Roman culture, but also from his community and colleagues.

> They went and hid in a cave. A miracle occurred: a carob tree and a spring of water were created for them. They would strip off their garments and sit [covered] up to their necks in sand. They studied all day long. When it was time to pray, they dressed and covered themselves, prayed, and then stripped off their garments again so that they would not wear out. [In this way,] they lived in the cave for twelve years.

R. Shimon takes his son, R. Elazar b. Shimon, with him into internal exile to be his study partner. The pair live a marginal, ascetic existence; here they have no need for Roman marketplaces, bathhouses, roads, and bridges. Their lives are stripped to the bare essentials: No house—just a cave. No clothing—except when they pray. God supplies their only nourishments: carob and water, food that does not require the cooperation of a civilized society.

Their days are spent engaged in Torah study and prayer—ostensibly an ideal life for a scholar such as R. Shimon, who will later extol this Spartan existence because, lacking distractions—including other human beings save his son—he is able to concentrate exclusively on Torah. To preserve their only set of garments, R. Shimon and R. Elazar bury themselves up to their necks in sand most of the time. Could there be a more graphic depiction of R. Shimon's rejection of the technologies and luxuries of Rome—or, indeed, of society? One wonders if any other scholar, regardless of how in love with Torah, would welcome these conditions as conducive to study and sufficient for life.

R. Shimon and R. Elazar live entirely alone for twelve years. No one knows where they are, and therefore when it finally becomes safe for them to emerge from the cave and return to society, their family cannot relay that message to them.

> Elijah came and stood at the entrance to the cave and said, "Who will inform the son of Yochai that the emperor is dead and his decree annulled?"
>
> They emerged. They saw people plowing and sowing. [R. Shimon] said, "They forsake eternal life and engage in the life of this world!" Wherever they cast their eyes was immediately incinerated.
>
> A *bat kol* ['heavenly voice'] rang forth and cried out, "Have you emerged to destroy My world? Return to your cave!"
>
> They returned and lived there [another] twelve months, a year. They said, "The punishment of the wicked in Gehinnom ['Gehenna'] is [limited to] twelve months."
>
> A *bat kol* rang forth and said, "Emerge from your cave!"

At the end of twelve years, God—the only one who knows where R. Shimon and his son are hiding—sends the prophet Elijah to inform R. Shimon that the emperor is dead and therefore the decree against him is no longer operative.[34]

When R. Shimon and his son emerge, their first sight is of people engaged in sowing and plowing to produce life-sustaining food. Pirkei Avot 3:21 attributes to R. Elazar b. Azariah this pillar of Rabbinic thought: "Without flour [i.e., sustenance] there is no Torah, and without Torah there is no flour." Nonetheless R. Shimon flies into a rage, exclaiming that by occupying themselves with the mundane activities of farming rather than devoting themselves full time to Torah study, these people prioritize life in this world over life in the world to come. Prior to his extended exclusion from society, R. Shimon had disparaged the technology and material culture of the Greco-Roman world; twelve years of exile appear to have hardened him against all human pursuits save Torah. His son, R. Elazar, who has been exposed exclusively to his father's views for twelve years, is equally incensed.

Their rage quickly turns to violence, facilitated by a colorful superpower worthy of a comic supervillain: Talmud tells us that both Rabbis' eyes are flamethrowers. Wherever they cast their condemning gaze, obliterating fire erupts. And so, in their fury at the simple people working the land, R. Shimon and R. Elazar commit murder.

We can imagine God's chagrin and horror. Is this not a testament to the danger of zealotry and fanaticism?

God's response is swift and unequivocal. A heavenly voice orders R. Shimon and his son back into the cave, lest they destroy the entire world. They are not fit for human society.

R. Shimon and his son return to the cave for yet another year, bringing their total elapsed time of exile to thirteen years. The additional year, however, is not a retreat to preserve their lives; the decree, after all, has elapsed. Rather, it is divine punishment for taking the lives of others.

The thirteenth year is also a preview of Gehinnom/Gehenna (purgatory) in this world. Rabbinic tradition holds that following death, the souls of all who have sinned are consigned to Gehinnom to atone for those sins for up to (but no more than) one year. Therefore, R. Shimon reasons, he should not be required to spend more than a year in the cave. At the end of the year, a heavenly voice, now heard for a second time, announces the end of their punishment.

Just as R. Shimon's withdrawal from society occurred in two stages (first, to the *bet midrash*, and second, to the cave), so, too, his reemergence and reintegration into society occurs in two stages. Whereas the stages of R. Shimon's withdrawal were marked by places, the phases of his reintegration are marked both by places and interactions with people. The story next tells us of the first stage.

They emerged. Wherever R. Elazar destroyed [by incinerating with his gaze], R. Shimon healed. [R. Shimon] said to him, "My son! You and I are sufficient for the world."

On the eve of Shabbat, they saw an old man holding two bundles of myrtle and running just at twilight. They said to him, "What are these for?"

He said to them, "[They are] in honor of Shabbat."

"But wouldn't one bundle suffice you?"

"One is for 'remember' and one is for 'observe.'"

[R. Shimon] said to his son, "See how precious the commandments are to Israel." Their minds were at peace.

R. Shimon and R. Elazar once again emerge into the light of day. But have they changed? R. Elazar, who has lived thirteen years of his young life with only his father, thereby hearing his father's views exclusively, strikes out against people engaged in the quotidian of life. This time, however, R. Shimon steps in and reverses the destruction wrought by his son.

How are we to understand R. Shimon's enigmatic comment, "My son! You and I are sufficient for the world"? Underlying his assertion is the Rabbinic assumption that the world was created by, and for, Torah, and hence those who study Torah sustain the world. Torah Sages are, therefore, superior to other people or superhumans—which in some sense may account for R. Shimon's and R. Elazar's superhuman powers. This understanding suggests that R. Shimon means that he and his son alone sustain the world by living completely immersed in Torah—the image of them buried up to their necks in sand all day studying Torah bolsters this interpretation—and that he now understands that two Sages so wholly devoted to Torah are sufficient to sustain the world. Therefore, R. Shimon counters his son's destructive and punishing outbursts with healing.

The focus of the story now shifts entirely to R. Shimon. R. Elazar is not heard from again. As the first Shabbat after exile approaches, R.

Shimon sees a man running while holding two bundles of myrtle in his hands. The man is on the verge of committing two Shabbat violations: running[35] and carrying.[36] On this occasion, unlike when R. Shimon first emerged from the cave, he does not rush to harsh judgment; rather, he asks the man his intentions. The man replies that he intends to use the sweet-scented myrtle to honor Shabbat. Myrtle is often used for the *Havdalah* (Separation) ceremony on Saturday night that bids goodbye to the holy time of Shabbat, separating it from the mundane weekdays to come. The second blessing of *Havdalah* is, "Blessed are you, Adonai our God, ruler of the universe, who creates various kinds of spices."

R. Shimon, perhaps struggling to suppress his judgmental tendency, points out that one bundle of myrtle would suffice. The man responds that he intends the two bundles for more than *Havdalah*: They will fulfill both versions of the commandment concerning Shabbat found in the two versions of the Decalogue in the Torah—Exodus 20:8, **Remember** *the Sabbath day and keep it holy*; and Deuteronomy 5:12, **Observe** *the Sabbath day and keep it holy*.[37]

Recognizing that the man is intent on honoring Shabbat, R. Shimon views his endeavors as noble and sacred, rather than as egregious violations.

> R. Pinchas b. Ya'ir, [R. Shimon's] son-in-law, heard and went out to meet him. He took him to the bathhouse and massaged his flesh. Seeing the cracks in his skin, he wept and the tears trickled from his eyes and caused him pain. [R. Pinchas] said to [R. Shimon], "Woe to me that I see you like this!"
>
> [R. Shimon] said to him, "You are fortunate to see me like this, for if you had not seen me like this you would not find me thus [learned]." For originally, when R. Shimon b. Yochai posed a [halakhic] question, R. Pinchas b. Ya'ir would respond with twelve answers. But at the end [of thirteen years in the cave], when R. Pinchas b. Ya'ir would ask a question, R. Shimon b. Yochai would respond with twenty-four answers.

A chance encounter with the anonymous man carrying myrtle for Shabbat constitutes the first stage of R. Shimon's reintegration with the world. The intentional meeting with his son-in-law, R. Pinchas b. Ya'ir, who comes to escort him back to his home, community, and society, marks the second stage. With unmistakable irony, R. Pinchas takes his father-in-law to nothing other than a Roman bathhouse to wash his body and begin healing the wounds of his thirteen-year ascetic existence. Where the way station between society and cave thirteen years ago was the *bet midrash*, the way station from cave back to society is the bathhouse. The bathhouse R. Shimon initially condemned is not now a place of hedonism; it is a place of healing.

We also learn that exile has multiplied both R. Shimon's physical pain and intellectual prowess. The cracks in R. Shimon's skin, the result of studying Torah each day buried in sand up to his neck, has severely damaged his body, inducing R. Pinchas to weep from pity and compassion. Yet, R. Shimon hardly seems to notice his own pain and suffering. He is focused on all the Torah he has learned in thirteen years without the distractions of the mundane world. Prior to his exile, R. Pinchas could answer each of R. Shimon's challenges with twelve responses; now, R. Shimon can answer each of R. Pinchas's challenges with twenty-four answers. Hence, over the course of his years in isolation R. Shimon's intellectual prowess has increased nearly 300-fold!

Does R. Shimon's impressive improvement translate into being a better Sage? Is he now capable of contributing to the flourishing of his society? We don't have to wait long for an answer.

[R. Shimon] said, "Since a miracle has occurred, let me go and amend something, for it is written, *and Jacob arrived whole [or: in peace] [to the city of Shechem]* (Genesis 33:18), and Rav said [concerning this verse], "Whole in his body, whole in his finances, and whole in his Torah learning." *And he encamped[38] outside the city* (Genesis 33:18). Rav said he established a new coin for them. Shmuel said he established marketplaces for them. R. Yochanan said he established bathhouses for them.

R. Shimon sets out to improve the lives of the community in thanksgiving for his miraculously surviving the emperor's attempt to kill him. He takes as his model the Patriarch Jacob, whom Torah tells us arrived in Shechem *shalem* (whole). As Rav considers what being *shalem* might entail, he recalls that despite Jacob's wrestling match with the angel,[39] during which his hip was wrenched at its socket (Genesis 32:25), Jacob healed. Further, despite giving Esau a significant sum of money prior to arriving in Shechem (Genesis 33:10–11), Jacob remains wealthy. As a bonus, Rav tells us that Jacob retained all his Torah learning, despite the trials and tribulations of his life in Haran, his travels back to *Eretz Yisrael*, and his reunion with Esau. The verse on which Rav bases his claim, Genesis 33:18, suggests that Jacob entered Shechem, but then immediately says he "encamped outside the city." Rav reads the word *va-yi-chan* (encamped) as coming from *chen*, meaning "grace." Hence, he concludes, because Jacob survived whole, he graced Shechem with improvements.

R. Shimon b. Yochai seeks to replicate Jacob's model behavior. With the greatest dose of irony yet, he forges improvements in precisely the areas that had inspired his caustic criticism of Rome, yet which three great Sages—Rav, Shmuel, and R. Yochanan—have deemed worthy of Jacob: coinage for commerce, marketplaces, and bathhouses. What R. Shimon once regarded as secular and hedonistic concerns of a corrupt Roman society, as well as egregious distractions from Torah learning, he now appreciates as facets of civic life that support society, and hence Torah learning as well. He realizes that mundane functions of civic society make the sacred obligations of study possible.

> [R. Shimon] said, "Is there something [else] that requires amending?"
>
> They said to him, "There is a place in doubt regarding ritual impurity and it is difficult for priests to go around it."

[R. Shimon] said, "Is there someone who knows of a presumption of ritual purity that once existed here?"

An old man said to him, "[Rabban Yochanan] b. Zakkai cut down lupines of *terumah* here."

So [R. Shimon] did likewise. Wherever [the ground] was hard he declared it *tahor* ['ritually pure'], and wherever it was loose he marked it off [as *tame*, 'ritually impure'].

Having attended to a marketplace and a bathhouse, R. Shimon now asks what more he might do to improve life in the community. The answer will afford him the opportunity to build a "bridge."

An old man tells R. Shimon there is an unresolved matter related to ritual purity. To understand the concern: Torah stipulates that those descended from *kohanim* (priests) are not permitted contact with the dead, lest they become ritually impure (*tame*). Thus, they may not enter a cemetery. When the Temple stood, the ashes of the red heifer purified one from *tumah* (ritual impurity, Numbers 19), but in R. Shimon's day it is no longer possible to undergo purification, so *kohanim* scrupulously attempt to avoid *tumah*.[40] One area in the city is rumored to have been a graveyard long ago. Hence, in order to avoid it, *kohanim* are taking an inconvenient, circuitous route around the questionable area each time they need to cross town.

R. Shimon seeks to solve this problem by examining the area. He learns that Rabban Yochanan b. Zakkai had planted lupines throughout the land. Since Rabban Yochanan was a *kohen*, he would not have trod on earth he considered *tame*—hence, in his time he must have deemed the entire area *tahor* and not a cemetery. Yet people are expressing concern about it, so we may presume they have seen bones subsequent to Rabban Yochanan b. Zakkai's time. R. Shimon b. Yochai sets out to survey the land to determine the location of these few, scattered graves. Where the earth is hard packed, he deems it pure and untouched; where he finds loosened soil, he presumes it was dug for graves, declares it *tame*, and marks it off as an area the *kohanim* must avoid. In effect, R. Shimon has built a "bridge" through town for the *kohanim*; now they can safely cross the city, avoiding the areas R. Shimon has marked off rather than going the long way around.

It appears that R. Shimon has fully reengaged with life. He has instituted civic improvements of both a secular and Jewish nature to improve people's daily lives—evidence that he values mundane matters and finally recognizes the importance of balance in life.

What is more, thus far two of the three exemplars of Roman engineering and culture (marketplaces, bathhouses, and bridges) that R. Shimon b. Yochai originally condemned have figured prominently in his physical recovery and rehabilitation: the bathhouse and his gift to the community (he created shortcuts, essentially "bridges," for the *kohanim*).

The final scene will incorporate the third element—the marketplace.

That old man said, "The son of Yochai has purified a cemetery!"

[R. Shimon] said to him, "Had you not been with us, or even if you had been with us but did not vote, what you say would be fine. But since you were with us and voted with us, [people who hear what you say] will say: '[Even] whores braid one another's hair; how much more so scholars [should respect one another]!'" [R. Shimon] cast his eyes upon him and he died.

[R. Shimon] went out to the marketplace. He saw Yehudah b. Gerim. "Is that man still in the world?" He cast his eyes upon him and turned him into a heap of bones.

The story ends on a disconcerting and disturbing note. After surveying the land and marking off the areas that are *tame* for the *kohanim*, the very same old man who suggested this improvement now objects and claims that R. Shimon has purified a cemetery, which cannot legitimately be done. R. Shimon retorts that the old man's criticism would be understandable had he not been present for the Rabbis' conversation or had he been present and raised an objection at the time the matter was discussed and voted on by the Rabbis. However, because the old man was present and had not raised an objection then, objecting now will encourage people to view the Rabbis' authority with skepticism, if not contempt. Even harlots, he says, treat one another with greater respect than the old man is treating his colleagues.

R. Shimon thereupon fires up his flamethrower eyes and the old man dies.

How are we to understand this shocking turn of events? Is it an act of retribution? Is R. Shimon violently asserting his authority over any and all dissenters?

In the next breath, Yehudah b. Gerim, whose indiscretion led to the Roman's decree against R. Shimon, passes by him in the marketplace — and meets the same end.

As much as a reader might wish to applaud R. Shimon's turnaround and welcome him back into the fold of rationality and reasonable accommodation to secular society, these two deaths take one's breath away. Was R. Shimon's repentance insincere? Is he reverting to his former extremism?

The Rabbis' final message here remains ambiguous. One reading is that reality often fails to deliver the satisfying outcomes we want. Talmud rarely delivers fairy-tale endings because life is messy and personal change comes slowly, incrementally — no less so in the second century than in the twenty-first.

Moreover, living as Jews in an essentially non-Jewish world will always entail conflicts. We often have to make uncomfortable choices as we prioritize one action above another. Searching for our own proper life balance, we may find temporary equilibrium, but then something may come along to rock our boat and make us feel unbalanced and unsure of our decisions. Even more so for the Rabbis living in the post-Temple world: then the whole universe was out of balance. Then, as now, many Jews struggled to live with one foot in each of two worlds.

Continuing the Conversation

1. Where Do You Plant Your Feet?

When and where do you experience tension or conflicts between living Jewishly and living in a larger, predominantly non-Jewish culture? How do you decide what to do? Are there conflicts you have not resolved?

2. Maintaining Balance

R. Elazar b. Azariah taught: If there is no Torah, there is no decency; if there is no decency, there is no Torah. If there is no wisdom, there is no piety; if there is no piety, there is no wisdom. If there is no understanding, there is no knowledge; if there is no knowledge, there is no understanding. If there is no sustenance [lit. 'flour'], there is no Torah; if there is no Torah, there is no sustenance [lit. 'flour'].[41]

R. Elazar b. Azariah recognizes the need for balance in our lives. His fourth example—flour and Torah—may speak to the farmers R. Shimon saw upon emerging the first time from the cave. How do you understand this and the other three points of symbiosis that R. Elazar teaches?

3. A Leopard's Spots?

Until the last two scenes of the story, R. Shimon's thirteen years of exile in the cave appear to have transformed him: he emerges the second time from the cave with a seemingly new outlook and executes community improvements supporting his new vision. Yet at the story's close R. Shimon ends the lives of both an unnamed old man, who accuses him of purifying a cemetery, and Yehudah b. Gerim, who informed on him to the Romans.

An old adage has it that the leopard cannot change his spots—a person cannot make substantial and enduring changes. In your view, did R. Shimon truly change? Were his contributions to the community reflective of a new attitude, or merely *kapparah* (atonement) for killing the farmers?

Do you believe people can, and do, change in substantive, meaningful, and enduring ways? What life experiences attest to your view?

4. Where Is the Teshuvah?

The term *teshuvah*, most often translated "repentance," literally means "turning" or "returning." Underlying the term is the perspective that in the course of life everyone makes mistakes—behavioral and relational—and that in most cases a course correction can repair the damage. *Teshuvah* is a major theme of the High Holy Days each autumn, but is needed throughout the year. Each of the three daily prayer services includes prayers of repentance.

Moses Maimonides (1135–1204) devoted an entire section of his *Mishneh Torah* to an in-depth discussion of the process of *teshuvah*. Rabbi Yonah b. Avraham of Gerondi (d. 1264), a Catalonian sage who disagreed with Maimonides on many matters, composed a treatise on *teshuvah* entitled *Sha'arei Teshuvah* (Gates of repentance). Both sages wrote in a similar vein about *teshuvah*, teaching that it is a process requiring these five elements: (1) acknowledgement and regret for having committed the wrongdoing; (2) confession and expression of regret to the person wronged and to God; (3) commitment to not repeating the wrong and a plan of action to ensure it will not be repeated; (4) atonement, meaning efforts to reverse the damage done (especially in cases of verbal or financial wrongdoing); (5) refraining from committing the sin again. The measure of successful *teshuvah* is not repeating the wrong.

Do you find evidence in the story that R. Shimon b. Yochai did *teshuvah* for killing the farmers? Was his *teshuvah* complete? Sufficient? What role might the extra year of exile in the cave have played in this process?

The Rabbis taught that no *teshuvah* we do in this life fully suffices for taking a life; only our own death atones for taking the life of another. How might that religious claim have informed R. Shimon's behavior toward the old man and Yehudah b. Gerim after he returned from exile?

How does *teshuvah* work in your life? Have you gone through the traditional steps of *teshuvah*? What has been the spiritual result for you?

The Rabbis were keenly aware that even after sincere *teshuvah*, people may backslide and commit the same wrongs again. Has this happened to you? Do you think "repeat offenses" derive from inadequate or incomplete *teshuvah* the first time, or is this simply part and parcel of human nature? What might help people refrain from backsliding?

5. The Blinding Power of Suffering

Yoda, the grand master of the Jedi order, famously taught his disciples: "Fear leads to anger. Anger leads to hate. Hate leads to suffering." But that is not the only pathway between such often overpowering feelings. Sometimes suffering leads to anger, and anger leads to hate. This seems to be the path R. Shimon bar Yochai traveled.

R. Shimon bar Yochai lived in the second century, only one or two generations after the Second Temple's destruction. In 118 CE, Hadrian became emperor of Rome. Initially he permitted the Jews to return to Jerusalem, where they expected to rebuild the Temple, but subsequently he reneged and deported many Jews to North Africa, instigating talk of rebellion. In 132, he began to construct a city he called Aelia Capitolina (combining his own name with that of the Roman god Jupiter Capitolinus) in Jerusalem on the site of the former Temple, igniting full-scale rebellion that coalesced under the leadership of a charismatic figure named Shimon bar Kokhba. The rebellion was initially successful, but the tide turned when Hadrian amassed twelve Roman legions in Judea. Ultimately, the revolt was a colossal failure: when it ended on the Ninth of Av in 135 CE, Hadrian's twelve Roman legions had defeated and destroyed nearly one thousand villages and fifty Jewish fortresses, including Bar Kokhba's stronghold in Betar. Hadrian subsequently instituted laws banning the principal practices of Judaism in order to punish the Jewish religious authorities; executed numerous Rabbinic leaders, among them R. Akiva; and banned Jews from entering Jerusalem.

Given this historical reality, R. Shimon's attunement to the Jewish people's suffering under Roman rule may have led him to anger; his anger then led him to hate what he considered quintessentially Roman (marketplaces, bathhouses, and bridges); and his expressed hatred consequently led to his exile—and later to murderous behavior. In this sense, could R. Shimon's actions be understood as the "blinding power of suffering"? Have you ever experienced the "blinding power of suffering"?

In the story's greatest irony, R. Shimon seeks healing in the very institution he condemned and celebrates his freedom by instituting community improvements that precisely parallel the Roman projects he reviled. What do you think the Rabbis are telling us? Have you experienced ironic parallels in your own life?

Summing Things Up

Each of us must navigate relationships with a variety of people and cultures. For those of us living in the Diaspora, this means our Jewish community and culture—its practices, priorities, and values—as well as the dominant, or host, culture. While a smooth integration of the two in our lives is desirable, some conflict is inevitable.

In the ancient world the Roman bathhouse was emblematic of both inherent and potential conflict. Infused with imagery and iconography that bespoke pagan culture, it was reasonable to ask if Jews should ever set foot in it. Yet the bathhouse was a significant feature of cultural life in the Greco-Roman cities of *Eretz Yisrael*—thus akin in its time to Friday night high school football games, Saturday weddings, and other social events that coincide with our celebrating Shabbat or festivals today; to popular secular events whose menus make adhering to kashrut impossible; and to Christian symbols in the public square. Where do and should we draw the line in our responses?

The astounding ending to the irony-laden story of R. Shimon leaves us with an uncomfortable and unavoidable truth. Personal change is an incremental and dogged endeavor, and no guarantee of future happiness. Life is messy, but it's the only playing field we're given.

7 Caring for Poor People

Babylonian Talmud, Tractate Bava Batra 10a

> If there is a needy person among you, one of your kin in
> any of your settlements in the land that Adonai your God
> is giving you, do not harden your heart and shut your hand
> against your needy kin. Rather, you must open your hand
> and lend whatever is sufficient to meet the need. . . . For
> there will never cease to be needy people in your land, which
> is why I command you: Open your hand to the poor and
> needy kin in your land.
>
> —Deuteronomy 15:7,8,11

Why Study This Passage?

The scourge of poverty has plagued humanity throughout recorded
history, burdening the lives of millions, including many people in afflu-
ent countries.[1] Is poverty an intractable feature of life, as Deuteronomy
15:11 avers, or can it be remedied? What is God's responsibility for the
continued, unabated prevalence of poverty, and what is ours?

Before we attempt to answer these questions, let us set the stage.

Torah opens with twin accounts of God's Creation of the universe. In
Genesis 1, God creates the world in six days; in Genesis 2, God plants

a garden in Eden. The two stories of Creation not only differ, but also contradict one another in fundamental ways, including the order in which the elements of the universe came into being and the manner in which people were created.[2] Yet the Torah's redactors included both accounts. Perhaps they chose to overlook the glaring contradictions because both stories embody deeply held religious values and address crucial religious questions, among them God's purpose in Creation and God's ongoing role in the universe as a whole, as well as in the lives of individuals in particular. Each story, in its own way, explains the deep imperfections we see in our world—and thereby lays the groundwork for thinking about poverty.

Traditional theology—Jewish, Christian, and Islamic—holds that God is omnipotent, omniscient, and omnibenevolent, but this troika of dogmatic divine attributes is not biblical.[3] It dates to the Middle Ages. The Bible evinces a far more nuanced view of God's mastery of the universe, God's knowledge, and God's "character." The focus here is on omnipotence, which we will explore through the two Creation accounts.

The first story affirms God as imposing order on the primordial watery chaos through a series of separations and boundaries. Bible scholar Jon D. Levenson notes that Hebrew Scripture does not claim that God engaged in *creatio ex nihilo* (creating out of nothing), but rather that God created *against something*: against disorder, injustice, affliction, and chaos.[4]

While the first Creation story (Genesis 1) suggests that after six days the world contained all the elements and processes necessary to sustain life, it is agnostic concerning God's control over all the elements of Creation.[5] Elsewhere, the Tanakh affirms the view that God never entirely masters the universe: pockets of chaos and evil persist. For example, Leviathan and the *behemot*[6] remain beyond God's control, at least temporarily. Another instance appears in Psalm 82: while imagining God standing among divine colleagues, the Psalmist beseeches God to assert divine power to render judgment against the wicked and protect the vulnerable from them—*Arise, O God, judge the earth, for all the nations are*

Your possession—strongly suggesting that, as yet, God had not achieved, or perhaps exercised, mastery.[7] Similarly, the prophet Jeremiah's challenge to God—to complete the Creation by mastering it and expunging evil—also suggests that God's control is incomplete:

You will win, Adonai, if I make claim against You,
Yet I shall present charges against You:
Why does the way of the wicked prosper?
Why are the workers of treachery at ease?
You have planted them, and they have taken root,
They spread, they even bear fruit.
You are present in their mouths,
But far from their thoughts.
Yet You, Adonai, have noted and observed me;
You have tested my heart, and found it with You.
Drive them out like sheep to the slaughter,
Prepare them for the day of slaying!
How long must the land languish,
And the grass of all the countryside dry up?
Must beasts and birds perish,
Because of the evil of its inhabitants,
Who say, "God will not look upon our future"?[8]

The second Creation story presents a close-up view of Creation that, taken together with the first Creation story, explains one way in which God's mastery is incomplete. In Genesis 2, the scope of God's Creation is not the universe, as with the first chapter's Creation story, but narrowly focused on life in the Garden of Eden, where two human beings live in paradise yet exercise their desire in a manner that God can neither foresee nor forestall.[9] Eve's decision to eat the fruit of the forbidden tree and Adam's compliance bespeak a realm of the universe God cannot control: human free will. God can only respond to what the people have done.

Despite the contradictions evident in these first two chapters, the Bible consistently envisions God as a powerful (if not omnipotent) commanding deity who orders the universe, brings the nation of Israel into existence, and demands Israel's loyalty. God rewards Israel's obedience with abundant rain in its proper season, fertile flocks and herds, children, and protection from enemies. When Israel disobeys, the Bible warns, God metes out punishments in the form of natural disasters (primarily drought and ensuing famine) and sets their enemies against them.

What is more, God intervenes directly in the world at critical junctures of history, performing miraculous "signs and wonders." In just a few chapters in Exodus, God visits the Ten Plagues on Egypt; parts the Sea of Reeds, enabling the Israelites to pass through safely and escape the pursuing Egyptian army; rains down quail and manna to nourish the Israelites in the wilderness; and brings forth water from a rock to quench their thirst. The Bible records many more miracles: God halts the sun in the sky for Gideon, enables Elijah to revive a dead child, protects Daniel from a den of lions, and shelters Jonah for three days in the belly of an enormous fish.

While God's power is prodigious, it is not unlimited. Standing between God's power and God's reserve are two barriers: the primordial forces of chaos and human free will. The creative order God imposes by making separations (light from dark, sky from water, water from land, and so forth) is set against the *tohu va-vohu* (primordial chaos) that continually threatens to reverse God's creative order.

The second limitation to God's power, human will, became a chief preoccupation of the Rabbis. Were God to exert divine will in every instance, there would be no room for humans to make decisions or follow their own consciences. Indeed without free will they could not choose to obey God, and hence the idea of covenantal loyalty would be meaningless.

Conversely, traditional Jewish beliefs concerning God's requirements for Israel (as articulated in Torah) and God's proclivity to intervene in the world (also described in Torah) — both essential elements of the received tradition inherited by the Rabbis—came into sharp conflict with the Rabbis' own lived experience. The calamity of the Second Temple's destruction in 70 CE and the failed rebellions that followed led to the loss of sovereignty over *Eretz Yisrael* and to enormous human deprivation and suffering. From the Sages' standpoint, God did not rush to intervene to save Israel from Roman ruin. On the contrary: the wars with Rome decimated the country, leaving a multitude living in penury. Could God be counted on to promote God's own agenda of caring for the poor, or did it now lie in Israel's hands alone?

What is more, with Alexander the Great's incursion into the ancient Near East in the latter half of the fourth century BCE, a raft of philosophical ideas deriving from Hellenistic culture and philosophy, and later Greco-Roman culture as well, entered the Jewish world of *Eretz Yisrael*. For Hellenists and their intellectual heirs, logic and reason were the arbiters of divine thought—and the mind of God was the immutable, natural order of the universe.

In this Greco-Roman world, there was a considerable clash—not only between Hellenistic ideas and biblical thought, but also between God's ideal world and the reality of the world the Rabbis inhabited. How, then, could the Rabbis balance God's will, forcefully in evidence throughout the Torah, with what Jews during the early Rabbinic period experienced as God's quiescence? How could they reconcile God's biblical promises to uphold moral law through reward and punishment[10] with God's passivity, or perhaps even indifference, in the face of grave injustice and suffering in the world?

Having inherited a tradition grounded in the claim of divine revelation expressed through Torah, the Rabbis expanded the notion of divine authority to encompass their own interpretations of Torah: in the Torah God was the author of truth and right, whereas the Rabbis' interpretations elucidated God's will far beyond the Torah's actual words.[11] Their new set of hermeneutical principles expounded and applied Torah to the many new and pressing exigencies of life in their day. While reason and logic were staples of their interpretative arsenal, consistency was never a *sine qua non* of halakhah.

The same questions the Rabbis struggled with frame the dilemma of theodicy in our day: If God is just, why is there so little justice in the world? Why do good people sometimes suffer undeservedly, and why do wicked people often prosper? How do we explain the magnitude of disease, poverty, and suffering around us?

These questions give rise, in turn, to an even thornier question: If suffering is a perpetual and intractable feature of human existence, should we not presume this is God's will? The Talmud phrases this painful question another way: *If God cares for poor people, why doesn't God take care of them?* In fact, Talmud boldly places this very question in the mouth of the Roman governor of Judea during the Bar Kokhba rebellion, the last Jewish revolt of 132–135 CE, which ended in immeasurably greater poverty and suffering for the Jewish people.

In our time, perhaps the most prevalent theological question Jews have asked—"Where was God during the Holocaust?"—presumes that God could have stopped the Nazi genocide, but did not. Not finding a satisfactory theological answer to this question, many Holocaust survivors turned their backs on God and Judaism.

Yet suffering need not occur on a colossal scale to warrant the question of God's role when injustice prevails. The death of even one child is sufficient to call God's justice into question, as the passage in this chapter reveals.

A Broad View to Begin

Sociologist of religion Peter L. Berger explains in *The Sacred Canopy* that human beings create society—its norms, rules, and symbols—and society in turn shapes people.[12] Those who wish to rule a society employ predictable methods to eliminate or sideline opposition, control the economy, and direct communication, but these alone will not suffice. In order to successfully exercise enduring control, rulers must not only legitimate their power using the norms, rules, symbols, and institutions the society has created, but also defend it against resistors who question the social norms and institutions. This is where religion enters the picture. As Berger explains, rulers employ a process of legitimation broader and more encompassing than religion, but religion powerfully conveys legitimation.

> [R]eligion has been the historically most widespread and effective instrumentality of legitimation. All legitimation maintains socially defined reality. Religion legitimates so effectively because it relates the precarious reality constructions of empirical societies with ultimate reality. The tenuous realities of the social world are grounded in the sacred *realissimum*,[13] which by definition is beyond the contingencies of human meanings and human activity."[14]

By claiming that humanly devised laws and doctrines were divinely promulgated and reflect the will of the Divine, Berger says that societal leaders can assert that earthly political institutions, laws, and customs reflect the heavenly realm in will and structure.[15] As a result, Berger advises analyzing religious systems with a "hermeneutic of suspicion" aimed at exploring the genuine motives behind religion's efforts to conceal the human origin of its power.

Applying Berger's thinking to constructions of power—how power was exerted and justified in ancient Israel in a conventional way vis-à-vis the Davidic line—Bible scholar Joshua Berman agrees that the hermeneutic of suspicion is warranted:

> Alongside these [Davidic constructions of power], however, we find many texts, particularly in the Pentateuch, in which the pattern is broken. The metaphors adopted from the experiences of day-to-day affairs to conceptualize the encounter between God and man do little, if anything, to buttress the earthly power structure. Moreover, they serve to attenuate the hierarchical stratification of society in a fashion unmatched in the other thought systems of the ancient Near East.[16]

Berman cites as an example the Mesopotamian cosmogony myth of Atrahasis.[17] A hierarchy of gods are engaged in creating the world, the higher status gods pressing the lower classes of gods to perform the menial labor and serve those above them. The oppressed gods call a strike, provoking those at the top to create human beings — a lower class of workers composed of flesh and blood mixed with clay — to relieve the drudgery of the lesser gods. Berman comments that in the tale of Atrahasis "[t]he divide between the dominant tribute-imposing class, and the dominated tribute-bearing class is granted religious sanction."[18] The political structures in the earthly domain are legitimated by conceiving of them as mirroring the upper divine realm.

While there are recognizable commonalities between Atrahasis and the Torah's two Creation stories — for example, in both accounts God fashions people from earth and infuses them with "the spirit of life" — Assyriologist Jean Bottéro points out a striking difference: "In Atrahasis, man is created to engage in backbreaking work on behalf of the gods. In Genesis 2, man is created to till the ground — but ultimately for his own nourishment and pleasure."[19] What is more, Berman notes, "[i]n Atrahasis, man is created in order to be a servant; in Genesis [chapter 1], all men are created to have dominion."[20]

When modern scholars consider the Torah's social institutions and economic laws, the "hermeneutic of suspicion" reveals many that fail to serve the interests of the powerful elite.[21] Berman points out that whether or not the Torah's laws comprised a normative law code in force during the biblical period, they reflect a world of values and ethics. He writes: "The laws of the Bible may be rightly viewed as reflections of wider systems of thought and ideology, as the indexes of the blueprint of a civilization."[22] In other words, Torah goes far beyond legitimating the political and economic control of those in power: it creates societal norms and institutions that break the ancient mold by prioritizing morality over power.

As a prime example that is crucial to our passage, Torah prominently proclaims that God commands Israel to care for the most vulnerable members of society. Again and again Torah forbids wronging or oppressing the strangers living among the Israelites (who are more likely to be unlanded and economically vulnerable). Torah charges—as a covenantal obligation—that the Israelites are to treat foreigners as citizens: *When a stranger resides with you in your land, you shall not wrong him. The stranger who resides with you shall be to you as one of your citizens; you shall love him as yourself, for you were strangers in the land of Egypt: I, Adonai, am your God* (Leviticus 19:33–34).[23] The community is instructed to identify and address the needs of poor people in its midst: *If there is a needy person among you, one of your kin in any of your settlements in the land that Adonai your God is giving you, do not harden your heart and shut your hand against your needy kin. Rather, you must open your hand and lend whatever is sufficient to meet the need* (Deuteronomy 15:7–8).[24]

To encode these values in practice, the Torah prescribed social institutions. The mitzvah of *pe'ah* required farmers to leave the corners of their fields unharvested so the poor could pick what they needed to sustain themselves and their families. The mitzvah of *leket* similarly required the owners of vineyards to leave some of their harvest for the less fortunate: *When you reap the harvest of your land, you shall not reap all the way to the edges of your field, or gather the gleanings of your harvest. You shall not pick your vineyard bare, or gather the fallen fruit of your vineyard; you shall leave them for the poor and the stranger: I, Adonai, am your God* (Leviticus 19:9–10).[25]

In addition, Torah mandated lending money to "kin" at no interest to prevent them from descending into debt and, as a result, sinking into indentured servitude: *You shall not deduct interest from loans to your countrymen, whether in money or food or anything else that can be deducted as interest* (Leviticus 23:20). Bible scholar Jeffrey H. Tigay explains that Israelites did not borrow money for commercial investment; loans were made to those who fell into poverty.[26] If, however, the situation became so dire that an Israelite had no choice but to work off a debt, Torah prescribed strict limits as to how the lender could treat the debtor.

If your kin, being in straits, come under your authority, and are held by you as resident aliens, let them live by your side: do not exact advance or accrued interest, but fear your God. Let your kin live by your side as kin. Do not lend your money at advance interest, or give your food at accrued interest. I, Adonai, am your God, who brought you out of the land of Egypt, to give you the land of Canaan, to be your God. (Leviticus 25:35–38)

Bible scholars Adele Berlin and Marc Zvi Brettler comment in *The Jewish Study Bible*, "What appears to be servitude is not; an Israelite forced to become indentured to another Israelite has the status of a hired laborer. Moreover, this servitude is temporary, and the option of remaining in slavery forever, available in the non-Priestly collections (Exod. 21:5–6; Deut. 15:16–18), is not provided [here]."[27] Berman notes that the prohibition "closed an avenue through which the rich could accrue greater wealth at the expense of the needy. It fostered a sense of community and shared responsibility."[28] This is altogether different from legitimating the control of the ruling elite.

Torah further establishes time limits for indentured servitude (debt slavery). The various mechanisms Torah institutes for responding to poverty—debt release, redemption, and manumission—operate during the *shemitah* (the sabbatical year, every seventh year) and the *yovel* (the jubilee year, every fiftieth year).[29] Berman observes that grounding the release of indentured servants and debt slaves in theological considerations serves to "neuter [relief edicts and releases] as tools of political manipulation."[30] They are not seen as the largesse of a human ruler; the king cannot abrogate them because they are moral legislation ordained by God.

While it is difficult to gauge the extent to which these laws were practiced in ancient Israel, there is no doubt how seriously they were considered to be God's moral law. The classical Hebrew prophets Isaiah and Ezekiel equated tzedakah with piety. Isaiah went so far as to berate the people of his day for the insincerity of their fasts because, while their body posture was visually pious, their less visible ethical behavior was the antithesis. And ultimately the continuing presence of "wretched poor" people reflected their failure to root out evil and oppression.

> Is such the fast I desire, a day for people to starve their bodies?
> Is it bowing the head like a bulrush and lying in sackcloth and ashes?
> Do you call that a fast, a day when Adonai is favorable?
> No, this is the fast I desire:
> To unlock fetters of wickedness, and untie the cords of the yoke,
> To let the oppressed go free; to break off every yoke.
> It is to share your bread with the hungry,
> And to take the wretched poor into your home;
> When you see the naked, to clothe him,
> And not to ignore your own kin. (Isaiah 58:5–7)

Ezekiel, for his part, tries to exhort the people of Judah in his day to greater generosity by comparing them unfavorably to the evil people of Sodom who, despite their plenty, refused to share their food with the poor,[31] and to those in Samaria (a metonymy for the Northern Kingdom), whom the Assyrians conquered and destroyed in punishment for their sins. In the prophet's mind the paramount sins of both Sodom and Samaria are the people's failures to support the poor and needy.

> Only this was the sin of your sister Sodom: arrogance! She and her daughters had plenty of bread and untroubled tranquillity; yet she did not support poor and needy people. In their haughtiness, they committed abomination before Me; and so I removed them, as you saw. Nor did Samaria commit even half your sins. You committed more abominations than they, and by all the abominations that you committed you made your sisters look righteous. Truly, you must bear the disgrace of serving as your sisters' advocate: Since you have sinned more abominably than they, they appear righteous in comparison.

So be ashamed and bear your disgrace, because you have made your sisters look righteous. (Ezekiel 16:49–52)

Just as the Torah and the prophets understand God to punish Israel for failing to attend to the poor, the Bible also suggests that there is divine reward for giving. The book of Proverbs twice proclaims: *Tzedakah saves from death.*[32] In both instances, Proverbs asserts that while wealth brings rewards in the short term, righteousness pays off in the long term. The Rabbis hold this phrase aloft. While tzedakah is correctly translated "righteousness" or "deeds that promote justice," when the Rabbis use the term, they most often have charity in mind.

If giving charity can save one from death—influencing the course of events—what, precisely, does that look like? In Tractate Shabbat, the Rabbis engage in a long conversation about the idea of fate and how tzedakah can alter it.[33] They ask whether the stars determine our destiny, as astrologers believed, or whether we can alter the course of our lives by our own choices. From there, they tell two stories to illustrate how righteous behavior is rewarded by heaven.

In the first story, Shmuel and an astrologer sit together people watching. As a man embarking on a journey walks past them, the astrologer comments, "He will not return alive." Shmuel replies, "He will if he is a Jew." Sure enough, the man returns safely. The astrologer thereupon checks the man's knapsack and discovers that it contains a poisonous snake, severed. Shmuel realizes that the man must have performed a righteous deed that resulted in his deliverance from life-threatening danger. He asks the man, "What [righteous deed] did you do?" The man explains that while away he shared food with a group of people. What is more, when one of the group was ashamed because he had nothing to share, the man pretended to accept bread from him to preserve his dignity. Shmuel nods in recognition and says, "You performed a mitzvah and it saved you: *tzedakah saves from death.*" The story illustrates the Rabbis' understanding of Proverbs 10:2: tzedakah literally saves the one who performs it from death.

The second story concerns R. Akiva's daughter. Astrologers predicted that on the day of her wedding she would die from a snakebite. On that day, as she was dressing for the ceremony, she stuck a brooch she intended to wear into a wall for safekeeping, and it penetrated the eye of a poisonous snake, killing it. When her father saw what had happened, he asked what she had done to deserve reprieve. She told him that a poor person had happened by the wedding banquet and everyone was ignoring him because they were absorbed in the festivities, so she brought him food. R. Akiva interpreted: *Tzedakah saves from death.*[34]

To the Sages, the obligation to give charity was so important they ruled that even one who receives tzedakah should give charity in turn to those who are less fortunate.[35] At first glance, this sounds illogical: how can those who need charity afford to give charity? Perhaps the Sages idealistically envisioned a world in which the community cared for its poor people so well that, at least on occasion, they had sufficient surplus to bestow charity on others.

The Sages discussed the obligation to give charity at length. They established guidelines concerning the minimum amount one ought to give, depending on one's economic circumstance.[36] They ruled that a court could compel selfish people to give charity, and even appropriate their property to pay their proper share.[37]

On the other side of the ledger, the Rabbis thoroughly discussed how much those in need should receive. Rather than specifying an amount, they determined that the amount should be sufficient to restore the dignity impoverishment had stolen from them.[38]

As the Sages made tzedakah a central fixture of Jewish life and thought, a communal system of charitable institutions arose,[39] resting on the foundational talmudic teachings concerning anticipating and address- ing the needs of poor people in a systematic manner: do not wait for God to intervene and feed those who are hungry today; rather, care for those in need and ensure that no one goes without the basics of life. In time, Jewish communities established funds to provide clothing, medicine, burial, wedding celebrations, business loans, education for children, and care for the aged. Giving charity became the queen of Jewish values.

Portraying Jewish life in the shtetl, anthropologist Mark Zborowski and social science writer Elizabeth Herzog describe how giving tzedakah beat out the rhythm of life:

> Life in the shtetl begins and ends with tsdokeh [tzedakah]. When a child is born, the father pledges a certain amount of money for distribution to the poor. At a funeral the mourners distribute coins to the beggars who swarm the cemetery, chanting, "Tsdokeh will save from death."
>
> At every turn during one's life, the reminder to give is present. At the circumcision ceremony, the boy consecrated to the Covenant is specifically dedicated to good deeds. Every celebration, every holiday is accompanied by gifts to the needy. Each house has its round tin box into which coins are dropped for the support of various good works. A home that is not very poor will have a series of such boxes, one for the synagogue, one for a yeshiva in some distant city, one for "clothing the naked," one for "tending the sick," and so on. If something good or bad happens, one puts a coin into a box. Before lighting the Sabbath candles, the housewife drops a coin into one of the boxes. . . .
>
> Children are trained to the habit of giving. A father will have his son give alms to the beggar instead of handing them over directly. A child is very often put in charge of the weekly dole at home, when beggars make their customary rounds. The gesture of giving becomes almost a reflex. When anything out of the ordinary happens, one says a blessing and one drops a coin into the box.[40]

These days, the answer to the first question posed in this chapter—*If God cares for poor people, why doesn't God take care of them?*—is hardly ever asked. Perhaps this is because in the second century R. Akiva answered it.

Exploring the Nooks and Crannies of Our Passage

The very question, *If God cares for poor people, why doesn't God take care of them?* was a fundamental challenge to the Rabbis' worldview, because it exploited a theological weakness. The Rabbis had inherited the biblical view that God is an active agent in the world and the Torah's assertion that God requires Jews to engage in acts to alleviate poverty. If God is the Creator and Commander, a powerful agent capable of miracles, the Rabbis asked, why doesn't God resolve seemingly intractable problems?

In our passage the Rabbis imagine this challenging question emerging not from one of their own, but from the mouth of a "classic" opponent — Turnus Rufus, the Roman governor of Judea at the time of the Bar Kokhba rebellion (132–135 CE) — who challenges the fundamentals of biblical and Rabbinic Judaism as well as the Rabbis' authority. Presenting a fictitious anecdotal exchange between a prominent Rabbinic leader and a powerful Roman official is a common Rabbinic literary technique. Both Talmud and Midrash record numerous legendary debates between R. Akiva and Turnus Rufus revolving around three topics: circumcision, God's love for Israel and abhorrence of idolatry, and Shabbat. These subjects both provided entrée into larger theological and philosophical issues and served to illustrate the unbridgeable chasm between Jewish and Roman values. For the Rabbis, Turnus Rufus personified Greco-Roman intellectual challenges to Jews and Judaism and provided literarily "tangible" proof that the Roman Empire, which had decimated Israel and destroyed God's altar, was callous and evil.

> It was taught [in a *baraita*]: R. Meir used to say: The opponent [of Judaism] may challenge you, saying, "If your God loves poor people, why does [God] not support them?" Say to him, "So that through them we may be saved from the punishment of *Gehinnom*."
>
> Turnus Rufus, the wicked one, put this very question to R. Akiva: "If your God loves poor people, why does God not support them?" [R. Akiva]

replied, "So that we may be saved through them from the punishment of *Gehinnom*."

The passage opens with a *baraita* attributed to R. Meir, who raises the question as a hypothetical challenge one should be prepared to answer. It would seem that he learned the proper response from his teacher, R. Akiva.

R. Akiva and R. Meir respond that God delegates the care of those who are hungry and in need to people so that through fulfilling the obligation of tzedakah they can offset whatever punishment in *Gehinnom* (purgatory) might be due after their deaths because of sins they committed while alive. This follows from the assertion that God allows people to languish in poverty so others can derive *zechut* (merit) through fulfilling the mitzvah of tzedakah. On its surface, the response suggests that the reason for feeding, housing, and clothing poor people is *not* to mitigate suffering or because God desires it, but for one's own benefit. It may even be construed to imply that poor people are not rewarded even in this world (as evidenced by their poverty), while the rich are rewarded both in this world (as evidenced by their wealth) and the world to come (for their tzedakah). Thus the answer R. Meir and R. Akiva offer is theologically and morally problematic.

Turnus Rufus shrewdly turns R. Akiva's answer against him with a parable.

[Turnus Rufus] said to [R. Akiva], "On the contrary. This is what condemns you to *Gehinnom*. I will illustrate with a parable. To what may the matter be compared? To a king of flesh and blood who became angry with his servant and put him in prison and ordered that he be given neither food nor drink, but a man went and gave him food and drink. When the king hears, is he not angry with [the man]? And you [Jews] are called 'servants,' as it is written, *For to Me, the Israelites are servants: [they are My servants, whom I freed from the land of Egypt, I, Adonai, your God]* (Leviticus 25:55).

It is often easier to decode Sages' parables than comprehend their meaning. In most every case, a "king of flesh and blood" (i.e., a human king) represents God. The "king's son," "prince," or "servant" is Israel. Turnus Rufus' parable can thus be translated: "When God is angry with people, God impoverishes them, intending for them to suffer as punishment for their behavior. One who alleviates their suffering thereby undoes God's punishment; this violates God's will and undermines God's design for the world. Logic suggests that doing so angers God. What is more, your own Scripture — Leviticus 25:55 — proves this applies to the Jews, for you Jews claim to be God's servants."

Certainly, the image of a Roman official quoting Torah is remarkable and imaginative in and of itself.[41] It is also a further indication that the Rabbis constructed this story to probe a sensitive theological question.

Turnus Rufus's argument operates on two levels. The surface level concerns the theoretical case of poor people, the seeming subject of the conversation. The deeper, more significant level concerns the nation of Israel. On this latter level, we might paraphrase the parable as follows: "You claim that you are God's special people, but I claim that your abject condition in the world proves that God is angry with you. Just like an earthly king who punishes servants who have angered him, God is punishing Israel with imprisonment and poverty: the Jewish people is currently imprisoned by Roman control of their country and suffering deprivation under Roman rule. And just as an earthly king resents someone who undermines his decrees of punishment and privation, so too one who alleviates Israel's suffering defies and angers God. What is more, this can be proven from your own Scripture."

Underlying this second, deeper level is a theological conundrum: if Israel's historical situation of debasement results from God's retribution for the people's sins, then Rome is merely God's instrument of punishment. This was not a new argument. The prophets and early Rabbis had already concluded that both Temples were destroyed because of Israel's sins. In the case of the First Temple, the prophets spoke of idolatry, sexual immorality, and murder and the Rabbis confirmed that view. In the case of the Second Temple, the Rabbis identified the sin of *sinat chinam* (gratuitous hatred) as a cause.[42]

Given that Turnus Rufus provides what could be construed as a logical deduction from the Rabbis' theology, we next find R. Akiva's response, in the form of an alternative parable.

> R. Akiva said to [Turnus Rufus], "I will illustrate with [another] parable. To what may the matter be compared? To a king of flesh and blood who became angry with his child and put him in prison and ordered that he be given neither food nor drink, but a man went and gave [the son] food and drink. When the king hears of it, does he not send [the man] a gift? And we [Jews] are called 'children,' as it is written, *You are the children of Adonai your God* (Deuteronomy 14:1).

R. Akiva says, in effect, "Okay, I'll play your game of parables. However, your parable is faulty. I will supply a superior parable to explain our situation." In R. Akiva's parable, the king becomes so furious with his child that he has him tossed into prison and then issues an order denying the child food and water—and both listener and reader understand that this is an absurd overreaction to a child's disobedience. Whereas Turnus Rufus's parable focuses on God as "stern ruler," R. Akiva's parable presents God as a loving, but emotionally overwrought, parent. Hence, when someone takes pity on the starving child and provides him with sustenance, the king is gratified because deep down he does *not* want his child to suffer, but rather to thrive. The parable preserves the notion that God is in control and the cause of privation, but asserts that when people feed one another, God is pleased.

R. Akiva's prooftext designates Israel "the children of Adonai" (Deuteronomy 14:1). The Talmud does not quote the entire verse, nor the verse that follows, because it is presumed that we know them, but here, as in a great many other instances, the parts the Rabbis do not quote are crucial to their arguments. God thinks of Israel as God's children. They are especially beloved of God and therefore God does not want them to suffer.

> You are children of Adonai your God. You shall not gash yourselves or shave the front of your heads because of the dead. For you are a people consecrated to Adonai your God: Adonai your God chose you from among all other peoples on earth to be [God's] treasured people. (Deuteronomy 14:1–2)

If we are to equate "God's child" with people suffering from poverty, the message is clear: God does not want poor people to suffer. God appreciates and rewards those who step in to help them.

R. Akiva's parable, like that of Turnus Rufus, operates on two levels. On the deeper level, where "God's child" is Israel, the conversation addresses the existential situation of Israel in the aftermath of the Second Temple's destruction in the early second century. To this, R. Akiva says that for some inexplicable reason God felt compelled to punish Israel, but it was a vast overreaction. Deep down, God does not truly want Israel to suffer privation. This addresses the possible claim that Rome is merely fulfilling God's will and therefore cannot be held morally culpable for the cruelty and oppression perpetrated against the Jewish people. In addition, R. Akiva's analogy affirms that, even in exile, Israel remains God's beloved child.

Torah supports both portrayals of Israel: God's "servant" and God's "child." Which, then, should dominate the conversation? Following the debate motif of the passage, Turnus Rufus proposes his view first, and R. Akiva responds.

> [Turnus Rufus] said to [R. Akiva], "You are called both 'children' and 'servants' [because] when you carry out the will of the Omnipresent you are called 'children,' and when you do not carry out the will of the Omnipresent, you are called 'servants.' And now [at the present time] you are not carrying out the will of the Omnipresent."

Turnus Rufus does not negate R. Akiva's parable. He undermines it. Tacitly affirming that both verses (Leviticus 25:55 and Deuteronomy 14:1) reflect God's perspective, he cleverly claims that the terms "servants" and "children" apply in different situations (or, to be more accurate, the Rabbis cleverly enable him to impressively interpret these sacred texts). Turnus Rufus argues that suffering is de facto evidence of God's displeasure with people; it is their just punishment for violating God's covenant.

Reading this on the two parallel levels of the story, Turnus Rufus argues: Poor people suffer deprivation because God desires them to be punished in this manner; Israel suffers deprivation because the people disobeyed God. This logic shines a spotlight on an inherent problem—a "Catch 22"—of Rabbinic theology concerning the Second Temple's destruction: if poor people are deservedly suffering because they displeased God, it follows that any attempt to help them change their circumstances violates God's will for them.

This claim is theologically devastating. Were we to accept it, we would be forced to conclude first, that all suffering is deserved, and second, that we humans have no responsibility to alleviate suffering.

R. Akiva recognizes the danger here. Using Isaiah 58:7 (quoted above, though it is worthwhile to review the entire passage), he attempts to resolve it.

> [R. Akiva] said to [Turnus Rufus], "Behold [Scripture] says, [The fast that God desires] is to share your bread with the hungry, and to bring the wretched poor into your home (Isaiah 58:7). When [should you] bring the wretched poor into your home? Right now! [That is why] it says, It is to share your bread with the hungry.

R. Akiva backs us out of Turnus Rufus's moral and theological corner by changing the terms of the conversation. He does not directly attack the theology; rather, he engineers a work-around. From Isaiah, we learn that although God commands Israel to fast (in particular, on Yom Kippur, a fast that Jews *choose* to keep in response to God's will), God considers their fasting hypocrisy rather than religiosity if it does not move them to feed those who fast involuntarily. Feeding the hungry is not only consistent with fasting; it is its purpose.

Ultimately, the Rabbis conclude, the obligation to take care of poor people overrides whatever judgments one might make concerning whether or not poverty is the consequence of violating God's mitzvot. As R. Akiva reads Isaiah, God requires Jews to mitigate the suffering of poor people regardless of whatever else one thinks God has in mind. Nor is it permissible to delay; those who are hungry must be fed "Right now!"

Does God feed poor people? Yes — by requiring us to attend to their needs. When we obey our covenantal obligations to God, we are an extension of God.

At the same time, in backing out of the conversation, the Rabbis do not fully resolve the thorny issue of whether poor people — and by extension all of us — are responsible for our own misfortunes. As the dual level of meaning attached to the R. Akiva-Turnus Rufus dialogue has alerted us, the answer to this question has painful implications for the plight of the Jewish people in history, as well.

Elsewhere in the Talmud the Rabbis voice tremendous anger at God for abandoning Israel to the Roman legions in 70 CE. In particular, four stories make it clear that the Rabbis see the Jewish people not as sinners, but rather as victims.[43] Employing provocative images (an imprisoned and sexually abused child, captive siblings bred like animals, a woman who is sexually battered and then sold in a marketplace, and a woman whose husband sells her into adultery) in disturbing parables, the Rabbis express their collective pain and anguish, and a measure of guilt, but also overwhelming anger toward God for failing to intervene and protect the nation from ruin.[44] In time, the contradiction between the Tanakh's portrayal of God as immanent and involved in the affairs of Israel and the actual lived experience of the Rabbis led them to view God as distant and uninvolved in most of history.

This passage does seem to suggest that we bear some responsibility for our own misfortunes, but on balance the Rabbis weigh in on the side of compassion, emphasizing good intentions over condemnation. After all, our passage ends by looking not backward but forward, focused not on castigating individuals or the collective for misdeeds, but speaking of the power of tzedakah to rebuild lives and build a better world. For R. Akiva—indeed for all the Sages—it was obvious that Torah establishes tzedakah as a foundational social value for the People of Israel. No amount of theological or textual manipulation, however clever, can mitigate the command to *share your bread with the hungry, and to bring the wretched poor into your home.*

Continuing the Conversation

1. *Saved from* Gehinnom

Many people expect the Rabbis to argue for the necessity of giving tzedakah to poor people because it is the right thing to do, or because they will feel good about themselves, or because God wants them to wipe away the scourge of poverty in the world. Instead, both R. Akiva and his student R. Meir offer a selfish motive: they tell us that God leaves taking care of poor people to us "so that through them we may be saved from the punishment of *Gehinnom*."

Is the interpretation that some people suffer privation in order to permit other people to reduce their time in purgatory the only way to understand this statement? Might it supply motivation for people who are not inclined toward generosity to support those in poverty? In other words, might the idea of being saved from the punishment of *Gehinnom* motivate people—including yourself—to behave generously? Alternatively, might it be construed as manipulative, as the threat of hell is sometimes perceived?

2. *"Servants" and "Children"*

What are the different implications of thinking of people who experience privation as either God's "servants" or God's "children"?

If you experience a relationship with God, are you more likely to view yourself as God's "servant" or God's "child"? What other metaphors would you suggest and why? Does your viewpoint ever change depending on circumstances?

3. Applied Tzedakah

Torah says: *If there is a needy person among you, one of your kin in any of your settlements in the land that Adonai your God is giving you, do not harden your heart and shut your hand against your needy kin. Rather, you must open your hand and lend whatever is sufficient to meet the need. . . . For there will never cease to be needy people in your land, which is why I command you: Open your hand to the poor and needy kin in your land* (Deuteronomy 15:7–8).

What do you think *sufficient to meet the need* means?

The Rabbis explained it by way of several stories, each followed by concerns the story raises.[45] How does each story and response speak to the problems of poverty in our day?

#1—Our Rabbis taught [in a *baraita*]: *Sufficient to meet the need* (Deuteronomy 15:8) [means] you are commanded to maintain [a poor person], but you are not commanded to make him rich. *Sufficient to meet the need* [means] even a horse to ride on and a servant to run before him. It was said about Hillel the Elder that he hired for a certain poor man who was of a good family a horse to ride on and a servant to run before him. Once, [Hillel] could not find a servant to run before him, so he himself ran before him for three miles.

Our Rabbis taught [in a *baraita*]: It once happened that the people of Upper Galilee bought for a poor member of a good family of Tzippori a pound of meat every day. A pound of meat?! What is so great about this? R. Huna replied, "[It was] a pound of fowl's meat. Or, if you prefer, I might say [they purchased] ordinary meat for a pound [of coins]." R. Ashi replied, "The place was a small village where every day a beast had to be wasted for his sake."

Hillel, focused on the lost dignity of a man who fell into acute poverty after having lived a life of means, goes to great lengths to restore his dignity. Do you believe Hillel is correct to focus on the element of dignity in the experience of poverty? Does he go too far?

The story also intimates that the generous attention the people of Upper Galilee devote to the needs of a previously wealthy, now poverty-stricken family led the community to be wasteful. Do you think that social welfare programs today strike the right balance vis–à–vis human dignity? How would you balance the human needs of food and dignity?

#2 — A certain man once came before R. Nechemiah [seeking funds]. [R. Nechemiah] said to him, "On what do you [customarily] dine?" [The man] said to him, "On fatty meat and aged wine [expensive delicacies]." "Would you [agree to] join me eating [meals of] lentils?" [The poor man] joined him [eating meals of] lentils and died. [R. Nechemiah] said, "Woe to this man whom Nechemiah has killed." To the contrary, he should have said, "Woe to Nechemiah who killed this one." Rather, [the poor man] should not have pampered himself so much.

The second story as well concerns a formerly wealthy man. In this instance, however, R. Nechemiah, upon ascertaining that the poor man is accustomed to a rich cuisine, asks him if he would be willing to live a more spartan lifestyle. The man agrees—when R. Nechemiah asks him to subsist on a low-grade, inexpensive diet, can the man really say no?—and for reasons we can only surmise, and indeed the story invites us to theorize, the simple diet of lentils causes his death.

How do you understand the man's demise? Does he die because he is unaccustomed to a harsh diet of lentils? Or, perhaps, is the cause of death the vast diminution of his lifestyle and dignity—in contrast to the man tended to by Hillel in the previous story?

R. Nechemiah reacts with pity for the man and assigns culpability to himself. An anonymous voice, acknowledging that R. Nechemiah caused the man's demise, says R. Nechemiah should be even harder on himself. A second anonymous voice, however, disagrees, saying the poor man was responsible for his own death; because he lived such an extravagant lifestyle, he could not subsist on anything less.

Do you think this discussion is about physical luxuries or dignity? Is society's responsibility toward people who have always lived in poverty different from its duty toward people who were once well off but have fallen into poverty?

R. Nechemiah was the *resh galuta* (exilarch) in his day, and hence a wealthy man in his own right. Does this influence your thinking concerning how he hosted the poor man?

> #3—A [poor man] once came before Rava [seeking funds]. [Rava] said to him, "On what do you [customarily] dine?" [The man] said to him, "On fattened hen and aged wine." [Rava] said to him, "Are you not concerned that [the funds necessary to support your expensive diet] will be a hardship to the community?" [The man] said to [Rava], "Am I eating what belongs to them? I am eating that which belongs to the Merciful One, for we learned [in a *baraita*]: *The eyes of all look to you, and you give them their food in his/its time* (Psalm 145:15). It does not say, 'in their time,' but rather 'in his time.' This teaches that the Holy Blessed One provides food for each in his time [i.e., according to each individual's need]." At that time, Rava's sister, who had not seen him for thirteen years, came by and brought for him a fattened hen and aged wine. [Rava] said, "What is this before me?!" [Rava] said to [the poor man], "I said too much to you [i.e., I apologize]. Rise and eat [with me]."

Encountering a poor man who, like the one R. Nechemiah met, is accustomed to expensive delicacies, Rava asks him directly if he believes he is entitled to expensive fare at the community's expense. The man replies that the food the community provides him is God's, not theirs, and

God has promised to give each creature the food God deems appropriate. At just that moment, Rava's sister, who rarely visits, arrives with precisely the menu the man requests—we are to understand that God has found a way to deliver fattened hen and aged wine to the man.

What is your takeaway from this story? Do you believe there is truth to the notion that poor people should be provided according to their perceived needs? How do you respond to the man's profession that God has promised to give each creature the food God deems appropriate?

Have you found that the kind and amount of financial help someone requests of you influences your own generosity? How might this story speak to that situation?

4. God's Influence on Human Events

If you believe in God, how have you understood God's ability to influence human events? Does this chapter's passage help you refine your own view of God?

What do you think of the Rabbis' contention that through the tool of Roman destruction, God is expressing anger about the people's disobedience, but in truth God's anger is overblown and belies God's genuine wish for Israel's wellbeing?

What do you think of the Rabbis' suggestion that God feeds those who are hungry by requiring and empowering us to provide food for them?

If someone were to ask you, "If your God loves the poor, why doesn't God support them?" how would you respond?

5. Turnus Rufus vs. Conservative Social Darwinists

The 1859 publication of Charles Darwin's *On the Origin of Species*, which introduced such concepts as "survival of the fittest" and "natural selection," ignited a revolution in scientific thinking in the fields of biology and geology.

Meanwhile, burgeoning industrialization, immigration, and urbanization in the latter half of nineteenth-century America ushered in giant corporations, enormous wealth in the hands of a few, class wars, cities with ever-growing slums, and high tides of poverty. In this environment, politicians, journalists, social-science scholars, and religious thinkers appropriated Darwinian language, misapplying what they called "Social Darwinism," first proposed by British social philosopher Herbert Spencer and advocated in the United States by sociologist William Graham Sumner, to social and economic life. Social Darwinists employed the terminology of biological evolution to explain the sharply increasing chasm between the rich and the poor: the rich, they claimed, were biologically and socially "fit" to survive, whereas the poor were "naturally weak" and "unfit" for society. Moreover, because poverty stemmed from hereditary characteristics, alleviating poor people's suffering through public assistance would never work. If anything, giving handouts to people who couldn't work would only corrupt the larger society's work ethic. At the core of "Social Darwinism" was laissez-faire capitalism and racism, two prominent features of the Gilded Age.

How would you compare the Social Darwinism and Turnus Rufus arguments concerning society's responsibilities toward the poor?

What do you believe should be the government's obligations to its poor citizens?

In our own time, with certain exceptions, the Jewish community does not play the same all-encompassing role it did in the Rabbis' day. To what extent do you believe that the Jewish community of today should be responsible for alleviating poverty within the Jewish community and beyond?

Summing Things Up

Ancient Judaism bequeathed the Rabbis a worldview in which a powerful, caring God either rewarded the people (for example, protected them from their enemies and natural disasters) or punished them (for example, impoverished them), depending on whether or not their behavior adhered to or violated the covenant. This raised the question,

"If God cares for poor people, why doesn't God take care of them?" In our passage, the Rabbis imagine Turnus Rufus, a Roman governor intent on challenging and denigrating Judaism, asking this question. His dialogue partner, the clever and wise R. Akiva, bests him by explaining why a God who is believed to intervene in the workings of God's Creation does not seem to alleviate the suffering of poor people. Simultaneously, R. Akiva answers an unvoiced question concerning why God has not come to Israel's rescue in the face of Roman oppression. The answer to the first question explicates the human role in God's affairs. God charges us to care for the poor as a term of the covenant; in this way, God attends to the needs of the poor through us. The answer to the second exposes Turnus Rufus's failure to correctly interpret the meaning of the historical events that have devastated Israel. God is angry, but God's anger is overblown and belies God's genuine wish for Israel's well-being.

The passage treads on some very painful turf—the suffering of those who live in poverty, and the suffering of the Jewish people who have been "impoverished" by the wars with Rome—yet the Rabbis avoid criticism and condemnation of human behavior that may have brought about both consequences in favor of cultivating generosity that will help rebuild lives.

GLOSSARY

aggadah (pl. *aggadot*): narrative, nonlegalistic exegetical commentaries on Torah that are a staple of Rabbinic literature in both Talmud and midrash; aggadic material consists generally of stories and parable

aliyah: lit. "going up"; the term is used in a number of ways, including moving to the Land of Israel or from within the Land of Israel to Jerusalem, as well as an individual "going up" to bless or read Torah in the synagogue

amah (pl. *amot*): "cubit"; a measure of length defined as the distance from the tip of the middle finger to the elbow, usually estimated as eighteen inches

Amidah: lit. "standing"; refers to the prayer also known as the *Shemoneh Esrei*, or "Eighteen Benedictions," which constitutes one of the pillars of statutory Jewish prayer; further referred to as the *Tefillah*, the *Amidah* is traditionally recited thrice daily; an additional *Amidah* is recited during the *Musaf* (or "additional") service on Shabbat and holy days

amora (pl. *amora'im*): one of the second stratum of Rabbis who lived and taught between 200 and 500 CE in Babylonia and the Land of Israel; the *amora'im* are the Sages who wrote the Gemara

amud (pl. *amudim*): one side of a talmudic folio (denoted "a" or "b")

av bet din: lit. "chief of the court," the second highest position in the Sanhedrin during the Second Jewish Commonwealth

baraita: lit. "outside"; refers to mishnaic-era Rabbinic teachings that are not included in the Mishnah or either Talmud—hence, are "outside" the canonical texts

bat kol: lit. "heavenly voice"; a literary device used in Torah to express God's viewpoint

Bavli/Babylonian Talmud: Talmud, lit. "teaching" or "learning," refers to the central text of Rabbinic Judaism that serves as the primary source for Jewish religious practice and ethics; the Babylonian Talmud is composed of two integrated texts: the Mishnah, a collection of first- and second-century oral traditions from *Eretz Yisrael* compiled by Rabbi Yehudah ha-Nasi at the end of the second century; and Gemara, an extended discussion and commentary on the Mishnah that features four centuries of complex discussions, debate, legal decisions, theological views, and Mishnah-inspired stories collected, organized, and redacted by the Sages in the Babylonian academies (primarily Sura, Pumbedita, and Machuza) between 200 and 600 CE; following the organization of the Mishnah substrate, the Talmud is divided into six *sedarim* (orders), which are, in turn, subdivided into *massekhtot* (tractates); this massive work, also known as the Bavli, and abbreviated BT, is typically published in twenty volumes, and in more recent editions with modern commentaries, many more volumes

bet midrash: lit. "study house" or academy

bikkurim: first fruits of the harvest, which were brought as a sacrificial gift to the Temple, in accordance with Exodus 23:16,19 and Deuteronomy 26:1–10

bikur cholim: lit. "visiting the sick"; helping take care of the sick is considered a mitzvah (religious obligation)

brit (pl. *britot*): lit. "covenant"

brit milah: "covenant of circumcision" performed on a boy's eighth day of life as prescribed in Genesis 17:9–14 and Leviticus 12:3

chag (pl. *chagim*): lit. "holy day"; the primary holy days are the three pilgrimage festivals: Sukkot, Pesach (Passover), and Shavuot; minor *chagim* include Tu B'Shevat, Purim, and Chanukah

chakham: lit. "wise"; a term applied to a Rabbi or Sage of the talmudic period who was learned in Torah

cheil: an area ten cubits wide that surrounded the courtyards of the Jerusalem Temple, demarcated by a fence called the *soreg*

chevruta: lit. "friendship" or "companionship"; refers to the traditional study partnership in the *bet midrash*, by which pairs of students studied, analyzed, discussed, and debated the Talmud

chilazon: a rare mollusk whose bodily fluid was used to produce the blue dye to make the blue thread attached to the fringes tied to the corners of a garment, as prescribed by Numbers 15:38

chuppah: wedding canopy under which the couple stands at their marriage ceremony

daf (pl. *dapim*): a folio of Talmud, consisting of the front and back of the folio (designated "a" and "b"); one *daf* comprises two *amudim* (single sides of a folio)

derekh eretz: lit. "the way of the earth"; kindness, courtesy, consideration

Eretz Yisrael: lit. "the Land of Israel"

exegesis: a critical explanation or interpretation of a text, usually a biblical text

galut: lit. "exile"

gaonic period: The period following the redaction of the Babylonian Talmud, from the seventh through the beginning of the eleventh century, named for the heads of the Rabbinic academies in Babylonia (the *Ge'onim*)

Gehenna/Gehinnom: purgatory; derived from the name of a valley outside Jerusalem (Valley of the Son of Hinnom) where, according to the Bible (2 Chronicles 28:3, 3:6; Jeremiah 7:31, 19:2–6), people sacrificed their children to the Canaanite god Molech

Gemara: the component of Talmud that comprises an extended discussion and commentary on the Mishnah, featuring complex discussions, debate, legal decisions, theological views, and Mishnah-inspired stories; there are two Gemaras, one composed in Babylonia (hence the "Babylonian Talmud") and one in the Land of Israel (the "Jerusalem Talmud")

gemilut chasadim: lit. "deeds of loving-kindness"; considered a mitzvah of paramount importance

gezerah shavah: lit. "similar law[s]"; a Rabbinic hermeneutical principle whereby a halakhic decision in one circumstance is inferred from a halakhic decision in a similar case; more specifically, when the same word or phrase appears in two scriptural passages, the halakhah applying to one is applied to the other because they share the same word or phrase

halakhah: lit. "the path" or "the way"; a term that has come to be used synonymously with "Jewish law," although its real meaning is the "path" or "way" decisions are made using sacred texts, classical hermeneutics, and reasoning; halakhah also refers to the corpus of Rabbinic legal texts

Hekhal: lit. "Sanctuary"; the Jerusalem Temple

kavanah: spiritual focus and intention in prayer; spontaneous prayer

kavod: honor, dignity, or glory

ketubah (pl. *ketubot*): a document that constituted a wife's legal lien on her husband's property, given to her at the time of marriage to ensure her economic viability should the marriage end through divorce or the husband's death; today *ketubot* have little economic force since civil laws in most locations protect women, but they tend to be more an expression of the couple's emotional and spiritual commitment to one another and, as illuminated documents, an art form

keva: fixed, statutory prayer

kibbud av va-em: lit. "honoring father and mother"; one of the Ten Commandments, found in Exodus 20:12 and Deuteronomy 5:16

Kodesh ha-Kodashim: lit. "Holy of Holies"; the inner sanctum of the Jerusalem Temple

kohen (pl. *kohanim*): lit. "priest"; those descended by family tradition from the line of Aaron, the first High Priest of Israel

k'vod ha-briot: human dignity

Ma'ariv: lit. "Evening"; the designation for the evening prayer service *machloket l'shem shamayim*: lit. "controversy for the sake of heaven"; debate and disagreement that generate insight and ideas and serve to promote Torah learning and practice

mamzer: a child conceived by a man and woman who were not halakhically permitted to marry one another at the time of conception; often translated "bastard," although the English term is not a perfect fit in meaning; the child's status is called *mamzerut*

massekhet (pl. *massekhtot*): lit. "tractate"; the organizational elements of talmudic literature, similar to chapters; there are sixty-three tractates in the Mishnah, organized in six "orders"

megillah (pl. *megillot*): lit. "scroll"; usually refers to the Five Scrolls: Song of Songs, Ruth, Lamentations, Ecclesiastes, and Esther, but during the Talmudic period referred to biblical books aside from Torah because they were written on scrolls

Mikdash: the "Holy" Temples in Jerusalem; the First Temple was built by King Solomon and destroyed by the Babylonians in 586 BCE, and the Second Temple, built after the Jews returned from exile in Babylonia, was destroyed by the Romans in 70 CE

mincha: lit. "present" or "meal offering"; refers to the daily afternoon sacrifice offered in the Temple in Jerusalem; today *Mincha* refers to the afternoon prayers, which replace the *mincha* offering

Mishkan: the "Tabernacle" in the wilderness

Mishnah: from the word meaning "to study" or "to review"; a collection of oral traditions of the *tanna'im* compiled by Rabbi Yehudah ha-Nasi (Judah the Prince, d. ~217 CE) at the end of the second century CE; it is divided into six *sedarim* (orders), with each order further divided into *massekhtot* (tractates); an individual oral teaching is also called a "mishnah," and the plural is *mishnayot*

Mishneh Torah: lit. "Repetition of the Torah"; law code written by Moses Maimonides between 1170 and 1180 in Egypt and subtitled *Sefer Yad ha-Chazakah* (Book of the strong hand)

mitzvah (pl. mitzvot): religious obligation or commandment

musaf: lit. "additional," referring to additional sacrifices offered in the Temple in Jerusalem on Shabbat, holy days, and Rosh Chodesh (the new month); *Musaf* also refers to a prayer service consisting primarily of an additional *Amidah*, recited on Shabbat, holy days, and Rosh Chodesh in many synagogues, usually following *Shacharit*

musar: Jewish ethics; in the nineteenth century Rabbi Yisrael Lipkin Salanter originated the Musar Movement, an educational and cultural movement focusing on the refinement of individual character traits; it is enjoying a resurgence in popularity today

nasi: "president" of the Sanhedrin (the assembly of Rabbinic authorities in the Land of Israel), a position that, according to tradition, was reserved for direct descendants of Hillel

olam ha-ba: lit. "the world to come"; in traditional Jewish eschatology, history will end when the Messiah comes, heralding an age of peace and tranquility, resurrection of the dead, and the afterlife (world to come)

Oral Torah (*Torah she-b'al peh*): refers to the Babylonian Talmud; the Rabbis who composed the Talmud claimed that it was "Oral Torah" given to Moses on Mount Sinai along with the "Written Torah" (the Five Books of Moses), but transmitted orally through the generations until Rabbi Yehudah ha-Nasi commissioned its writing at the end of the second century CE

pasul: unfit or disqualified for use to fulfill a mitzvah

pe'ah: lit. "corner"; refers to the portion of the crop that must be left standing in the field for the poor to harvest for themselves as their due, in accordance with Leviticus 19:9 and 23:22; Pe'ah is also the name of a tractate of the Mishnah and the Talmud

Pentateuch: lit. "five books"; refers to the Five Books of Moses that the Written Torah comprises: Genesis, Exodus, Leviticus, Numbers, and Deuteronomy

Rabban: title of the *nasi* (president, patriarch) of the Sanhedrin (the assembly of Rabbinic authorities in the Land of Israel)

resh galuta: exilarch, lit. "head of the exile"; the Jewish leader representing the Jewish community to the government in Babylonia; the exilarchs traced their family line to King David

Rosh Chodesh: the "new moon" marking the beginning of the lunar month in the Jewish calendar

Sanhedrin: the "council" of Rabbinic judges that constituted the courts of justice in Israel from the late Second Temple period until 358 CE; the Great Sanhedrin consisted of seventy-one Rabbis convened in cases of national significance, such as declaration of war or the trial of a king; a Lesser Sanhedrin court of twenty-three heard criminal and civil cases

satan: "the adversary"; originally conceived as a position in the heavenly court approximately equivalent to the prosecuting attorney, filled by angels on a rotating basis; later, the position came to be conceived as the name of a particular angel, Satan, who was given the job of being the prosecuting attorney or adversary in the heavenly court

seder (pl. sedarim): lit. "order"; the broader organizing element of the Mishnah; orders were subdivided into tractates

sefer Torah (pl. *sifrei Torah*): scroll of Torah, written on parchment, for use in public Torah readings

Shacharit: the morning prayer service, so called because *shachar* means "dawn"

Shekhinah: God's indwelling Presence in the world, from the verb meaning "dwell" or "live"

shemitah: the biblical sabbatical year, every seventh year, during which the land lies fallow, debts are cancelled, and indentured servants are released (see Exodus 23:10–11, Leviticus 25:1–7,18–22, Deuteronomy 15:1–6)

Shemoneh Esrei (see *Amidah*): lit. "Eighteen Benedictions"; the central prayer of the evening, morning, and afternoon prayer services

shivah: the seven days of mourning following burial observed by a parent, spouse, sibling, or child of the deceased

siddur: the Jewish prayer book; from the word meaning "order," because there is a prescribed order to the prayers that are recited thrice daily

sinat chinam: baseless or gratuitous hatred

Stamma'im, stammaitic: the term *Stamma'im* refers to the unnamed redactors of the Talmud who followed the *amora'im*; stammaitic refers to the activity of these unnamed redactors and the stratum of Talmud they edited

sugya: literary unit of the Talmud

tagin: decorative "crowns" that some scribes add to certain letters of a Torah scroll

tahor/taharah: lit. "pure/ritual purity"; according to the Torah, a priest had to be in this state in order to offer sacrifices

talmidei chakhamim: lit. "students of the Sages"; full-time students of Torah in the academies of Babylonia and *Eretz Yisrael*

tame/tumah: lit. "impure/ritual impurity"; according to Leviticus, the primary source of ritual impurity is contact with the dead; others include being present in a building or under a roof where a dead body lies, contact with certain carrion (including many insects and all lizards), childbirth, a group of skin afflictions under the umbrella term *tzara'at*, and contact with certain body fluids; the rules concerning purification varied with the cause of *tumah*

tamid: lit. "continuous"; the daily sacrifice made in the Temple, morning and afternoon, also called the *olat tamid* (daily burnt offering), as set out in Exodus 29:38–42 and Numbers 28:1–8; Tamid is also the title of a Talmudic tractate that discusses the priests' activities and responsibilities from early morning through the offering of the *tamid*

Tanakh: Hebrew Scripture; "Tanakh" is an acronym for the three major sections that constitute the Hebrew Bible: Torah (Five Books of Moses), Nevi'im (Prophets), and Ketuvim (Writings)

tanna (pl. *tanna'im*): A Sage (pl. the Rabbinic Sages) of the first and second centuries CE, whose opinions are recorded in the Mishnah (the collection of oral traditions that serves as the substrate of the Talmud)

Tefillah: lit. "prayer"; refers both to prayer in general and to the central prayer of the formal prayer service, the *Amidah*, also called the *Shemoneh Esrei* (Eighteen Benedictions)

tefillin: phylacteries consisting of two small black lacquer boxes containing scriptural passages that are affixed to the head and arm with leather straps and worn during weekday morning prayer, a literal enactment of *Bind them as a sign on your hand and let them be as a frontlet between your eyes* (Deuteronomy 6:8)

tekhelet: Numbers 15:38 and Exodus 25:4 prescribe that a *p'til tekhelet* (thread of blue) be attached to the required fringes on the corners of a garment; also the term for the blue dye used to produce the threads for the fringes and in the High Priest's vestments; this dye was made from the bodily fluid of a rarely found (and consequently expensive) mollusk called a *chilazon*; the term has come to refer to the dye that produces the blue color

teshuvah: lit. "return"; repentance

tokhachah: rebuke or admonition; the term connotes a litany of curses that will befall Israel if they fail to keep God's law (see Leviticus chapter 26 and Deuteronomy 28:15–68)

Torah she-bi-khetav: the "Written Torah"; the Five Books of Moses (Genesis, Exodus, Leviticus, Numbers, and Deuteronomy)

Tosafot: medieval commentaries on the Talmud in the form of critical glosses (marginal annotation) composed in the eleventh and twelfth centuries by Rashi's students, sons-in-law, grandsons, and others in France and Germany

Tosefta: lit. "supplement"; a compilation of Jewish Oral Law from the period concurrent with the Mishnah (second century CE) that corresponds closely to the Mishnah but is not identical to it; Tosefta provides attributions for many laws that Mishnah reports anonymously and includes aggadic material and discussions not found in the Mishnah; tradition attributes the redaction of Tosefta to R. Chiyya and his student R. Oshayah; modern scholars disagree about its origins

tzedakah: righteousness or charity

tzitzit: ritual fringes attached to the four corners of a garment, as instructed in Numbers 15:37–41 and Deuteronomy 22:12; the tallit (prayer shawl) was produced to facilitate the observance of this mitzvah once clothing no longer had natural corners—by attaching tzitzit to the tallit's corners

world to come (see *olam haba*)

Written Torah (*Torah she-bi-khtav*): the Five Books of Moses: Genesis, Exodus, Leviticus, Numbers, and Deuteronomy

Yerushalmi/The Jerusalem Talmud: Like the Babylonian Talmud, the Jerusalem Talmud has two components: the Mishnah that was compiled at the end of the second century CE, and a discussion and commentary on the Mishnah written by the Sages in the Land of Israel (primarily in the academies in Tiberias, Tzippori, and Caesarea) from the end of the second century CE through the fifth century CE; the Yerushalmi, abbreviated JT, was completed earlier and is shorter than the Babylonian Talmud

yissurim shel ahavah: lit. "chastisements of love"; the belief that certain undeserved suffering is a gift from God through which the one who chooses to accept the *yissurim* atones in this world for sins committed and is thereby entitled to a larger reward in the world to come

yovel: jubilee year; occurring every fiftieth year, the jubilee year was biblically designated as a time when debts were annulled and land returned to its original owners (see Leviticus 25:8–17,25–28)

NOTES

Introduction

1. The Hasidic teacher Reb Bunam told a similar story of a man named Yitzhak b. Yakil. The motif of this story is found in the folklore of many cultures; it conveys a universal message.

2. The tractate of Talmud known as Pirkei Avot (often translated Ethics of the Ancestors) tells us, "Shimon ha-Tzaddik was one of the last survivors of the Great Assembly. He used to say: The world is sustained by three things — by Torah [study], by worship, and by deeds of loving-kindness" (Pirkei Avot 1:2).

3. Shaye Cohen, *Maccabees to the Mishnah*, 219.

4. Stuart Cohen, *Three Crowns*, 3.

5. Holtz, *Rabbi Akiva*, 1.

6. Sukkot, celebrated in the autumn after the last crops are brought in, expresses thanksgiving at the end of the harvest. Passover, in early spring, marks the time of year when new lambs are born and the wheat is planted. Shavuot, in early summer, marks the early barley harvest.

7. Passover is associated with the Exodus from Egypt, the liberation of the Jews from servitude to Pharaoh, as told in the book of Exodus. Shavuot, seven weeks later, commemorates the giving of the Torah to Israel at Mount Sinai. Sukkot recalls the forty years the Israelites wandered through the wilderness after leaving Egypt before they entered *Eretz Yisrael*. Thus, the story of the people's redemption from Israel, covenant with God at Mount Sinai, and journey to reclaim and settle the land of their ancestors is told — indeed, relived — each year through the festivals.

8. Often translated "charity," tzedakah actually means "righteousness" and refers to a wide range of behaviors considered righteous, chief among them generosity toward those who have less than we do.

9. *Gemilut chasadim* means "deeds of loving-kindness." The distinction between tzedakah and *gemilut chasadim* is described beautifully in the Bavli: "Tzedakah can be achieved only with one's money, but *gemilut chasadim* can be accomplished with one's person [i.e., through an action] or one's money. Tzedakah can be given only to the poor; *gemilut chasadim* can be done for both the rich and the poor. Tzedakah can be given only to the living; *gemilut chasadim* can be done both for the living and for the dead" (BT Sukkot 49b).

10. *Derekh eretz*, literally, "the way of the land," means treating others with proper decency and courtesy, essential to a civilized and functional society.

11. Pirkei Avot 5:19.

12. They are often called "School/House of Hillel" and the "School/House of Shammai" or simply Bet Hillel and Bet Shammai.

13. BT Eruvin 13b.

14. Emerson, *Works*, 2:11.

15. This may be an urban legend, but at least it's entertaining.

16. *JPS Hebrew-English TANAKH*.

17. Stein, *Contemporary Torah*, 2006.

1. Maintaining Self-Control

1. Although written after the Bavli, *Avot de-Rabbi Natan* (a compilation of midrashim on Pirkei Avot from the eighth- and ninth-century CE gaonic era) is sometimes termed a "minor tractate" of the Talmud and often printed together with Pirkei Avot in standard publications of the Babylonian Talmud, holding the place that Gemara on Pirkei Avot, if it existed, would hold.

2. Ecclesiastes 4:13–14: "Better a poor but wise youth than an old but foolish king who no longer has the sense to heed warnings. For the former [a 'poor but wise youth'] can emerge from a dungeon to become king; while the latter [an 'old but foolish king'], even if born to kingship, can become a pauper." Ecclesiastes (*Kohelet*, in Hebrew), one of the books in the third section of the Tanakh, is among the books designated as Wisdom Literature. *Kohelet* explores questions about mortality and the transitory nature of life and offers advice concerning living a meaningful life. In 4:13–14 the author notes that one who is lacking age and experience, as well as wealth and position, but who is possessed of wisdom, is better positioned to ascend in the world

than one who seems to "have it all" but lacks wisdom; a fool lacking wisdom can only descend.

3. Midrash Ecclesiastes Rabbah 3:11.

4. M Pirkei Avot 4:1.

5. Ritual fringes attached to the corners of a garment, as instructed in Numbers 15:37–41 and Deuteronomy 22:12. In time, Jews developed a special garment with four corners to facilitate the fulfillment of the mitzvah of tzitzit: the tallit. While we usually term a tallit a "prayer shawl," it is basically a simple four-cornered garment. A tallit is worn for morning prayers throughout the year except on Tisha B'Av, and it is additionally worn throughout the evening and day of Yom Kippur. The blessing recited before putting on the tallit is "Blessed are You, Adonai our God, ruler of the universe, who makes us holy with mitzvot and has commanded us to wrap ourselves in the tzitzit." Since the tallit is worn only for morning prayer, and since our usual clothing does not have corners, a *tallit katan* ("small tallit," sometimes called simply "tzitzit") was invented to be worn under normal clothing to facilitate the fulfillment of the mitzvah of tzitzit throughout the day. A *tallit katan* is a rectangular garment with a hole for the head and tzitzit tied on the corners that is worn as an undershirt.

Torah itself does not limit the mitzvah of tzitzit to men. The Rabbis exempt women from "time-bound, positive mitzvot" (M Kiddushin 1:7), which is not the same as barring them from wearing tzitzit. Talmud mentions two Sages who considered women obligated: R. Yehudah (BT Menachot 43a) and R. Amram the Pious (BT Sukkot 11a). Similarly, Midrash *Sifrei*, citing Numbers 15:37 (*And Adonai said to Moses: Speak to the Israelite people and instruct them to make for themselves fringes . . .*), concludes, "Thus women are obligated as well" because *b'nai Yisrael* (the Israelite people) includes women as well as men.

6. BT Menachot 43b.

7. E.g., Chen-Bo Zhong, Vanessa K. Bohns, and Francesca Gino, "Darkness Increases Dishonest Behavior," *Psychological Science* (March 2010). "Darkness increases dishonest behavior, study shows," Science Daily, March 1, 2010, https://www.sciencedaily.com/releases/2010/03/100301122344.htm; Kevin J. Haley and Daniel M. T. Fessler, "Nobody's Watching? Subtle Cues

Affect Generosity in an Anonymous Economic Game," *Evolution and Human Behavior* 26 (2005): 245–56; Brandon Randolf-Seng and Michael E. Nielsen, "Honesty: One Effect of Primed Religious Representations," *The International Journal for the Psychology of Religion* 17 (2007): 303–15.

8. Norenzayan, *Big Gods*, 23.

9. BT Menachot 43b.

10. Lempriere, *A Classical Dictionary*, 394.

11. A gold *dinar*, the Roman coin known as an Aureus, weighed 0.257 oz. (gram) gold and was equivalent to twenty-five silver *dinarim*. In the first century CE, a day laborer's wage was one or two silver *dinarim* (*Avot de-Rabbi Natan*, Version B, 26). Hillel earned a half silver *dinar* each day (BT Yoma 35b). In the second century, a worker might be paid one silver *dinar* to pick vegetables for the day (BT Avodah Zarah 62a). R Meir, who was an excellent scribe, earned two silver *dinarim* per day (Ecclesiastes Rabbah 2:17). To convert these amounts to gold-*dinar*-equivalents, divide by 25. Four hundred gold *dinarim* was an enormous sum.

12. Perhaps a model for this tale was the legend of Flora that underlies the festival of Floralia, first introduced in 238 BCE. Lactantius, the third-fourth century Christian advisor to Emperor Constantine, wrote about a woman named Flora who became enormously wealthy through prostitution. Flora bequeathed her wealth to the people and established an endowment to fund a yearly celebration of her birthday marked by licentious displays of behavior that came to be called Floralia. The woman in our story is an anti-Flora. She earns her living practicing the same profession, but distributes some of it to those who supported her and uses the remainder for charity and her marriage—the antithesis of licentiousness.

13. Gino and Norton, "Why Rituals Work."

14. "Weaving Together Ritual and Ethics," My Jewish Learning, accessed March 30, 2017, http://www.myjewishlearning.com/article/ritual-and-ethics-a-holy-blend/.

15. *Tekhelet* is mentioned at least four dozen times in the Bible. The precise identity of the *chilazon*, a marine creature that is the source of the dye required to produce it, is not known, though some believe they have identified it. BT Shabbat 75a describes "smashing" the *chilazon* to extract its blood to make

the dye; this suggests it has a hard shell. BT Sanhedrin 91a identifies the *chilazon* as a snail. In BT Ketubot 5b, Tosafot say one can extract its blood from a sac without killing it, which seems to contradict BT Shabbat 75a. Hence, many believe it to be a snail, cuttlefish, or some type of squid. BT Bava Metzia 61b identifies the color of the dye as indigo, but that hardly comports with the description in BT Menachot 43b, which compares the color to the sea, the sky, and God's sapphire throne. Today, some identify the *chilazon* as a cuttlefish; others believe it be the murex snail. In the case of the cuttlefish, the "blood" mentioned in the Talmud would refer to the ink it uses in self-defense against predators; in the case of the murex snail, the "blood" is mucous it produces.

16. Pirkei Avot 4:2.
17. Rabbi Isaac Luria (1534–72), also known as Ha-Ari, was the most influential thinker among the community of mystics in Tzfat (Safed) in the sixteenth century that formulated what is known today as the Kabbalah. Luria's esoteric teachings were recorded by his disciple, Rabbi Chaim Vital, who, at his teacher's request, shared them only with the small circle of his students. Nonetheless, his novel ideas — and in particular his mystical cosmology — were circulated beyond this circle and, by the seventeenth century, were widespread and popular.
18. Rabbenu Yonah is Rabbi Yonah ben Avraham Gerondi (d. 1264), who lived in Catalonia and wrote a popular commentary on the Mishnah, of which Pirkei Avot is a tractate.
19. De Uzeda, *Midrash Shmuel*, 230.

2. Respecting Human Dignity

1. In a letter to Bishop Mandell Creighton, April 5, 1878, published in J. N. Figgis and R. V. Laurence, eds., *Historical Essays and Studies* (London: Macmillan, 1907).
2. Hicks and Tutu, *Dignity*, 2.
3. Hicks's definition of dignity: "Dignity is our inherent value and worth. We all come into the world with it . . . Each of us is equally worthy of having that dignity honored." From her TEDx talk at https://www.youtube.com /watch?v=GPF7QspiLqM&t=25s, accessed April 3, 2017.

4. Hobbes, *Leviathan*, ch. 10.

5. Kant spent virtually his entire adult life in the society of the University of Königsberg. A philosopher first and foremost, he also studied mathematics, astrophysics, geography, and anthropology. His most influential tomes are *Groundwork of the Metaphysics of Morals* (1785), *Critique of Pure Reason* (1781), and *Metaphysics of Morals* (1797). Kant stressed that what is morally right is independent of context. Kant was not claiming that the moral imperative to respect another's dignity also necessarily requires respecting that person's actions, but the distinction is sometimes difficult to make.

6. In Kantian ethics, a "maxim" is a subjective principle that is part of an agent's thought process that guides his or her action. Today we would be inclined to use the terms "intention" or "rationale." The "categorical imperative," central to Kantian ethics, serves as a litmus test to determine whether the maxims in one's head lead to behavior that is right or wrong. (One might think of the categorical imperative as an uber-maxim.) Here is another way to understand the categorical imperative: "What would happen if everyone did what I'm about to do? If the result is good, then I should act according to my maxim; if the result would be detrimental, then I should not act according to my maxim." Using the categorical imperative, people can evaluate their own thinking as well as their own acts.

7. The "Universal Declaration of Human Rights," United Nations, accessed April 3, 2017, http://www.un.org/en/universal-declaration-human-rights/, adopted by the United Nations on December 10, 1948, was drafted by, among others, the Jewish French jurist René Samuel Cassin, who wrote concerning it: "The expression: 'God created Man in his own Image' characterizes both that *prise de conscience* and the religious form which it adopted initially. Secularization followed. The dignity of man has been reaffirmed by philosophers, sociologists, and statesmen regardless of religious beliefs, and has been detached from religious credos or cults. What is incontestable is the permanence of the idea through the centuries and despite the most profound divergences of interpretation of the doctrine. The Decalogue, one of the most ancient documents of Israel's tradition, is essentially religious and monotheistic in its first commandments, and subsequently lays down principles of morals and justice. The

first commandment states the monotheistic principle: 'I am the Lord thy God . . . Thou shalt have no other Gods before me.' The Decalogue then dictates to man rules of conduct, some positive ('Remember the Sabbath day, to keep it holy . . . ,' 'Honour thy father and thy mother . . .') and some negative ('Thou shalt not murder,' 'Thou shalt not steal,' 'Thou shalt not bear false witness,' 'Thou shalt not covet . . .'). Although we can infer from these commandments that other human beings (ordinary men, parents, spouses, servants, property-owners, etc.) must be respected, there is no direct formulation in the Decalogue of a correlative prerogative, or of any subjective right. It is only 'duty' which the legislator of Israel stresses in man's relationship to man" (Cassin, "From the Ten Commandments to the Rights of Man," April 19, 2011, http://renecassin.over-blog.com/article -from-the-ten-commandments-to-the-rights-of-man-72080499.html).

8. This inspires a question: if human beings lack autonomy, the ability to reason, and/or a moral compass—as do people lying in a coma—do they forego the right to human dignity?

9. *And God said, "Let us make humankind in our image, after our likeness . . ." And God created humankind in the divine image, creating it in the image of God— creating them male and female* (Genesis 1:26–27).

10. At the same time, human dignity is positioned beneath divine dignity, the higher priority. *You have made him little less than divine, and adorned him with glory* [kavod] *and majesty* (Psalm 8:6).

11. Many translators and commentators understand "you impale him on a stake" to be an imperative. I understand it as an option: the verse instructs that *if* the executed person is impaled on a stake, the body must be taken down before nightfall.

12. *Mekhilta de-Rabbi Yishmael, Mishpatim, parashah 12. Mekhilta* was written around 400 CE.

13. The Talmud supplies numerous examples of human dignity superseding Rabbinic injunctions, among them: BT Shabbat 81 permits a type of carrying on Shabbat that preserves human dignity, but otherwise would be Rabbinically (but not biblically) impermissible; in BT Shabbat 94b Rav Nachman permits a corpse to be removed from a house on Shabbat for the sake of human dignity.

14. E.g., in JT Nazir 56a, a Nazirite is permitted to walk with a crowd on an impure road—risking violation of his vow—so that he does not have to walk alone; the Yerushalmi explains, "for R. Zeira says, 'So great is human dignity that it temporarily supersedes a negative commandment.'" Note that the suspension of biblical law is temporary, not permanent.

15. *Tanna* (pl. *tanna'im*) is an Aramaic term equivalent to the Hebrew *shana* meaning "one who repeats/learns," since all learning was accomplished first and foremost through repetition. *Tanna* is a term applied to a Sage of the first and second centuries of the Common Era, until the compilation of the Mishnah (under the auspices of R. Yehudah ha-Nasi) at the end of the second century.

16. In addition, the Rabbis tell us in BT Berakhot 26b that each set of prayers was instituted by a Patriarch: Abraham was the first to say *Shacharit*, the morning prayers; Isaac initiated *Mincha*, the afternoon prayers; and Jacob inaugurated *Ma'ariv*, the evening prayers. This claim is supported by citing verses from Torah that are interpreted to portray each Patriarch praying at the corresponding time of day.

17. Pirkei Avot 1:2: "Shimon ha-Tzaddik was among the last members of the Great Assembly. He used to say: The world rests on three things: on [study of] Torah, on worship of God, and on deeds of loving-kindness." Midrash comments: Once, as Rabban Yochanan b. Zakkai was coming forth from Jerusalem, R. Yehoshua followed after him and beheld the Temple in ruins. "Woe to us!" cried R. Yehoshua, "that this, the place where the iniquities of Israel were atoned for, is laid to waste!" Rabban Yochanan said to him, "My son, do not grieve. We have another atonement as effective as this. And what is it? It is acts of loving-kindness, as it is said, *I desire goodness, not sacrifice*" (*Avot de-Rabbi Natan*, ch. 4).

18. *Musaf*, on Shabbat and festivals, corresponds to the additional offering made in the Temple on Shabbat and festivals. It consists largely of an additional *Amidah* with a special *k'dushat ha-yom* (sanctification of the day) that speaks to the meaning and importance of the occasion.

19. BT Bava Metzia 59b.

20. Ezra, a priest-scribe, led a contingent of Jews from exile in Babylonia back to *Eretz Yisrael* in the fifth century BCE.

21. The expression "to pay homage at the Caesar's court" suggests a variety of functions that R. Elazar b. Azariah would be expected to fulfill, given his family's wealth: serve as the Jewish people's representative to the Roman government; negotiate and lobby on Israel's behalf; provide gifts and pay taxes, bribes, and extortions as the need arose.

22. The first incident, retold in BT Rosh Hashanah 25a (see ch. 3 of this vol.), concerned a difference of opinion on how the calendar was intercalated, and hence the calculation of when Yom Kippur occurred. Rabban Gamliel ordered R. Yehoshua to appear before him on the day the latter calculated to be Yom Kippur, carrying his money bag and staff (which one may not carry on a holy day). The second incident, recounted in BT Bekhorot 36a, concerned how one gauges the trustworthiness of a priest who is also a Rabbi compared with one who is not. The second story follows a similar pattern: R. Tzaddok asks R. Yehoshua a question and receives an affirmative response. He then queries Rabban Gamliel and, upon receiving a negative response, reports that R. Yehoshua had answered the question in the affirmative. Rabban Gamliel says, "Wait until the champions enter the *bet midrash*," and the confrontation plays out much as the one in the Berakhot account, with Rabban Gamliel treating R. Yehoshua in virtually the same manner, and R. Yehoshua responding that telling the truth is inescapable when the witness is alive and present. Here, as well, those present end Rabban Gamliel's humiliation of R. Yehoshua by silencing Chutzpit the Translator.

23. BT Sukkah 28a waxes poetic about Yochanan b. Zakkai and his connection to Hillel, testifying to his extraordinary qualifications: "Our Rabbis taught: Hillel the Elder had eighty disciples, thirty of whom were worthy of the *Shekhinah* resting upon them as it did upon Moses our teacher, thirty of whom were worthy that the sun should stand still for them as it did for Joshua the son of Nun (Joshua 10:12–14), and twenty of whom were ordinary. The greatest of them was Yonatan b. Uzziel. The youngest was Rabban Yochanan b. Zakkai. They said of Rabban Yochanan b. Zakkai that he did not leave [unmastered] Scripture, Mishnah, Gemara, halakhah, *aggadah*, minutiae of the Torah, minutiae of the scribes, *a fortiori* inferences and verbal analogies, calendrical calculations, numerology [i.e., gematria], the conversation of

the ministering angel, demons, and palm-trees, launderers' parables and fox fables, and matters great and small" (BT Sukkah 28a).

24. In an earlier mishnah of this tractate, R. Elazar enigmatically said, "I am like one who is seventy years old" (BT Berakhot 12b). The comment attributed to him here is understood to explain the earlier comment.

25. The numbers here are undoubtedly hyperbole. Hayim Lapin (*Rabbis as Romans*) writes that in the first and second centuries the *tanna'im* were small discipleship circles, only arising to the level of a "Rabbinic movement" with the third-century *amora'im*. Their numbers would have been far smaller than those reported in stories such as this one.

26. The talmudic Tractate Eduyot (Testimonies) records many disputes between Sages, beginning with Hillel and Shammai. A majority of the *mishnayot* in *Eduyot* are found in other tractates as well. The Gemara here claims that the conflict between Rabban Gamliel and R. Yehoshua over the matter of *Ma'ariv* gave rise to Tractate Eduyot.

27. In M Yadayim 4:4.

28. BT Yoma 22b teaches this principle that someone or something can be elevated to a higher level of sanctity but may not be degraded to a lower level of sanctity.

29. BT Chagigah 3a.

30. BT Shabbat 21b. Bet Shammai's opinion, which was rejected, was to light eight candles the first night and reduce the candles by one each night of the festival.

31. Maimonides, *Mishneh Torah, Hilkhot Matanot Aniyim* 10:7–14.

3. Creating Consensus in Community

1. Neusner, "Mishnah Viewed Whole," 8.

2. The primary myths of Torah are that (1) God created the universe, imposing order on chaos, establishing humanity as the stewards of the earth, and adopting Israel as God's chosen people; (2) God redeemed Israel from bondage in Egypt so that the people could serve God; and (3) God revealed the Torah to Israel at Mount Sinai to be the constitution that would establish them as a nation of priests and a holy people in the land of their ancestors, the Land of Israel.

3. No doubt, profit was among Weems's motives. The myth of Washington's honesty in revealing that he had chopped down a cherry tree contributed to the popularity of the biography Weems was attempting to sell, *The Life of Washington* (Augusta GA: George P. Randolph, 1806). The ease of passing on legendary stories about famous people is illustrated by P. T. Barnum's claim in 1835 that Joice Heth, a slave who toiled in his circus as a sideshow attraction, was the "nursing mammy" who had raised George Washington, although he was born more than a century earlier. Barnum claimed Heth had been born in 1674 and was (in 1835) 161 years old.

4. Geertz, *Interpretation of Cultures*, 90.

5. Langer, *Philosophy in a New Key*, 287.

6. Gillman, *Doing Jewish Theology*, 34–35.

7. Gillman, "Problematics of Myth."

8. May, *Cry for Myth*, 15.

9. Gillman, "Problematics of Myth."

10. Goody, *Logic of Writing*, 95.

11. Titus Livius (Livy), *The History of Rome*, book 9, ch. 46.

12. M Rosh Hashanah 2:5 (23a).

13. M Sotah 15:18 informs us, "Since Rabban Gamliel the Elder died, there has been no more reverence for the law, and purity and piety died out at the same time."

14. The extent of the Jewish political spectrum in this period is attested in numerous stories, nowhere as clearly as BT Gittin 55–57.

15. Halakhah specifies that one may travel only two thousand cubits from home on Shabbat (or outside one's town or city). This is called the *techum* (boundary). BT Eruvin 41b stipulates that one who exceeds the *techum* on Shabbat, as would be the case for one who arrived in Bet Ya'azek on Shabbat to give testimony concerning the new moon, was limited to four cubits until Shabbat ended. Enforcing this restriction discouraged people from expending the effort and expense of coming to give testimony, so Rabban Gamliel enacted a leniency, permitting them to travel two thousand cubits in any direction from Bet Ya'azek after they arrived.

16. A lunar month is the time between subsequent conjunctions of the moon with the sun, equal to 29.5306 days. Hence, if no one has seen the new moon

by the thirtieth day, there is no question that the following day must be considered Rosh Chodesh.

17. R. Akiva's role here is unsurprising in light of several other stories in which he serves as peacemaker. See, e.g., BT Bava Metzia 59b, where R. Akiva's colleagues nominate him to placate R. Eliezer b. Hyrcanus, who has been excommunicated from the *bet midrash* headed by Rabban Shimon b. Gamliel.

18. In a review of Hayim Lapin's *Rabbis as Romans*, Jewish historian Steven Fine observes that scholarship on the *tanna'im* has tended to view them through whatever lens those doing the research view their own generation. He notes that, "[w]here for Saul Lieberman 'How Much Greek in Jewish Palestine?' (1963) was the question of the day, one that fit a mid-century religious culture," the pressing question for scholars in "the later third of the twentieth century was something like: 'what was the status of the rabbis in Jewish society?'" Lapin points out that this new focus parallels declines in Jewish endogamy, birth rates, and synagogue affiliation as well as questions about Rabbinic authority that were transforming the American Jewish community. Today, Fine notes, "the very nature of 'Jewish identity' is a preoccupation," and historical scholarship reflects this, including Lapin's *Rabbis as Romans*, which "reorients the 'rabbinic authority' question to the issue of the place of the rabbis on the wide stage of the Roman world" (2013, Society of Biblical Literature, accessed April 24, 2017, https://www.academia.edu /3412357/Review_of_Lapin_--Rabbis_as_Romans_The_Rabbinic_Movement _in_Palestine_100_400_CE).

19. Kraemer, *Jewish Eating and Identity through the Ages*, 40.

20. Hezser, *Social Structure of the Rabbinic Movement*, 492.

21. Hezser, *Social Structure of the Rabbinic Movement*, 493.

22. Hezser, *Social Structure of the Rabbinic Movement*, 493.

23. Consider, e.g., the image in the story in chapter 2 of this volume (BT Berakhot 28a) in which the doors of the study house are opened to all comers, and four- to seven hundred benches must be added to accommodate them.

24. The Gemara (BT Bava Metzia 58–59) recounts an occasion when R. Eliezer b. Hyrcanus refuses to accede to the majority opinion on the matter of a contaminated oven's purity. In defiance of his colleagues' decision, he performs several miracles to demonstrate the superiority of his view. When

miracles fail to persuade them, R. Eliezer calls on heaven to directly confirm that he is correct and, indeed, a heavenly voice rings out, "Why do you dispute with R. Eliezer, inasmuch as the halakhah agrees with him in all matters!" This provokes R. Yehoshua—the same R. Yehoshua who appears in this chapter—to rise and declare, "It is not in heaven!" meaning that since the time Israel received the Torah at Mount Sinai, halakhic decisions are not made in heaven, but rather in the *bet midrash* by the Rabbis. Hence, the majority view of the Rabbis *is* God's will. Lest the reader harbor any reservations, the account in Bava Metzia continues: "Rabbi Nathan met Elijah and asked him, 'What did the Holy Blessed One do in that hour?' [Elijah replied,] 'God laughed [with joy] saying, "My children have defeated Me! My children have defeated Me!"'"

25. There are three instances in Leviticus (23:2, 4, and 37) that say, *the festivals of Adonai; declare* **them** *as fixed times*, where the word *otam* (them) is written without the letter *vav* and can therefore be vocalized *atem* (you).

26. In chapter 2 of this volume, R. Yehoshua's poverty is directly contrasted with Rabban Gamliel's wealth.

27. Langer, *Philosophy in a New Key*, 176.

28. Langer, *Philosophy in a New Key*, 180.

29. Lapin, *Rabbis as Romans*, 56.

30. Mark Lukens, "The False Choice Between Top-Down and Bottom-Up Leadership," Fast Company *Work Smart Newsletter*, February 11, 2016, https://www.fastcompany.com/3056551/the-false-choice-between-top-down-and-bottom-up-leadership.

31. BT Bava Metzia 58–59.

32. Hartman, *Living Covenant*, 130.

33. See n. 25.

34. No claim is being made here concerning the legitimacy or quality of either method. Exegesis is appropriate in the academic world and to understanding biblical texts in their context (*P'shat*). However, much of midrash falls into the category of eisegesis and has proven deeply meaningful throughout Jewish history. In academia, only strict exegesis by accepted academic hermeneutical principles is considered legitimate study of Hebrew Scripture, but Jewish eisegesis is, itself, a fascinating topic of academic study. For the

purposes of extracting religious and spiritual meaning, both for homiletics and study, eisegesis is common fare.

4. Clashing Titans

1. Christine Porath and Christine Pearson, "The Price of Incivility," *Harvard Business Review* (January–February 2013): 116. Porath and Pearson conducting their research with interviews, questionnaires, and experiments, reported that in 2011 98 percent of respondents experienced incivility in the workplace and 78 percent reported that these experiences diminished their commitment to their organizations. Another group of researchers, extending the work of Porath and Pearson, noted, "Although incivility is pervasive at work (Porath & Pearson, 2013), our findings indicate that it does not always translate into [ego] depletion nor subsequent [retaliatory] acts of incivility. Practically speaking, our results indicate that incivility is depleting when it is experienced in work contexts that are perceived as political" (Christopher C. Rosen, Joel Koopman, Allison Gabriel, and Russell E. Johnson, "Who Strikes Back? A Daily Investigation of When and Why Incivility Begets Incivility," *Journal of Applied Psychology* [August 8, 2016]: 11). The context of the story told in this chapter is akin to the workplace in that the Rabbis mentioned spend the majority of their time in the *bet midrash*. It is also a decidedly political realm whose actors view themselves as communal leaders.
2. Whether the Sanhedrin existed after 70 CE is a matter of debate. Many scholars, including Shaye Cohen, see its mention in talmudic texts of the tannaitic and amoraic periods as a projection of the governing religious body during the Second Temple period into the era of the early Rabbis, a means of legitimating their authority. When I use the term "Sanhedrin" in this chapter, I use it as the Rabbis did to describe their proceedings.
3. Kokhba, meaning "star," can be transliterated in English as Kokhba and Kochba.
4. JT Ta'anit 4:5 (24a–b).
5. Usha had been the seat of the patriarchate in 80 CE under Rabban Gamliel II. In 116, the patriarchate returned to Yavneh, and then moved back to Usha. Jack Lightstone, a historian of ancient Judaism, writes: "Rabbinic evidence points to the southern Galilee as the principal base in Roman

Palestine of the rabbinic guild or class after the Bar Kohkba rebellion. Indeed, early third- through fifth-century Palestinian rabbinic sources consistently portray that principal base as co-located with the court of the Patriarch at Usha (with Simeon B. Gamaliel II [Rabban Shimon b. Gamliel II], if Patriarchal powers are not anachronistically assigned to Simeon by rabbinic sources), at Bet She'arim and subsequently at Sepphoris [Tzippori] (both with Judah I), and finally at Tiberias (with Judah I's successors through the first quarter of the first century)" (*Mishnah and the Social Formation of the Early Rabbinic Guild*, 192).

6. Stuart A. Cohen, *Three Crowns*, 186.

7. Both Talmuds consider Hillel the Elder to be a direct descendant of King David. JT Ta'anit 4:2, 68a, contains a report in the name of R. Levi. The Bavli (Ketubot 62b–63a) as well as Midrash Genesis Rabbah 98:8 claim Hillel is descended from David on his paternal side. The Yerushalmi (Kila'im 9:4, 32a–b, and Ketubot 12:3, 34d–35b) as well as Genesis Rabbah 33:3 claim his mother was descended from Judah, a direct ancestor of David. (Another source, BT Sanhedrin 37b–38a, seems to claim that the patriarch and exilarch are not descended from David.) See discussion in Goodblatt, *Monarchic Principle*, 146–69.

8. Pirkei Avot 4:17.

9. "On matters of constitutional relevance . . . early rabbinic perspectives on the distribution and exercise of Jewish political authority were informed by the notional existence of three ordained clusters of Jewish governmental instrumentalities, each endowed with its own Divine mandate to participate in national rulership. Eventually designated the three *ketarim* (literally translated as 'crowns'), those domains were together understood to comprise an administrative matrix; within the framework laid down by the *ketarim* Jewish polities shared and distributed whatever autonomous powers they were permitted—under God—to command" (Stuart A. Cohen, *Three Crowns*, 3).

10. Stuart A. Cohen, *Three Crowns*, 187.

11. Shaye J. D. Cohen, *Maccabees to the Mishnah*, 220.

12. Genesis Rabbah 61:3, Theodor-Albeck edition, 600.

13. The list of seven includes the five elders ordained by Yehudah b. Bava between Usha and Shefar'am during a time when the Roman government

under Hadrian outlawed ordination, according to BT Sanhedrin 13b–14a. This, too, speaks to the story's theme of survival under duress.

14. Baumgarten, "Akiban Opposition," 180–81.
15. Baumgarten, "Akiban Opposition," 180.
16. Stuart A. Cohen, *Three Crowns*, 3.
17. Stuart A. Cohen, *Three Crowns*, 3, 186.
18. David Goodblatt, "From History to Story to History: The Rimmon Valley Seven," in Schäfer, *Talmud Yerushalmi and Graeco-Roman Culture*, 177.
19. Friedman, "La'aggadah hahistorit batalmud habavli," 122.
20. Goodblatt suggests that the story might reference a stone quarry where broken chisels remained in the rock face, a location the storyteller knew to be associated with the assembly of the seven Sages. Goodblatt, "From History to Story to History," 194–95.
21. The term "Sanhedrin" itself may well be a historical anachronism, harkening to the Second Temple era, used to affirm and reinforce the authority of both the Rabbis and the patriarch.
22. BT Bava Metzia 86a.
23. R. Meir was buried in Tiberias near the shores of the Kinneret. To this day, his tomb is a pilgrimage site.
24. BT Berakhot 27b in ch. 2 of this volume.
25. The Sanhedrin moved to Usha under the presidency of Rabban Gamliel II in 80 CE; in 116, it returned to Yavneh, and then moved back again to Usha. Rabban Shimon b. Gamliel II (the *nasi* at the time of the incident recounted in our passage) moved the Sanhedrin to Shefar'am in 140. Rabbi Yehudah moved it to Bet She'arim, and later to Tzippori in 163. Rabban Gamliel III moved the Sanhedrin to Tiberias in 193, where it remained while R. Yehudah ha-Nasi, compiler of the Misnhah, presided as *nasi*.
26. BT Shabbat 13b.
27. Pirkei Avot 4:1.
28. As, e.g., in Psalm 145.
29. BT Bava Metzia 58b.
30. "Learning," in the first and second century, consisted in large measure of memorization. Without written texts, mastery of the moral teachings meant memorizing them. Adin Steinsaltz has written, "The work of preserving and

codifying the vast body of oral law went on for several generations, but its importance waned as the main focus of Torah scholarship shifted elsewhere. Those scholars who engaged in memorization of the vast number of *baraitot* were still known as *tannaim*, but the term took on new significance. *Tannaim* were no longer creators of the oral law but individuals gifted with phenomenal memories who did not always comprehend the full significance of what they were memorizing. They were to be found in many generations in the larger academies, serving as living archives utilized by the sages in order to clarify and elucidate various problems that cropped up in the course of the study of the Mishnah" (*Essential Talmud*, 41). Jacob Neusner points out that memorization enacts the religious claim that Mishnah is Oral Torah: "The Mishnah wants to be memorized for a reason. . . . This was to act out the claim that there are two components of the one whole Torah that 'Moses, our rabbi,' received from God at Sinai, one transmitted in writing, the other handed on by tradition, in oral form only. True, the claim for the Mishnah, laid down in Abot [Pirkei Avot], the Mishnah's first and most compelling apologetic, is that the authority of the Mishnah rests upon its status as received tradition of God. It follows that tradition handed on through memory is valid specifically because, while Self-evidently not part of the written Torah, which all Israel has in hand, it is essential to the whole Torah. Its mode of tradition through memory verifies and authenticates its authority as tradition begun by God, despite its absence from the written part of Torah" (*The Mishnah*, 240).

31. Consider, e.g., the dreams of Joseph (Genesis 37) and Pharaoh (Genesis 41).
32. Stuart A. Cohen, *Three Crowns*, 180, notes that the patriarchate in *Eretz Yisrael* claimed descent from the maternal line of David, while the exilarchs of Babylonia claimed descent from the paternal line. He further notes in *Three Crowns*, 206n3: "Where acknowledged, that *cachet* may indeed have been sufficiently evocative to bestow upon its owners the kind of respect which contemporary culture was wont to invest in proprietary dynasticism. But, even so, it could not entirely mask the novelty and limitations of their offices. . . . For all the antiquity of their titles and assumed patrimony, neither Patriarchs [in *Eretz Yisrael*] nor exilarchs [in Babylonia] constituted true institutional reincarnations of Israel's ancient monarchy. Rather, they represented extensions of Jewry's gentile overlords."

33. Rabbi is teaching his son BT Bekhorot 60.

34. BT Ketubot 103b.

35. R. Shimon, the son of Rabbi, was revered for his kindness (BT Bava Batra 8a). His father called him "the light of Israel" (BT Arakhin 10a and Menachot 88b).

36. Pirkei Avot 4:1.

37. May, *Power and Innocence*, 247.

38. The author of the tract entitled his book *Sefer ha-Middot* (Book of moral qualities) but a later copyist retitled it *Orchot Tzaddikim*. It was first published in Hebrew in Prague in 1581, but an earlier and incomplete version was published in Yiddish in 1542. The book appears to be a compilation of earlier writings, including those of Solomon ibn Gabirol, Moses Maimonides (Rambam), Yonah b. Avraham of Gerondi (Rabbenu Yonah), and Bachya ibn Pakuda.

39. *Orchot Tzaddikim*, ch. 2.

5. Moving to the Land of Israel

1. BT Sotah 37a.

2. The debate concerning how to define Judaism and the Jewish people—nation, religion, peoplehood, culture, ethnicity—dates to the Enlightenment, as Jews sought to integrate and participate in Christian Europe. Some thinkers, such as the German reformers (including Moses Mendelssohn, Abraham Geiger, and Hermann Cohen), adhered to the Protestant model of religion as a set of private beliefs and practices. Heinrich Graetz argued for a far broader understanding of Judaism that could not be contained in the narrow category of "religion."

3. Leora Batnitzky, *How Judaism Became a Religion*, 45.

4. Members of Naturei Karta in Israel and elsewhere actively campaign against Israel, burn the Israeli flag, and send emissaries to Iran and Hezbollah to pledge their support. The *Jerusalem Post* reported in August 2013 that a member of Naturei Karta was arrested in Israel after he flew to the Iranian Embassy in Berlin on January 11, 2011, and offered to spy on Israel for Iran. Returning four days later, he "kept up his connection with the Iranian officials by email, using Internet cafes, and via telephone calls made from public phones near his

place of residence in Jerusalem," according to the Shin Bet (the Israeli Security Agency) and the indictment against him. The article further notes: "The Shin Bet said that under questioning, the man confessed that he worked 'out of a hatred for the State of Israel and in exchange for financial compensation'" (Yonah Jeremy Bob and Ben Hartman, "Haredi from Anti-Zionist Naturei Karta Sect Charged with Trying to Spy for Iran," *Jerusalem Post*, August 1, 2013, http://www.jpost.com/National-News/Haredi-from-anti-Zionist-Naturei -Karta-sect-charged-with-trying-to-spy-for-Iran-321751).

5. "Why Orthodox Jews Are Opposed to a Zionist State," Naturei Karta, 2003, http://www.nkusa.org/aboutus/zionism/opposition.cfm.

6. Members of Naturei Karta are often termed *haredim*, but here I use the term to refer to those who self-identify as *haredim*.

7. Gilad Malach, Maya Choshen, and Lee Cahaner, "Statistical Report on Ultra-Orthodox Society in Israel" (Israel Democracy Institute and Jerusalem Institute for Israel Studies, 2016), 19, accessed July 12, 2017, https://en.idi.org.il /media/4240/shnaton-e_8-9-16_web.pdf.

8. An article in the *Times of Israel* suggests a rosier picture, with more *haredi* men interested in acquiring working skills and entering the workforce, but the gap remains large (Aron Heller, "In Israel, a New Generation of Orthodox Jews Seek Integration," *Times of Israel*, March 20, 2016, http:// www.timesofisrael.com/in-israel-a-new-generation-of-ultra-orthodox-jews -seek-integration/).

9. God's commandment to Abram is first articulated in Genesis 12:1–2 in combination with the promise to build Abram's family into a great nation and bless them. The promise is reconfirmed to his son Isaac (Genesis 26:2–3) and Isaac's son Jacob (Genesis 35:9–12). The redemption from Egypt is integrally connected with the Israelites' return to the land: *Adonai continued, "I have marked well the plight of My people in Egypt and have heeded their outcry because of their taskmasters; yes, I am mindful of their sufferings. I have come down to rescue them from the Egyptians and to bring them out of that land to a good and spacious land, a land flowing with milk and honey . . ."* (Exodus 3:7–8). The promise is reiterated to Joshua and the boundaries of the land specified when, following their four-decade sojourn in the wilderness, the Israelites enter *Eretz Yisrael* under his leadership (Joshua 1:2–4).

10. The trope of a "land flowing with milk and honey" is found more than twenty times in the Tanakh, in Exodus through Deuteronomy, Joshua, Jeremiah, Ezekiel, and Job. It gives rise to this amusing *aggadah* in the same section of Talmud as our passage: "Rami b. Yechezkel traveled to B'nei B'rak. There he saw goats grazing under the fig trees. Honey was dripping from the figs, and milk was flowing from the goats, and they mingled together. He exclaimed, 'This is indeed [a land] flowing with milk and honey!'" (BT Ketubot 111b).

11. I recommend googling images of the interchange.

12. M Kelim 1:6.

13. Leviticus Rabbah 13:2.

14. The translation of Tosefta 4:5 is from Neusner, *Jeremiah in Talmud and Midrash*, 3.

15. M Kelim 1:6–9 records ten degrees of holiness from the outside in: "[1:6] The Land of Israel is holier than any other land. . . . [1:7] Walled cities [within the Land of Israel] are holier than these. . . . [1:8] Within the walls [of Jerusalem] is holier than these. . . . The Temple Mount is holier than this. . . . The *Cheil* [the area surrounding the temple courtyards] is holier than this. . . . The Women's Courtyard is holier than this. . . . The Israelites' Courtyard is holier than this. . . . The Priests' Courtyard is holier than this. . . . [1:9] Between the Outer Portico of the Sanctuary and the altar is holier than this. . . . The *Hekhal* [Sanctuary] is holier than this. . . . The *Kodesh ha-Kodashim* [Holy of Holies] is holier than this."

16. Seth Daniel Kunin, "Judaism," in Holm and Bowker, *Sacred Place*, 116. (Reprinted in Kunin, *Themes and Issues in Judaism*, 23.)

17. A ketubah is a contract between a man and a woman that establishes their legal connection and stipulates the rights and responsibilities of the man toward the woman. It is a lien on the man's money and property held by his wife in case the marriage ends either through divorce or his death; the ketubah stipulates how much the wife is to be paid should the marriage end. The Rabbis insisted that every married woman should have a ketubah to protect her from becoming financially destitute if her husband dies or divorces her. As the mishnah makes clear, the ketubah also functioned as a disincentive for a man to divorce his wife: he would have to pay her the amount stipulated in her ketubah.

18. Cappadocia, located in present-day central Turkey, is in Asia Minor. It was a tributary to Rome until 17 CE, when Tiberius reduced it to a Roman province.

19. This permission contrasts with the prohibition, articulated in the prior mishnah (13:10), against a man compelling his wife to move from one province within *Eretz Yisrael* to another, though he could compel her to move to a new home within a province. The Rabbis had designated what areas were to be considered provinces, e.g., Judea, Transjordan, Galilee. The concern here seems to be that moving from one province to another would impose undue hardship on the wife when she wanted to return home to visit her family.

20. A *baraita* in the Gemara that follows this mishnah ruled that if a woman wishes to move from the Diaspora to the Land of Israel but her husband refuses to accompany her, he divorces her and pays her ketubah; conversely, if a man wishes to move to the Land of Israel but his wife does not, he divorces her but is not required to pay her ketubah.

21. Translation by Nina Salaman in Brody, *Selected Poems of Jehudah Halevi*, 2.

22. BT Yoma 80a, on the basis of Leviticus 27:34, the verse that closes out the book of Leviticus — *These are the commandments that Adonai gave Moses for the Israelite people on Mount Sinai* — established that "no prophet is permitted to introduce any new law," although prophets could reestablish forgotten laws. *Sifra* (a halakhic midrash to the book of Leviticus), commenting on Leviticus 27:34, confirms: "All [the mitzvot] were proclaimed from Sinai."

23. The complex rituals carried out by the *kohanim* in the Jerusalem Temple employed a wide variety of vessels and utensils, including implements to slaughter the animals, vessels used to collect their blood, libation cups, censors for incense offerings, gold bowls and jugs for sanctified oil for the menorah, utensils to prepare the meal offerings, shovels to remove ashes, and silver-plated *shofarot*. Most likely among the items brought to Babylonia were numerous fixtures, including the incense altar, the lampstand, the showbread table, and the golden altar.

24. M Yadayim, which addresses impurities related to the hands, discusses which books render one's hands ritually impure (*tame*) through contact. A Torah scroll, which is holy, conveys *tumah* (ritual impurity). The Song of Songs,

we are told in M Yadayim 3:5, was a matter of dispute (in fact, the mishnah records that there was a dispute about whether there was a dispute concerning Song of Songs). The mishnah then quotes R. Akiva as saying, "Heaven forbid! No one in Israel ever disputed that Song of Songs renders the hands ritually impure, since the entire world is not worth as much as the day on which Song of Songs was given to Israel, for all Scripture is holy, but Song of Songs is the Holy of Holies! If they did disagree, it was only about Ecclesiastes."

25. Song of Songs: 2:7, 3:5, and 8:4. A fourth instance, 5:8, also exists. The first two are identically worded and 8:4 is very similar. While this fourth instance begins like the others, it ends differently, and therefore the Rabbis did not view it as equivalent to 2:7, 3:5, and 8:4.

26. Most likely, on the basis of a *baraita* in BT Rosh Hashanah 20b that refers to the "secret of intercalation," the complex calculations and methods for setting the Jewish calendar.

27. The Chatam Sofer lifted this phrase out of its context in M Orlah 3:9, where it only concerns the tithing of new grain grown outside the Land of Israel. The statement says nothing about new ideas and behaviors, let alone the establishment of a third Jewish commonwealth.

28. Wisse, *Jews and Power*, 4.

29. Wisse, *Jews and Power*, 76.

30. Gordis, *Saving Israel*, 180.

31. Renee Garfinkel and Hannah Rothstein, "Authority or Authoritarianism? Dynamics of Power in the Contemporary Orthodox Rabbinate," *Conversations, the Journal of the Institute for Jewish Ideas and Ideals* 7 (May 2010), https://www.jewishideas.org/article/authority-or-authoritarianism-dynamics-power-contemporary-orthodox-rabbinate-0.

32. Shavit, *My Promised Land*, 131.

33. Mairav Zonszein, "Israel Defends Gaza Conflict as 'Moral War,'" *The Guardian*, June 14, 2015, https://www.theguardian.com/world/2015/jun/14/israel-defends-gaza-conflict-as-moral-war.

34. Robert Tait, "Israeli Soldiers Describe 'Losing Their Sense of Morality' during the Gaza Conflict," *The Telegraph*, May 4, 2015, http://www.telegraph.co.uk/news/worldnews/middleeast/gaza/11580539/Israeli-soldiers-describe-losing-their-sense-of-morality-during-the-Gaza-conflict.html.

6. Straddling Two Worlds

1. Mahfouz, "America's Melting Pot," 2.

2. Schwartz, "Gamliel in Aphrodite's Bath," 205–6.

3. Lapin, *Rabbis as Romans*, 31.

4. Aramaic was the daily vernacular language of the Jews of *Eretz Yisrael* in the first and second centuries. Many spoke and wrote Greek as well, as attested by epigraphic evidence: inscriptions (most famously, the synagogue at Kfar Nachum/Capernaum, as well as an abundance of sepulchral inscriptions that also attest that Jews took Greek names); Greek documents found in a cave at Wadi Murabba'at (the second of the Qumran caves), including letters written by Shimon bar Kokhba and his lieutenants, marriage contracts, deeds of land sale, and philosophical and literary texts (Fitzmyer, "Languages of Palestine," 501–31). M Sotah 9:14 comments: "During the war of Quietus they forbade . . . that one should teach his son Greek." The Gemara on BT Sotah 49b (and a substantially similar version in BT Bava Kamma 83a) wants to distinguish between Greek language and Greek wisdom and asserts that the latter, not the former, is forbidden: "But is Greek philosophy forbidden? Rav Yehudah said that Shmuel taught in the name of Rabban Shimon b. Gamaliel, 'There were one thousand students in the house of my father [Rabban Gamliel]; five hundred studied Torah and five hundred studied Greek wisdom, and of these the only ones who remain are me here and the son of my father's brother in Assia [a village near Tiberias].' It was different with the household of Rabban Gamaliel. . . . [T]hey permitted the household of Rabban Gamaliel to study Greek wisdom because they had close associations with the Government."

5. Urbach, "Hilkhot avodah zarah v'ha-metziut ha-arkiologit v'ha-historit be'me-ah ha-sh'niyah u'v'me-ah ha-shlishit" (The laws of idolatry and archaeological and historical reality in the second and third centuries), in *Mei-olamam shel Chakhamim*, 125–78.

6. Noam Zohar, scholar of moral and political philosophy, points out that this is essentially a psychological procedure whereby a gentile makes a minor physical defect in the idol, thereby foreswearing it as a god ("Avodah Zarah and Its Annulment," 63–77).

7. Siegfried Stein, "Symposia Literature," 33–44.

8. Bokser, *Origins of the Seder*, 4. See also Bokser, "Ritualizing the Seder," 443–71.

9. Among the specific differences Bokser notes in the Passover seder are (1) standardized practice (*symposia* were less structured and more fluid); (2) requiring everyone present to participate, including women and children; (3) attaching the drinking of wine to specific moments in the meal; (4) dipping the hors d'oeuvres and ascribing ritual value to them (they are not mere hors d'oeuvres); and (5) prohibiting postprandial frivolous singing and revelry.

10. Lapin, *Rabbis as Romans*, 4–5.

11. Eliav, "Bathhouses," 609.

12. Lapin, in *Rabbis as Romans*, 3, argues: "The emergence of the rabbinic movement is comparable to the identity politics of other provincials."

13. Lapin argues that the "Rabbis are best seen as an urban, provincial social grouping, deeply embedded in their provincial contexts. Third- and fourth-century Rabbis flourished in Palestinian cities, where they constituted a landholding subelite . . . located in cities. Some features of the urban landscape, such as baths, seem to have been naturalized, while others, such as the presence of images, are the subject of recurrent discussion in the texts." This is not to say that the Rabbis were merely recapitulating the culture of the Roman East, although there is evidence that they absorbed much from that culture. "Rabbis were also developing a literature, modes of piety, and a cultural praxis all their own that would ultimately transform the practice of Judaism in their image" (Lapin, *Rabbis as Romans*, 3, 97).

14. The Roman historian Tacitus wrote a book in c. 98 CE on the life and character of his father-in-law, Julius Agricola, an eminent Roman general who conquered the Britons and subdued them with a unique methodology: "Agricola gave private encouragement and public aid to the building of temples, courts of justice and dwelling-houses, praising the energetic, and reproving the indolent. Thus an honourable rivalry took the place of compulsion. He likewise provided a liberal education for the sons of the chiefs, and showed such a preference for the natural powers of the Britons over the industry of the Gauls that they who lately disdained the tongue of Rome now coveted its eloquence. Hence, too, a liking sprang up for our style of dress, and the 'toga' became fashionable. Step by step they were led to things which

dispose to vice, the lounge, the bath, the elegant banquet. All this in their ignorance, they called civilization, when it was but a part of their servitude." (From Alfred John Church and William Jackson Brodribb, eds., *The Life of Cnæus Julius Agricola*, book 1, ch. 21, in *Complete Works of Tacitus*, edited by Sara Bryant [New York: Random House, 1876, repr. 1942], accessed August 11, 2017, http://www.perseus.tufts.edu/hopper/text?doc=Perseus%3Atext %3A1999.02.0081%3Achapter%3D21.)

15. Lapin, *Rabbis as Romans*, 128.
16. Eliav, "Bathhouses," 606.
17. M Makhshirim 2:5. The expressed concern is not the use of the bath per se, but rather the need to fuel the fire to heat the water on Shabbat. The Yerushalmi (JT Shabbat 3:1, 6a) permits Jews to use the bathhouse on Shabbat, but halakhah eventually ruled it impermissible.
18. M Ta'anit 1:6.
19. M Pesachim 2:6.
20. Eliav, "Bathhouses," 610. Eliav further claims, "Similar conclusions regarding the neutral, uncontested status of public bathhouses emerge from the halakhic traditions relating to ritual purity" (p. 611) to the extent that T Mikvaot 6:4 permits the use of the cold water pool of a bathhouse for the purpose of ritual purification; the only concern expressed relates to *mikvaot* outside the boundaries of the Land of Israel, not with the use of the bathhouse pool itself. In agreement with this view are Schwartz, *Imperialism and Jewish Society*, 162–77; and Halbertal, "Coexisting with the Enemy," 159–72.
21. Eliav, "Bathhouses," 611
22. Discussing figurative art (statues, friezes, busts) installed at the entrance to, and inside, bathhouses, Eliav notes: "As elsewhere in the Roman urban landscape, the function of these artefacts extended beyond their decorative value. Public sculptures were the 'mass media' of the Roman world. They occupied urban centres throughout the empire, serving what art historians call a 'plastic language' that communicated political, religious, and social messages" (Eliav, "Bathhouses," 612).
23. M Avodah Zarah 1:7: "One may not sell to [non-Jews] bears, lions, or anything that can harm the public. One may not build with them a basilica, gallows, stadium, or dais, but one may build with them pedestals and bathhouses

such that when they reach the arched chamber in which they install an object of idolatry, it is forbidden to [help] build."

24. BT Avodah Zarah 3:4.

25. Talmudic stories frequently imagine non-Jews well versed in Torah and halakhah asking Rabbis challenging questions or, as in this case, challenging their views or activities, as a way of exploring an area of disagreement among the Rabbis themselves.

26. While the Rabbis might well have derided the bath as a technological and social import from Rome, interestingly Pliny, Seneca the Younger, Tacitus, and quite a few Roman emperors decried and disdained the baths. What seems to concern the Rabbis is the culture of the baths—what happens and is discussed there—as well as the possibly idolatrous ornamentation, not the fundamental fact of bathing there, which its Roman critics considered decadent.

27. M Avodah Zarah 3:4.

28. Proklos son of Plosfos, a fictional character, may be intended to sound like Proklos, son of a philosopher.

29. Urbach was first to point out that the tannaitic Rabbis transformed the biblical requirement to destroy idols and their appurtenances to a prohibition against deriving benefit from them, "Laws of Idolatry," 125–78.

30. Seth Schwartz and Moshe Halbertal also argue that the bathhouse was construed as "neutral space" for the Rabbis and their followers (Schwartz, *Imperialism and Jewish Society*, 162–77, and Halbertal, "Coexisting with the Enemy," 159–72).

31. BT Sanhedrin 14a.

32. Pirkei Avot 3:21.

33. Tzippori deserves historical notice as the location where R. Yehudah ha-Nasi compiled the Mishnah. At the end of the second century, R. Yehudah ha-Nasi relocated, along with the Sanhedrin, from Bet She'arim to Tzippori. He dwelled there for seventeen years before moving on to Tiberias. During his sojourn in Tzippori he compiled the Mishnah that serves as the core of both the Bavli (Babylonian Talmud) and Yerushalmi (Jerusalem Talmud).

34. Elijah, in his time, also retreated to a cave when he fled from Ahab, the king of Israel, and his wife, Queen Jezebel, who sought to kill him. Scripture

describes how Elijah went to Beer-sheba in Judah, and from there retreated into the wilderness. An angel supplied him with meager nourishment, as God supplied R. Shimon and R. Elazar with food, and from there Elijah journeyed forty days to *the mountain of God at Horeb. There he entered a cave and spent the night* (1 Kings 19:9). The following day, however, God summoned him to leave the cave. When Elijah appears at the entrance of the cave that has hidden and sheltered R. Shimon and his son for twelve years, he does not cross the threshold, as if even for Elijah the cave is too far to retreat from the world.

35. The imperative to enjoy Shabbat, as well as to refrain from activities of the workweek, derives from these verses in Isaiah: *If you refrain from trampling the Sabbath, from pursuing your affairs on My holy day; if you call the Sabbath "delight," Adonai's holy day "honored"; and if you honor it and go not your ways nor look to your affairs, nor strike bargains—then you can seek the favor of Adonai. I will set you astride the heights of the earth, and let you enjoy the heritage of your father Jacob—for the mouth of Adonai has spoken* (Isaiah 58:13–14). A more literal translation of Isaiah is "If you restrain your foot on Shabbat . . . ," which the Rabbis understood to mean, "Your walking on Shabbat should not be like your walking on the weekdays"—it should be slow and relaxed, precluding running except to perform a mitzvah, or to avoid danger" (BT Shabbat 113b). The line between *oneg Shabbat* (delighting in Shabbat) and *Shabbat menuchah* (resting on Shabbat) is often a fine one, and sometimes contradictory, as anyone who loves running and looks forward to a good, long run on Shabbat knows. The Rabbis understood this. The Hasidic master Ya'akov Yitzhak Rabinowicz of Przysucha (1766–1813, known affectionately as "The Holy Jew") observed, "It is nearly impossible to not desecrate Shabbat in some minor way, unless one were bound hand and foot. Yet this would offer no solution since it would prevent *oneg Shabbat*" (Rabinowicz, *Nifla'ot Hayehudi*, Rokatz ed., 62).

36. The prohibition against carrying on Shabbat is based on Exodus 36:6: "Moses thereupon had this proclamation made throughout the camp: 'Let no man or woman make further effort toward gifts for the sanctuary!' So, the people stopped bringing." BT Shabbat 96b understands this proclamation to have been made on Shabbat.

37. *Aseret ha-Dibrot* (the Ten Commandments) appear in both Exodus and Deuteronomy. In Exodus 20:8, the commandment concerning Shabbat is couched "*zakhor*/remember the Sabbath day"; in Deuteronomy 5:12, the commandment is to "*shamor*/observe the Sabbath day."

38. The Gemara reads the word "encamped" as "he was gracious to" based on its sound.

39. Concerning the "angel," Genesis 32:25 actually employs the term *ish* (man), but since the verse also stipulates that Jacob was alone that night, it is commonly presumed that Jacob's visitor was an angel who appeared to him in the guise of a man.

40. The red heifer can only be sacrificed and burned to ashes in the presence of the Temple. Once the Temple was destroyed in 70 CE, it was no longer permissible to produce the ashes.

41. Pirkei Avot 3:21.

7. Caring for Poor People

1. The World Bank report "Poverty and Shared Prosperity 2016: Taking on Inequality" states that while both extreme poverty and inequality between all people worldwide have declined, nearly eight hundred million people lived on less than $1.90 a day in 2013, and the income gap has widened in thirty-four of the eighty-three countries the World Bank monitored for the report. The report points out that population growth—a major factor in poverty and famine today—has offset reductions in poverty in a number of countries (see http://www.worldbank.org/psp, accessed July 17, 2017).

2. The two stories recount the order of Creation differently. In Genesis 1, plants are created before people because they serve as food for the people. In ch. 2, however, a man is created first and only subsequently the garden into which he is placed. As another example, ch. 1 considers humanity— males and females—to have been created simultaneously on the sixth day, and God declares that humans' ability to procreate is an inherent aspect of their being. Chapter 2, in contrast, posits that God initially created one man, and subsequently created a woman from his rib. While in the garden, they are immortal; only after they are expelled from the Garden of Eden

and separated from the Tree of Life, the source of their immorality, do the man and woman reproduce.

3. See Levenson, *Creation and the Persistence of Evil*. Also, while Aristotle laid the groundwork for some of these ideas, the seeds of the notion that God is the sole creator of the universe and has unlimited power (omnipotence), knowledge (omniscience), and extension (omnipresence), as well as moral perfection—often termed "theism"—are found in the writings of the Church Father Augustine of Hippo (354–430). E.g., Augustine writes that God is "the most powerful, most righteous, most beautiful, most good, most blessed" (*On the Trinity*, 15:4). Medieval Christian theologians developed this claim far more extensively, and it became an accepted tenet in many Western religious expressions.

4. Levenson writes: "In my view, the overall effect of these three ways of thinking [i.e., omnipotence, omniscience, and omnibenevolence] has been to trivialize creation by denying the creator a worthy opponent. Creation becomes self-referential, a tautology, a truism: no serious alternative can be entertained, since chaos or cosmic evil has been identified with nonbeing and unreality." *Creation and the Persistence of Evil*, xxv.

5. It could reasonably be argued that Genesis 1 describes the shaping of a self-sustaining universe whose Creator has no need to micromanage: all forms of life reproduce themselves, and the world provides the environmental venues and food supplies required by each species. This suggests that God does not expect to exert continual control, but begs the question of whether God can exert control in every domain or instance.

6. Leviathan is a mythical sea monster (see Psalm 74:12–17) whom God will ultimately crush when God at last gains dominion over the entire world (see Isaiah 27:1–2). *Behemah,* or the plural *behemot* (in English, the term "behemoth" comes from the plural Hebrew form), is a mythical land animal. Both Leviathan and *behemot* are mentioned in Job 40. Troubled by the notion of the existence of creatures beyond God's control, the Rabbis declared variously that they were created on the fifth day (*Yalkut,* Genesis 12) and that originally God created both a female and a male Leviathan, but to prevent them from procreating and destroying the world, God slew the female and reserved her flesh for a banquet that will be held for the righteous when the Messiah

comes (BT Bava Batra 74a). Hence, in the imagination of the Rabbis the mythical creatures that represented aspects of chaos that God had not yet tamed and controlled came to be fully God's creations and under God's control.

7. Levenson, *Creation and the Persistence of Evil*, 6, argues that the psalm celebrates God's ascent to cosmic mastery the moment God assumes command over the heavenly pantheon of divine powers.

8. Jeremiah 12:1–4.

9. The first Creation story is agnostic concerning God's omniscience, but in the second Creation story God's inability to foresee Adam and Eve's disobedience — even if one claims that free will is a divine endowment — confirms that the author did not consider God omniscient. Similarly, while God loves goodness and promulgates a Torah to inculcate goodness in the People of Israel, it would be difficult to argue from the evidence of the Tanakh that God does only good. The flood story, a tale of divinely ordained genocide, is but one story of God's violent retribution.

10. See, e.g., Exodus 34:6–7, Deuteronomy 7:9–11, Jeremiah 9:12–15, Ezekiel 18:20–32, Proverbs 13:6, Ezra 9:13–15, and the book of Job.

11. In *How the Bible Became Holy*, religious historian Michael Satlow argues that the origins of the Sadducees and Pharisees are quite different than conventionally presented: Pharisees, he writes, upheld the authority of traditions the people observed, following the status quo. The Sadducees, in contrast, promoted the notion that scriptural texts should have the normative authority to set religious practice. In the ether of the Hellenistic world, where texts were culturally determinative, Jews adopted their own normative texts — Scripture — but even beyond this, they developed a culture based on texts. In the third century the ideas of the Sadducees and the Pharisees merged with the Hellenistic reliance on culturally defining texts that created group identity to produce the Rabbinic concept that the Torah "was not a collection of oracles but the source of all true knowledge . . . the very place at which God continued to reveal to his people" (267–68). This belief paved the way for Oral Torah, a living, breathing document with divine authority.

12. Berger wrote: "Every human society is an enterprise of world-building. Religion occupies a distinctive place in this enterprise. . . . Society is a dia-

lectic phenomenon in that it is a human product, and nothing but a human product, that yet continuously acts back upon its producer. Society is a product of man. It has no other being except that which is bestowed upon it by human activity and consciousness. There can be no social reality apart from man. Yet it may also be stated that man is a product of society. Every individual biography is an episode within the history of society, which both precedes and survives it. Society was there before the individual was born and it will be there after he has died" (*Sacred Canopy*, 3).

13. *Realissimum* is a Latin term for God, the ultimate reality or the most real being.

14. Berger, *Sacred Canopy*, 31.

15. An example of this is found in the Rabbis' claim that, like Jews, God dons tefillin and prays daily. *Talmud of Relationships*, vol. 1, ch. 2.

16. Berman, *Created Equal*, 17–18.

17. Pritchard, *Ancient Near Eastern Texts*, 104–6.

18. Berman, *Created Equal*, 21.

19. Bottéro, *Religion in Ancient Mesopotamia*, 207.

20. Berman, *Created Equal*, 22.

21. Some scholars (among them: Joshua Berman, Raymond Westbrook, Jean Bottéro, and Michael LeFebvre) contend that ancient Near Eastern law codes were literary, rather than juridical, in nature. This is to say, ancient law codes functioned not as normative law but rather as (1) the ruler's proof to the gods that he was qualified to rule with divine approval; (2) training texts for judges, containing sample laws to consider when rendering their decisions; and (3) a collection of judicial problems and solutions for judges to consider.

22. Berman, *Created Equal*, 85.

23. See also Exodus 22:20; 23:9; Numbers 15:14–16; Deuteronomy 24:14,17; 26:11; 27:19.

24. See also Deuteronomy 24:14.

25. See also Deuteronomy 24:19–22.

26. Tigay, *Deuteronomy*, 217.

27. Berlin and Brettler, *Jewish Study Bible*, 272.

28. Berman, *Created Equal*, 97.

29. Leviticus 15:12–16; Deuteronomy 15:1.

30. Berman, *Created Equal*, 101.

31. Genesis 19.

32. Proverbs 10:2 and 11:4.

33. There was not unanimity of thought on this matter. In BT Shabbat 156a, R. Chanina claims that the heavenly bodies influence wisdom, wealth, and Israel's fortunes, but R. Yochanan summarily rejects this notion, claiming that Israel is immune from their influence. The two stories that follow, recounted here, are brought to support R. Yochanan's claim.

34. BT Shabbat 156b.

35. BT Gittin 7a.

36. BT Ketubot 50a.

37. BT Ketubot 49b.

38. BT Ketubot 67a.

39. Moses Maimonides describes two communal institutions that cared for the needs of those in the community experiencing hunger. The *kupah* (basket) held enough food to feed a family for a week. The *tamkhui* (plate) held food sufficient to feed a family through Shabbat. Each community was responsible for maintaining a *kupah* and a *tamkhui*. Officials (*gabba'im*) were appointed to collect money from members of the community and distribute the *kupah* and *tamkhui* each Friday to individuals and families in need. On the basis of BT Ketubot 49b, *gabbai'im* even had the authority to assess people and require contributions because tzedakah is an obligation.

40. Zborowski and Herzog, *Life Is with People*, 193–94.

41. It is not, however, unusual. The Rabbis often told stories of Jews holding conversations with prominent Romans who quoted Scripture, which in a way affirms the truth and importance of Scripture.

42. BT Yoma 9b explains that the First Temple was destroyed because of the three cardinal sins: idolatry, sexual immorality, and murder. BT Gittin 55–56 tells the story of an incident marked by *sinat chinam* (baseless hatred) that led directly to the destruction of the First Temple.

43. BT Gittin 58a.

44. Scheinerman, "Giving Voice to the Unspeakable," 109–23.

45. BT Ketubot 67b.

BIBLIOGRAPHY

Alter, Robert, and Frank Kermode, eds. *The Literary Guide to the Bible*. Cambridge MA: Belknap Press, 1990.

Batnitzky, Leora. *How Judaism Became a Religion: An Introduction to Modern Jewish Thought*. Princeton: Princeton University Press, 2013.

Baumgarten, A. I. "The Akiban Opposition." *Hebrew Union College Annual* 50 (1979): 179–97.

Ben-Shahar, Tal. *The Pursuit of Perfect: How to Stop Chasing Perfection and Start Living a Richer, Happier Life*. Columbus OH: McGraw-Hill Education, 2009.

Berger, Peter L. *The Sacred Canopy: Elements of a Sociological Theory of Religion*. New York: Anchor Books, 1990.

Berlin, Adele, and Marc Zvi Brettler. *The Jewish Study Bible*. Oxford: Oxford University Press, 2004.

Berman, Joshua A. *Created Equal: How the Bible Broke with Ancient Political Thought*. Oxford: Oxford University Press, 2008.

Blidstein, Gerald. *Honor Thy Father and Mother: Filial Responsibility in Jewish Law and Ethics*. New York: Ktav, 1975.

Bokser, Baruch M. *The Origins of the Seder: The Passover Rite and Early Rabbinic Judaism*. Berkeley: University of California Press, 1984.

———. "Ritualizing the Seder." *Journal of the American Academy of Religion* 56 (1988): 443–71.

Bottéro, Jean. *Religion in Ancient Mesopotamia*. Translated by Teresa Lavender Fagan. Chicago: University of Chicago Press, 2004.

Boyarin, Daniel. *Carnal Israel: Reading Sex in Talmudic Culture*. Berkeley: University of California Press, 1993.

Brody, Heinrich, ed. *Selected Poems of Jehudah Halevi*. Philadelphia: Jewish Publication Society, 1924.

Bruns, Gerald L. "Midrash and Allegory: The Beginnings of Scriptural Interpretation." In Alter and Kermode, *Literary Guide*, 625–46.

Cahill, Thomas. *The Gifts of the Jews: How a Tribe of Desert Nomads Changed the Way Everyone Thinks and Feels*. New York: Anchor Books, 1999.

Cohen, Getzel. "Travel between Palestine and Mesopotamia." In Geller, *The Archaeology and Material Culture of the Babylonian Talmud*.

Cohen, Shaye J. D. *From the Maccabees to the Mishnah*. 3rd ed. Louisville KY: Westminster John Knox, 2014.

Cohen, Stuart A. *The Three Crowns: Structures of Communal Politics in Early Rabbinic Jewry*. Cambridge: Cambridge University Press, 1990.

Coogan, Michael D. *God and Sex: What the Bible Really Says*. New York: Twelve, 2011.

De Uzeda, Shmuel. *Midrash Shmuel: A Collection of Commentaries on Pirkei Avot*. Translated by Moshe Schapiro and David Rottenberg. Jerusalem: Haktav Institute, 1994.

Dratch, Mark. "Honoring Abusive Parents." *Hakirah* 12 (2011): 105–19.

Ehrman, Bart. *God's Problem: How the Bible Fails to Answer Our Most Important Question — Why We Suffer*. San Francisco: HarperOne, 2009.

Eilberg-Schwartz, Howard. *God's Phallus: And Other Problems for Men and Monotheism*. Boston: Beacon, 1994.

———. *The Savage in Judaism: An Anthropology of Israelite Religion and Ancient Judaism*. Bloomington: Indiana University Press, 1990.

Eliav, Yaron Z. "Bathhouses as Places of Social and Cultural Interaction." In *The Oxford Handbook of Jewish Daily Life in Roman Palestine*, edited by Catherine Hezser, 605–22. Oxford: Oxford University Press, 2010.

Emerson, Ralph Waldo. *Works of Ralph Waldo Emerson*. Vol. 2. Boston: Houghton, Osgood, 1880.

Engel, Beverly. *Divorcing a Parent: Free Yourself from the Past and Live the Life You've Always Wanted*. Brattleboro VT: Echo Point Books & Media, 2014.

Fine, Steven. "Review of Lapin, Rabbis as Romans: The Rabbinic Movement in Palestine, 100-400 CE." *Society of Biblical Literature*, 2013. Accessed April 24, 2017. https://www.academia.edu/3412357/Review_of_Lapin_--Rabbis_as_Romans_The_Rabbinic_Movement_in_Palestine_100_400_CE.

Fisch, Menachem. *Rational Rabbis: Science and Talmudic Culture*. Bloomington: University of Indiana Press, 1997.

Fitzmyer, Joseph. "The Languages of Palestine in the First Century A.D." *Catholic Biblical Quarterly* 32 (1970): 501–31.

Fox, Everett. *The Five Books of Moses: Genesis, Exodus, Leviticus, Numbers, and Deuteronomy*. New York: Schocken, 1983.

Friedman, Shamma. "La'aggadah hahistorit batalmud habavli." In *Saul Lieberman Memorial Volume*, edited by Shamma Friedman. New York: Jewish Theological Seminary, 1993.

Geertz, Clifford. *The Interpretation of Cultures*. New York: Basic Books, 1973.

Geller, Markham J., ed. *The Archaeology and Material Culture of the Babylonian Talmud*. Leiden: Brill, 2015.

Gillman, Neil. *The Death of Death: Resurrection and Immortality in Jewish Thought*. Woodstock VT: Jewish Lights, 2011.

———. *Doing Jewish Theology: God, Torah & Israel in Modern Judaism*. Woodstock VT: Jewish Lights, 2008.

———. "Problematics of Myth." *Sh'ma: A Journal of Jewish Ideas*, January 1, 2002. http://shma.com/2002/01/the-problematics-of-myth/.

Gino, Francesca and Michael I. Norton. "Why Rituals Work." *Scientific American* (May 14, 2013). https://www.scientificamerican.com/article/why-rituals-work/.

Gold, Michael. *God, Love, Sex, and Family: A Rabbi's Guide for Building Relationships That Last*. Lantham MD: Jason Aronson, 1998.

Goodblatt, David. *The Monarchic Principle: Studies in Jewish Self-Government in Antiquity*. Tübingen: Mohr Siebeck, 1994.

———. *Rabbinic Instruction in Sasanian Babylonia*. Leiden: Brill, 1975.

Goody, Jack. *The Logic of Writing and the Organization of Society*. Cambridge: Cambridge University Press, 1987.

Gordis, Daniel. *Saving Israel: How the Jewish People Can Win a War That May Never End*. Hoboken NJ: John Wiley, 2009.

Halbertal, Moshe. "Coexisting with the Enemy: Jews and Pagans in the Mishnah." In *Tolerance and Intolerance in Early Judaism and Christianity*, edited by G. N. Stanton and G. G. Stroumsa. Cambridge: Cambridge University Press, 1998.

Hartman, David. *A Living Covenant: The Innovative Spirit in Traditional Judaism*. Woodstock VT: Jewish Lights, 1998.

Heschel, Abraham J. *Man's Quest for God: Studies in Prayer and Symbolism*. New York: Scribner, 1954.

Hezser, Catherine. *Jewish Travel in Antiquity*. Tübingen: Mohr Siebeck, 2011.

———. *The Social Structure of the Rabbinic Movement in Roman Palestine*. Tübingen: Mohr Siebeck, 1997.

Hicks, Donna. *Dignity: Its Essential Role in Resolving Conflict*. New Haven: Yale University Press, 2013.

Holm, Jean, and John Bowker, eds. *Sacred Place*. New York: Continuum, 1994.

Holtz, Barry. *Rabbi Akiva: Sage of the Talmud*. New Haven: Yale University Press, 2017.

Hume, David. *Dialogues concerning Natural Religion*. Indianapolis: Hackett, 1998.

Jacobs, Louis. *The Jewish Religion: A Companion*. Oxford: Oxford University Press, 1995.

JPS Hebrew-English TANAKH. 2nd ed. Philadelphia: Jewish Publication Society, 1999.

Kaplan, Mordecai M. *The Meaning of God in Modern Jewish Religion*. Detroit MI: Wayne State University Press, 1995.

Katz, Michael, and Gershon Schwartz. *Swimming in the Sea of Talmud: Lessons for Everyday Living*. Philadelphia: Jewish Publication Society, 1997.

Kol Haneshamah: Shabbat Vehagim. 2nd ed. Wyncote PA: Reconstructionist Press, 1995.

Kraemer, David C. *Jewish Eating and Identity through the Ages*. Routledge Advances in Sociology. New York: Routledge, 2007.

Kunin, Seth Daniel. *Themes and Issues in Judaism*. New York: Cassell, 2000.

Langer, Susanne K. *Philosophy in a New Key: A Study in the Symbolism of Reason, Rite, and Art*. Cambridge: Harvard University Press, 1967.

Lapin, Hayim. *Rabbis as Romans: The Rabbinic Movement in Palestine, 100–400 CE*. New York: Oxford University Press, 2012.

Lempriere, J. *A Classical Dictionary*. London: Forgotten Books, 2017.

Levenson, Jon D. *Creation and the Persistence of Evil: The Jewish Drama of Divine Omnipotence*. Princeton: Princeton University Press, 1994.

Levine, Étan, "Biblical Women's Marital Rights." *Proceedings of the American Academy for Jewish Research* 63 (1997–2001).

———, ed. *Marital Relations in Ancient Judaism*. Wiesbaden: Harrassowitz Verlag, 2009.

Lichtenstein, Aharon. "Study." In *20th Century Jewish Religious Thought*, edited by Arthur A. Cohen and Paul Mendes-Flohr. Philadelphia PA: Jewish Publication Society, 2009.

Lightstone, Jack N. *Mishnah and the Social Formation of the Early Rabbinic Guild: A Socio-Rhetorical Approach.* Waterloo ON: Wilfrid Laurier University Press, 2002.

Mahfouz, Safi Mahmoud. "America's Melting Pot or the Salad Bowl: The Stage Immigrant's Dilemma." *Journal of Foreign Languages, Cultures & Civilizations* 1, no. 2 (December 2013): 1–17.

May, Rollo. *The Cry for Myth.* New York: Norton, 1991.

———. *Power and Innocence: A Search for the Sources of Violence.* New York: Norton, 1998.

Nachman of Breslov. *The Gentle Weapon: Prayers for Everyday and Not-So-Everyday Moments,* adapted from *Likutei Mohoran* 1:54 by Moshe Mykoff and S. C. Mizrahi. Woodstock VT: Jewish Lights, 1999.

Neusner, Jacob. *Development of a Legend: Studies on the Traditions concerning Yohanan ben Zakkai.* Leiden: Brill, 1970.

———. *Jeremiah in Talmud and Midrash: A Source Book.* Lanham MD: University Press of America, 2006.

———. *Judaism: The Evidence of the Mishnah.* Chicago: University of Chicago Press, 1981.

———. *Judaism and Story: The Evidence of The Fathers According to Rabbi Nathan.* Chicago IL: University of Chicago Press, 1992.

———. *The Mishnah: Religious Perspectives.* Leiden: Brill, 2002.

———. "The Mishnah Viewed Whole." In *The Mishnah in Contemporary Perspective: Part One,* edited by Alan J. Avery-Peck and Jacob Neusner. Boston: Brill, 2002.

———. *Rabbinic Traditions about the Pharisees before 70.* Eugene OR: Wipf & Stock, 2005.

Norenzayan, Ara. *Big Gods: How Religion Transformed Cooperation and Conflict.* Princeton: Princeton University Press, 2015.

Nouwen, Henri J. *Out of Solitude: Three Meditations on the Christian Life.* Notre Dame IN: Ave Maria Press, 2004.

Paul, Shalom M. *Studies in the Book of the Covenant in the Light of Cuneiform and Biblical Law.* Leiden: Brill, 1970.

Porath, Christine and Christine Pearson. "The Price of Incivility." *Harvard Business Review* (January–February 2013). https://hbr.org/2013/01/the-price -of-incivility.

Pritchard, James B., ed. *Ancient Near Eastern Tests Relating to the Old Testament.* 3rd ed. Princeton: Princeton University Press, 1969.

Raveh, Inbar. *Feminist Rereadings of Rabbinic Literature.* Translated by Kaeren Fish. Waltham: Brandeis University Press, 2014.

Rieser, Louis. *The Hillel Narratives: What the Tales of the First Rabbi Can Teach Us about Our Judaism.* Teaneck NJ: Ben Yehuda Press, 2009.

Rubenstein, Jeffrey L. *Creation and Composition.* Tübingen: Mohr Siebeck, 2005.

———. *The Culture of the Babylonian Talmud.* Baltimore: Johns Hopkins University Press, 2003.

———. *Rabbinic Stories.* New York: Paulist Press, 2002.

———. *Stories of the Babylonian Talmud.* Baltimore: Johns Hopkins University Press, 2010.

———. *Talmudic Stories: Narrative Art, Composition, and Culture.* Baltimore: Johns Hopkins University Press, 1999.

Sarna, Nahum M., ed. *JPS Torah Commentary: Exodus.* Philadelphia: Jewish Publication Society, 1991.

Satlow, Michael L. *How the Bible Became Holy.* New Haven: Yale University Press, 2014.

Schäfer, Peter, ed. *The Talmud Yerushalmi and Graeco-Roman Culture.* Vols. 1 and 3. Tübingen: Mohr Siebeck, 1998.

Scheinerman, Amy. "Giving Voice to the Unspeakable: Rabbinic Responses to Disaster." CCAR *Journal: The Reform Jewish Quarterly* (Fall 2015): 109–23.

Schwartz, Seth. "Gamliel in Aphrodite's Bath: Palestinian Judaism and Urban Culture in the Third and Fourth Centuries." In Schäfer, *The Talmud Yerushalmi and Graeco-Roman Culture,* 1:203–17.

———. *Imperialism and Jewish Society, 200 B.C.E. to 640 C.E.* Princeton: Princeton University Press, 2001.

Shavit, Ari. *My Promised Land: The Triumph and Tragedy of Israel.* New York: Spiegel & Grau, 2013.

Skibell, Joseph. *Six Memos from the Last Millennium: A Novelist Reads the Talmud.* Austin: University of Texas Press, 2013.

Slapper, Gary, and David Kelly. *The English Legal System.* 2nd ed. London: Routledge-Cavendish, 2003.

Slonimsky, Henry. *Essays.* Cincinnati: Hebrew Union College, 1967.

Stein, David E. S., ed. *The Contemporary Torah: A Gender-Sensitive Adaptation of the JPS Translation*. Philadelphia: Jewish Publication Society, 2006.

Stein, Siegfried. "The Influence of Symposia Literature on the Literary Form of the Pesah Haggadah." *Journal of Jewish Studies* 8 (1957): 33–44.

Steinsaltz, Adin. *The Essential Talmud*. New York: Basic Books, 1976.

——. *The Talmud: A Reference Guide*. Jerusalem: Koren, 2014.

Stern, Chaim, ed. *Gates of Prayer*. New York: Central Conference of American Rabbis, 1975.

Tigay, Jeffrey H. *JPS Torah Commentary: Deuteronomy*. Philadelphia: Jewish Publication Society, 1996.

Urbach, Ephraim E., ed. *Mei-olamam shel Chakhamim* (From the world of the sages). Jerusalem: Magnes, 1988.

Weber, Max. *Economy and Society*, vol. 1. Berkeley: University of California Press, 1978.

——. *The Sociology of Religion*. Translated by E. Fischoff. Boston: Beacon, 1993.

White, Roger M. *Talking about God: The Concept of Analogy and the Problem of Religious Language*. London: Routledge, 2010.

Wisse, Ruth R. *Jews and Power*. New York: Schocken, 2007.

Zborowski, Mark, and Elizabeth Herzog. *Life Is with People: The Culture of the Shtetl*. New York: Schocken, 1962.

Zohar, Noam. "Avodah Zarah and Its Annulment" (Heb.). *Sidra* 17 (2002): 63–77.